Austerity Across Europe

Lived Experiences of Economic Crises

**Sarah Marie Hall, Helena Pimlott-Wilson
and John Horton**

Routledge
Taylor & Francis Group

LONDON AND NEW YORK

First published 2021
by Routledge
2 Park Square, Milton Park, Abingdon, Oxon OX14 4RN

and by Routledge
52 Vanderbilt Avenue, New York, NY 10017

Routledge is an imprint of the Taylor & Francis Group, an informa business

British Library Cataloguing-in-Publication Data
A catalogue record for this book is available from the British Library

Library of Congress Cataloging-in-Publication Data
A catalog record for this book has been requested

ISBN: 978-0-367-19251-8 (hbk)
ISBN: 978-0-429-20133-2 (ebk)

Typeset in Times New Roman
by Apex CoVantage, LLC

Austerity Across Europe

Drawing together multidisciplinary research exploring everyday life in Europe during times of economic crisis, this book explores the ways in which austerity policies are lived and experienced – often alongside other significant social, political and personal change. With attention to the inequalities produced by these processes and the measures used by individuals, families and communities to help them 'get by', it also envisages hopeful, affirmative socio-political futures. Arranged around the themes of intergenerational relations and exchanges, ways of coping through crises, and community, civic and state infrastructures, *Austerity Across Europe* will appeal to social scientists with interests in everyday life, family practices, neoliberal state policy, poverty and socio-economic inequalities.

Sarah Marie Hall is based in the Department of Geography at the University of Manchester, UK. Her research sits in the broad field of feminist political economy: understanding how socio-economic processes are shaped by gender relations, lived experience and social difference. Recent research projects focus on everyday life and economic change, including empirical work in the context of austerity, Brexit and devolution. She is currently Co-Editor of the international academic journal *Area*.

Helena Pimlott-Wilson is based in Geography and Environment at Loughborough University, UK. Her research focuses on the shifting importance of education and employment in the reproduction of classed power. Recent work investigates the aspirations of young people from socio-economically diverse areas in the UK, international mobility of students for higher education and work placements, and the alternative and supplementary education industries.

John Horton is based in the Faculty of Education and Humanities at the University of Northampton, UK. His research explores the spaces, cultures, politics, playful practices and social-material exclusions of contemporary childhood and youth in diverse international contexts. He is currently Editor of the international academic journals *Social & Cultural Geography* and *Children's Geographies*.

Contents

Figures

Tables

Contributors

Sofia N. Andreou is Senior Researcher at the Economics Research Centre of the University of Cyprus and an Adjunct Lecturer at the Open University of Cyprus. She completed her undergraduate studies in Economics at the University of Macedonia, Thessaloniki (2004), and received her MSc in Economics from the University of Essex (2005) and PhD in Economics from the University of Cyprus (2011). Previously, she worked as a postdoctoral research officer at the Economics Research Centre (2011–2013) and as a visiting and adjunct lecturer at the Department of Economics, University of Cyprus. Her research interests are in the area of applied economics and econometrics with emphasis on public and welfare economics. Most of her work was based on the consumer behaviour theory and demand analysis approaches aiming to extract conclusions for policy-making regarding efficiency, equity and distributional implications of empirical findings. Since September 2018, she serves as an EU Independent Expert on Poverty and Social Exclusion for Cyprus.

Mireia Baylina is Senior Lecturer in Geography at the Universitat Autònoma de Barcelona (UAB). She researches on social and economic issues from a gender perspective. Her research and publications are related to women's work and daily life in rural areas, representation of gender and rurality, women and public space and geographies of children and youth from a gender and intersectional perspective. She has been editor of the journals *Documents d'Anàlisi Geogràfica* and *European Urban and Regional Studies* and a member of the steering committee of the Commission of Gender and Geography of the International Geographical Union (2003–2009). She was co-founder and coordinator of the Interuniversity Doctorate Program on Gender Studies: Cultures, Societies and Policies at the UAB (2013–2019) and is coordinator of the Doctorate Program in Geography at the UAB (since 2014).

Julia Brannen is Emerita Professor of the Sociology of the Family, Thomas Coram Research Unit, UCL Institute of Education and a Fellow of the Academy of Social Sciences. She has an international reputation for research on the family lives of parents, children and young people and work-family issues in Britain and Europe, intergenerational relationships and food in families. She is well known for her methodological expertise and innovative practice in the development of mixed methods and for her use of biographical approaches and comparative research. Her latest book, *Social Research Matters*, was published in November 2019 by Bristol University Press.

Kostas Dimopoulos is Professor in the Department of Social and Educational Policy, University of Peloponnese. He has served as vice president of the Institute of Education Policy (a national agency supervised by the Ministry of Education responsible for education planning in primary and secondary education). His current research interests concern the analysis of education programs of various forms and levels, as well as understanding how the Greek school works under the current socio-political circumstances. He has written 98 articles and conference papers and two books on these issues. Among the international journals he has published are *International Journal of Learning, Educational Studies, International Journal of Leadership in Education, Leadership & Policy in Schools* and the *Curriculum Journal*. His published work has been cited by hundreds of peers from 48 different countries. He has also participated (as member of the working group or as coordinator) in 15 national and 17 European R&D projects.

Richard Filčák is Head of the Institute and Senior Researcher at the Slovak Academy of Sciences/CSPS-Institute for Forecasting. His work and research interests are focused on environmental and social policy development and trends in the transitional countries of Central and Eastern Europe, particularly in the context of the EU economic and social cohesion policies vis-à-vis industrial development, decarbonisation and climate change.

Irene Hardill is Professor of Public Policy in the Department of Social Sciences, Northumbria University. She has extensive experience in researching geographies of ageing, including digital exclusion and theorising work (paid and unpaid work) and active citizenship.

Eleanor Jupp is Senior Lecturer in Social Policy at the University of Kent. She works between the social policy and human geography disciplines and researches on community, activism and care, especially in the context of austerity.

Abigail Knight is Honorary Senior Research Associate at the Thomas Coram Research Unit, UCL Institute of Education, University College London, where she worked for over 20 years as a qualitative researcher with children and families. Her research interests include the experiences of looked-after children, disabled children and their families, and the impact of poverty on the lives of children, young people and their families. She has published in a variety of journals such as *Children and Society, Child and Family Social Work* and *Families, Relationships and Societies*. She now works as an independent social worker.

Kirsten Koop is Associate Professor of Geography at the University of Grenoble Alps (UGA) in France and a member of the research centre PACTE.

She works on development studies epistemology, globalisation, poverty, post-development and transition across the north-south divide. Her recent research projects focus on disruptive social innovations and their potential for social and spatial transformation. She is currently a member of the steering committee of the interdisciplinary research project Innovation and Transitions in Mountain Territories (ITTEM) at UGA and president of Modus Operandi, an association dealing with constructive conflict transformation.

Christos Koutsampelas is Assistant Professor in the Department of Social and Educational Policy of the University of Peloponnese. He holds a BSc degree in economics, a MSc degree in international economics and finance (2004) and a PhD in economics (2009), awarded by Athens University of Economics and Business. His scientific interests revolve around measuring and understanding socio-economic and educational inequalities as well as assessing public policy. He has been involved in several research programmes, published articles in peer-reviewed academic journals and collective volumes, served as reviewer in academic journals and co-authored a large number of policy reports published by the European Commission.

Cecília Kovai is Cultural Anthropologist and Research Fellow at the Centre for Social Sciences, Hungarian Academy of Sciences Centre of Excellence. Recently she has conducted fieldwork in Roma communities in Hungarian rural areas. Her main research interests include the role of ethnicity in the organisation of local societies, the connection between ethnicity and class position, the organisation of Roma communities and the working of intersectionality within Roma communities. Since 2017, she has been working as a postdoctoral scholar. Her new research focuses on development activities in poor neighbourhoods of small towns in Hungary, with a particular interest in poor Roma communities.

Sally Lloyd-Evans is Associate Professor in human geography at the University of Reading with research interests in cities, community development, relationality and participation from social justice perspectives. She specialises in using participatory action research to empower urban communities to act for social change, facilitating local people to undertake research that enables them to tackle poverty and social exclusion from the grassroots. She co-founded the University's Participation Lab and directs an award-winning participatory action research collective in Reading called the Whitley Researchers (https://research.reading.ac.uk/community-based-research/).

Rebecca O'Connell is Reader in the Sociology of Food and Families at the Thomas Coram Research Unit, UCL Institute of Education. She is co-author of *Food, Families and Work* (with Julia Brannen, 2016) and *Living Hand to Mouth: Children and Food in Low-Income Families* (with Abigail Knight and Julia Brannen, 2019). She is co-editor of a new collection, *What Is Food? Researching a Topic with Many Meanings* (2019). From 2011 to 2017 she was co-convenor of the British Sociological Association Food Study Group. In addition to her substantive interests, she has expertise in research methodology, particularly mixed and multi-methods research.

Anna Ortiz Guitart is Feminist Geographer as well as Senior Lecturer at the Department of Geography of the Autonomous University of Barcelona. She is a member of the Research Group on Geography and Gender and collaborates with the Research Group on Immigration, Mixedness and Social Cohesion (INMIX). Her research is within social and cultural geography. Particular interests are identity processes; children's and youth geographies, planning; urban transformation in Barcelona; student migration and skilled migration in Mexico; and experimental qualitative methods. She has published in academic journals such as *Cities, Children's Geographies, Journal of Youth Studies, Journal of Ethnic and Migration Studies* and *Population, Space and Place*.

Roger O'Sullivan is Professor and Director of Ageing Research & Development at the Institute of Public Health and Visiting Professor at Ulster University. He is a member of the UK Faculty of Public Health and a fellow of the Gerontological Society of America.

Evangelia Papaloi is Adjunct Lecturer for Postgraduate Courses in Educational Management at various universities in Greece (Hellenic Open University, University of Thessaly, University of the Peloponnese, University of Western Macedonia). She received a PhD with a cross-disciplinary focus on education sciences, social organisational psychology and adult learning and development from University Toulouse II (France). She is a research associate and a trainer at various public research institutes and training centres in Greece and has conducted cross-disciplinary research in the areas of organisational behaviour, educational leadership, leadership ethics, social justice, social inclusion and stereotypes. She serves as a reviewer at the Academy of Management Conference in Organisational Behaviour (OB) and in Organizational Development & Change (ODC) Departments and sits on the editorial board of the international journal *Business Ethics and Leadership* (*BEL*). She has published papers in scientific journals and has written chapters in collective volumes both in Greece and abroad (Cambridge Scholars).

Maria Prats Ferret is Senior Lecturer at the Department of Geography and Director of the Observatory for Equality at Universitat Autònoma de Barcelona. She is a member of the research group on Geography and Gender. She teaches undergraduate and master's courses on geography and gender. She has been visiting scholar at the University of Reading, Universidade de Lisboa and the City University of New York (CUNY). She is a member of the Editorial Board for the journals *Documents d'Anàlisi Geogràfica* and *Revista Latinoamericana de Geografía y Género*. Her research interests are geographies of gender, geographies of children and youth, and qualitative methodologies. She has published in academic journals and co-authored works in edited collections for Routledge and Springer.

Rebecca Reynolds was Research Fellow in the School of Social Work & Social Policy at the University of Strathclyde, working on the Getting By project between 2017 and 2018.

Serena Romano has a PhD in sociology and social research and is interested in social policy, poverty, welfare and social inclusion. She has been a postdoctoral fellow at the University of Salerno (Italy), a research fellow at University of Naples Federico II (Italy) and a Jemolo Fellow at the University of Oxford (UK).

Daniela Sime is Professor of Youth, Migration and Social Justice in the School of Social Work & Social Policy at the University of Strathclyde. Her current research examines the impact of migration on families and sense of belonging, issues of social justice affecting children and young people and approaches to tackling social inequalities in service provision. She was a British Academy Mid-Career Fellow in 2017–2018, and the data collected for her grant, Getting By: Young People's Experiences of Poverty and Stigma at the Intersection of Ethnicity, Class and Gender, form the basis of her chapter in this volume.

Daniel Škobla is Senior Researcher at the Institute of Ethnology and Social Anthropology of the Slovak Academy of Sciences in Bratislava. As a researcher he is focused mainly on ethnicity, social inclusion and the labour market. He provided technical assistance for the Slovak government regarding the EU Framework for National Roma Integration Strategies 2020. He has also been involved in Roma advocacy on an international level, participating in numerous meetings throughout Europe, and has cooperated with the European Roma Rights Centre, Amnesty International and the Open Society Institute. He has written academic articles in journals as well as chapters in books on social inclusion and Roma integration.

Silje Elisabeth Skuland is Sociologist and Senior Researcher at Consumption Research Norway (SIFO) at Oslo Metropolitan University. She has worked at SIFO since 2009 on topics related to food consumption including food poverty, healthy eating, sustainable food consumption and food safety. She has recently worked on topics such as young people's consumption, lone parents and consumption inequalities and debt problems.

Anna Tarrant is Associate Professor in Sociology at the University of Lincoln, UK, and is a UKRI Future Leaders Research Fellow. Her research interests include men and masculinities, family life, the life course and methodological developments in qualitative secondary analysis. Her current research, Following Young Fathers Further, is a qualitative longitudinal and participatory study exploring the lived experiences and support needs of young fathers.

Sander van Lanen is Lecturer in Human Geography and Planning at the Faculty of Spatial Sciences, University of Groningen. His research focuses on the everyday urban geographies and experiences of social exclusion, poverty and inequality with a specific focus on austerity and labour precarity.

Tünde Virág is Sociologist and Senior Research Fellow at the Centre for Economic and Regional Studies, Hungarian Academy of Sciences Centre of Excellence. Her research focuses on poverty and ethnicity, social and spatial inequalities and socio-economic transformation. She has conducted and participated in numerous national and international research projects in different Roma communities focused on spatial and social inequalities and social stratification.

The Whitley Researchers collective is a partnership between the University of Reading, the Whitley Community Development Association, local residents and schools that trains and employs local residents and young people in conducting action research and devising innovative solutions to local issues. The co-authors and contributors to the research presented include John Ord (community project manager); Lorna Zischka (postdoctoral research assistant); Paul Allen (arts teacher and Young Researcher lead); Liz Ashcroft, Aneta Banas, Sandra Clare, and Naomi Lee (community researchers); Sonia Duval (community administrator); and students at the John Madejski Academy.

1   Introduction

Austerity across Europe: lived experiences of economic crises

Sarah Marie Hall, Helena Pimlott-Wilson and John Horton

In January 2014 *The Guardian*, a leading British newspaper and media outlet, issued a call to its younger readership to send in pictures of their bedrooms. The reason? There was evidence that growing numbers of young people in the UK aged 20–34, three million in fact, were living at home with their parents (ONS 2014) as a result of direct and indirect austerity policies affecting access to jobs, welfare and housing (Heath and Calvert 2013; MacLeavy and Manley 2018; Wilkinson and Ortega-Alcázar 2017). Similar trends can be seen across Europe, with reports of 'over three-quarters of young adults aged 18–24 in the EU usually live with at least one of their parents' (Eurofound 2019, p. 56). As *The Guardian* story explained, this was 'the highest number since records began' and an increase of 25% since 1996 (*The Guardian* 2014a). The interest here was specifically in young people who were still living at home or had gone back home and were living in their childhood bedroom: 'Has it changed at all since you were at school? Or have you still got the same posters up as you had 10 years ago?'

The challenge, it seems, was accepted. Viewers replied in their droves, and the website still carries some of these images and quotations about their experiences of living at home (*The Guardian* 2014b). The photographs have common themes, including the careful arrangements of soft furnishings, furniture, storage boxes, more than often stuffed awkwardly into small or ill-fitting spaces, with just about enough room for a single bed (also see Horton and Kraftl 2012). The quotations carry tales of job losses, high rents, leaving university and indebtedness. And when placed in tandem with short vignettes, these images also tell a stark and profound story of the lived and felt impacts of austerity on the ground.

As editors of this collection and scholars with research interests in this field, we have together and individually been working in this space for what seems like a very long time. Significant proportions of our careers have been dedicated to questioning, interrogating and quietly observing the ongoing ramifications of austerity policies for communities, families and society at large (e.g. see Hall 2019; Horton 2016; Horton et al. in press; Pimlott-Wilson 2017). This is not to say austerity is a new problem, rather that austerity is highly contextual and situated, while at the same time can represent shared experiences. Moreover, austerity is not a flash-in-the-pan event or policy; over the last ten years, it has become the new normal for state and personal finances alike across many European countries.

With this collection we explore the multitude of ways in which austerity and economic crises are experienced in everyday life across Europe. We connect and place into conversation emerging, cutting-edge social science research evidencing everyday experiences of austerity and crisis across diverse European contexts. With a pan-European perspective, the collection explores the geographically differentiated, regionally distinctive and personally provoking nature of these experiences via case studies from different states, regions, localities, cities and communities. In doing so, we aim to offer key thinking and evidence of the multiscalar nature of personal, local and family experiences of austerity and crisis, and so too the relational impact of austerity and crisis on lived experiences.

Furthermore, we are interested in not just what everyday experiences of austerity look like, but also in how they are imagined and lived with over time, including how they shape and are shaped by socio-spatial inequalities. We ask: How is austerity lived in and lived with? How is it felt on the ground, and by whom? And what can we learn from taking a European perspective? In what follows, we outline key scholarship across the social sciences on austerity from throughout Europe, as well as that which has focused on lived experiences. We also provide a summary of the contributions within the collection and the themes by which they are arranged.

Austerity across Europe

Austerity comes in many forms, with local, regional and national particularities in how austerity policies are adopted and the impact they have (see Farnsworth and Irving 2012). However, what connects approaches and fiscal measures that come under this umbrella is that they involve the retraction of public spending with the specific aim of reducing a national deficit. There is a general consensus within social and political science literatures that austerity cuts have been pursued with most enthusiasm in some parts of Europe, namely Southern Europe (Italy, Greece, Portugal, Spain), the UK and Ireland (see Farnsworth and Irving 2012; Knight and Stewart 2016; Matsaganis and Leventi 2014). Here, the impacts of these fiscal measures are deep and pervasive across employment, housing, health, social care, welfare, education and more, as well as having implications for marginalised groups and communities (see Bassel and Emejulu 2017; Eurofound 2017). Furthermore, while the socio-spatial differentiations in austerity policies are highly interesting, with this collection our interest lies in the *everyday* impacts of austerity, or rather how austerity is *lived with*, across a range of European contexts.

Although austerity is a global phenomenon, the case of Europe is an interesting one and provides our collection with parameters for discussion. Trends across Europe, while contextually significant, can be seen through increases in unemployment, growing wealth and intergenerational inequalities, and changing living circumstances and family arrangements (Christophers 2018; MacLeavy and Manley 2018). There are also important cross-European issues to consider, including but not limited to migration and refugee flows shaped by national and international economic policy and humanitarian disasters (Carastathis 2015); a rise in right-wing, authoritarian political movements, considered by some to be a backlash against migration and austerity cuts (Hall and Ince 2018; Moore and Forkert 2014); and growing dissatisfaction with governance by the European Union with related class and race tensions, including of course the recent Brexit referendum (Burrell and Schweyher 2019). Europe – here loosely defined according to cultural affiliation, various bodies of membership, and as a physical continent – is a highly topical and vibrant context by which to examine the impacts of austerity and economic crises.

Moreover, while there have been suggestions that austerity is 'ending' (see Raynor 2018), what this means in practice is lesser known. Not only have recent policies across Europe offered little in the way of reversing austerity cuts, but this also has been coupled with a lack of reinvestment in public services (Hall 2019). As emerging commentaries suggest, more focus should be placed on what ends in austerity: 'the absent, as well as the silenced and the muted' (Raynor 2018). And at the time of writing this introductory chapter, the unfolding crisis surrounding the COVID-19 pandemic is exposing the damage caused by years of austerity measures that have left public services underfunded and under-resourced (see Flesher Fominaya 2020). We are, therefore, particularly interested in the difference that the recent and ongoing era of austerity has made for the everyday lives and futures of people living in Europe.

Lived experiences of austerity and economic crises

There has been increased interest among social scientists in how recent years of austerity and economic crises have shaped everyday lives. This has also led to reconceptualisations of what is meant by austerity. In the preceding section we drew on a definition that refers mainly to state financial policy. However, austerity has another meaning: it is understood as a condition of severe simplicity and restraint. Understanding austerity as having these interconnecting meanings then allows us to think through austerity as simultaneously a condition of the personal and the social (Hall 2019; Hitchen 2016; Stenning 2020). These definitions also hint at the multi-scalar nature of austerity (Pimlott-Wilson and Hall 2017), an intimacy that is at once local and global in its effects (also see Oswin and Olund 2010). Here we are also reminded of Dyck's (2005, p. 234) observations that 'attention to the local . . . provides a methodological entry point to theorising the operation of processes at various scales – from the body to the global'. With this collection, we establish dialogue and discussion between these multiple scales of austerity politics and experiences across Europe.

A growing body of scholarship across human geography, sociology, education, social policy and more illustrates the importance of examining austerity as a multi-scalar, lived experience. Examples include García-Lamarca and Kaika (2016) on mortgage debt and the financialisation of housing in Spain, which they conceptualise as a form of biopolitics, and mortgages as a biopolitical tool. As they explain,

> mortgage debt securitisation significantly changed the performance of mort-gage contracts as biopolitics, mutated what used to be experienced as an embodied and often personalised debt relationship (usually with a clerk or director of a local bank branch) into a disembodied debt relationship with an opaque and unreachable global financial entity.
>
> (García-Lamarca and Kaika 2016, p. 314)

Garthwaite (2016a, p. 148) makes similar observations about the traversal of spa-tial politics from her ethnographic research in a UK foodbank. She notes how media stories 'are fuelling the idea that foodbank users are in some way to blame for having to ask for a foodbank parcel', and that such dichotomous representa-tions of poverty (i.e. the deserving and undeserving poor) then 'manifest them-selves in the lived experiences of people using the foodbank'. Arampatzi (2017, p. 2156), writing from the Greek context, argues that residents are rethinking the outcomes and possibilities of the recent global financial crisis via solidarity tactics and community organising 'from below' – itself a direct reference to scales of austerity resistance.

What these and many other rich contributions (too many to name, in fact!) illustrate is that statistics can only tell a partial story, and there is real value in developing approaches and methodologies to elicit detail on such lived experi-ences. They also remind us of how interconnected austerity experiences can be. For instance, it is hard, if unnecessary, to separate findings on housing or employ-ment, either from one another or from other concerns such as intergenerational wealth or increasing care burdens (also see Holloway and Pimlott-Wilson 2016; MacLeavy 2011). In part because of the depth and breadth of these lived experi-ences, and that austerity does not appear to be going away any time soon, the subject matter of this book remains a burgeoning area of research interest. This collection therefore brings together writings by scholars who have been research-ing this topic for a long time with new voices and analyses. We aim to synthesise this work, to provide distinctly European perspectives and thereby to consolidate this vibrant and significant field of research.

Intergenerational relations and exchanges

The intergenerational features of austerity are of intense interest and debate in academic, policy and media forums. Whether in discussions about cuts to social care provision for the elderly and children alike (Power and Hall 2018), con-cerns about generations sandwiched by caring responsibilities (Pearson and Elson 2015) or tensions between the politics of young and older voters (Team Future et al. 2017), intergenerationality is a common theme across austere international contexts (also see Horton et al. in press). Entanglements of intergenerational-ity and austerity emerge in many forms, through the day-to-day experiences, conditions and impacts of austerity; in the form of dreams, hopes and imaginaries shaped by austerity; and are produced by formal and informal political processes and decisions (Kretsos 2014). That is to say, the intergenerational features of austerity are plural and plentiful and are 'lived' in various ways. Furthermore, cross-generational relations and exchanges may in some cases engender a sense of interdependence and solidarity, whereas in others they may unearth tensions and resentments. The intergenerational implications of austerity cannot therefore be understood out of place or in isolation, given the multitude of intersectionalities with other social categories and experiences according to race, class, gender, sexuality, disability and so forth (see Ginn 2013; Hopkins and Pain 2007; McDowell 2012; Tarrant 2018).

The chapters in the first themed section of this collection interrogate ideas about intergenerationality in different ways, but all mobilise around an understanding of generational relations beyond simply exploring dualistic, book-end approaches (also see Tarrant 2013; Vanderbeck 2007). The authors work through complex accounts of austerity in the present, but also as to how this connects to previous cycles of crisis, recession and poverty, and how these might be used as life-course markers for current generations reflecting back upon such experiences (see Hörschelmann 2011; Jupp et al. 2019; Knight and Stewart 2016). Moreover, intergenerational differences can be understood as more than individualised and personal experiences, but also as providing insight into deep-seated structural inequalities in matters such as housing, wealth and employment (Christophers 2018; MacLeavy and Manley 2018; Pimlott-Wilson 2017). An intergenerational perspective then also offers an insight into the temporality of austerity, or rather, austeri*ties* (see Horton 2016). Moreover, the intergenerational relations and exchanges that form the focus of these chapters can be noted in various guises. Whether in the provisioning of material things, the sharing of political sentiments, or in co-presence in community spaces, intergenerational concerns are provoked within all lived experiences of austerity.

In Chapter 2, Rebecca O'Connell, Abigail Knight, Julia Brannen and Silje Elisabeth Skuland open the section with their discussion of food, family and poverty. Drawing on data collected using mixed methods across the UK and Norway, they examine the experiences of children and young people in low-income families eating out with friends and the challenges and exclusions they face. They identify a complex but significant relationship between food and sociability, and that austerity measures can limit important avenues for young people to engage in social participation. In Chapter 3, Daniela Sime and Rebecca Reynolds also hone in on youth experiences of poverty and hardship, this time focused on the Scottish context. Focus groups with young people from within some of Glasgow's most deprived communities reveal how austerity policies have led to everyday humiliations and degradations for this group. However, as they illustrate, stigma can become internalised as a personal attribute, leading to the creation of a certain genre of neoliberal selfhood.

Writing from the context of urban Ireland, in Chapter 4 Sander van Lanen explores the particularities of city life for disadvantaged young people in Dublin and Cork. A comparative approach, involving interviews with young people living in deprived neighbourhoods, reveals the necessity to consider place-specific experiences in the urban landscape of austerity. Class, age and place are shown to work together to mediate young people's experiences of austerity and reveal poignant feelings of not-belonging due to structural urban inequalities related to housing and costs of living. Taking a relational approach to intergenerationality, in Chapter 5 Maria Prats Ferret, Mireia Baylina and Anna Ortiz Guitart explore the impact of economic crisis on children in Catalonia. With data from reports from non-governmental organisations and governmental institutions, they illustrate how the lives of many families in the region have been subject to severe forms of poverty and social exclusion. In particular, it is telling how all the data they analyse acknowledge the significant impacts on children, both directly and indirectly. Together, these four chapters identify how an intergenerational lens is one which speaks to broader societal trends and concerns around social relations and exchanges but which are manifest in personal and collective lives.

Ways of coping through crises

The impacts of austerity are characterised by social and spatial unevenness (Greer-Murphy 2017), which has raised questions about the ability of different groups and communities to deal with or 'get by' during austere conditions. Structural inequalities mean that access to resources – whether material, practical, financial or emotional – during times of austerity are also socially and spatially differentiated (Hall 2019). However, poverty and hardship remain tightly interwoven with stigma and shame, individualisation and responsibilisation (Garthwaite 2016b; Holdsworth 2017; Valentine and Harris 2014). These political and personal concerns can become reified and normalised through the uses and re-uses of certain terminologies. Recent years, especially since the introduction of austerity policies across Europe, have seen the rise in discourses about 'resilience', referring to the ability to weather unfortunate circumstances (economic, environmental, social). People and communities are encouraged to be resilient and to take responsibility for their own resilience as opposed to relying on state support (Harrison 2013). The concept of resilience then takes on a new life in austerity, because the literal meaning of austerity is the retrenchment of state spending, to pay off the national debt, and with it a retrenchment of state responsibility.

Similar sentiments and debates can be traced back to heated dialogues about 'coping strategies' over 20 years ago. Social scientists levelled sharp critiques at the uses (and misuses) of this type of language as militaristic and masculinist, and presuming a type of calculated logic that does not map onto everyday practices (Edwards and Ribbens 1991; Morgan 1989). Furthermore, as Edwards and Ribbens (1991, p. 480) succinctly explain, it 'imputes objectives which the individuals within a situation themselves would not recognise'. Alternative phrases, such as 'ways of coping' (Edwards and Ribbens 1991) and 'getting by' (Harrison 2013; McCrone 1994) have been suggested as a means of conveying the various possibilities of living in and through experiences of poverty and hardship.

Nevertheless, the *ways* in which people cope (or not), how and if they survive or thrive, remain of particular interests to scholars and policy makers alike. This is not so much in a bid to responsibilise citizens for their own actions and choices, but more to trace the lived impacts of austerity as they bear down on some of society's most marginalised groups.

In Chapter 6, Serena Romano explores urban solidarity in Naples, Italy, with economic recession as the backdrop. The spontaneous transformation of a former hospital as a space for solidarity and self-help provides an inspirational reading about how communities get by through collective action and interdependence. The author argues, however, that such spaces have become pillars of the community, when austerity measures served to accelerate poverty and deprivation in the city, and that founders are calling out for sustainable, state-led alternatives. Chapter 7 considers men's hidden participation in family caring responsibilities in the UK. Anna Tarrant argues that austerity provides a space for re-gendering care, with revised distributions of reproductive labour. Using the novel method of qualitative secondary analysis, her findings challenge long-held stereotypes of men in low-income families and localities as being uncaring, showing how varied engagements of fatherhood are a key resource for families getting by in austerity. Chapter 8 by Christos Koutsampelas, Sofia N. Andreou, Evangelia Papaloi, and Kostas Dimopoulos explores the case of economic crisis and fiscal episodes in Cyprus, with a focus on affected families with children. With their analysis of European data sources, they identify three key drivers that lead to some children and families being most affected and how they get by: parents' participation in the labour market, the generosity of income support to families with children and household structure. As well as offering a narrative for the impacts of austerity in Cyprus, the authors also gesture towards best practice and anti-poverty policies to actively address and counteract the adverse effects of economic crises on children and their families.

Chapter 9 by Sally Lloyd-Evans and the Whitley Researchers explores the politics and realities of 'beyond coping'. With particular focus on entanglements of neighbourhood identities, relationality and socio-spatial stigma in times of austerity, they draw on a wealth of data collected as part of a creative, grounded participatory project. Deploying these rich findings, they illustrate how entrenched place-based stigmatism can also provide a space for a politics of resistance. Building on this discussion, in Chapter 10 Kirsten Koop examines how hopeful alternative lifeworlds have emerged in France. Where arguably less impacted by austerity cuts than many other European countries due to a different policy approach, it is contended that community-led projects and grassroots organising have led to forms of resistance via a politics of degrowth and postcapitalism. With findings from alternative collectivities in rural mountain regions in the southeast of France, the chapter proposes how economic crises can be moments for contemplating and transmitting alternative values and practices to the incumbent (capitalist, neoliberal) system. Through rich empirical examples, the chapters in this section also reveal how crises are felt on multiple fronts, and that austerity can work as both a backdrop and a catalyst for these processes.

Community, civic and state infrastructures

The impacts of austerity on everyday life are felt at a range of scales and across various spaces, including the domestic, institutional and community. Public spending cuts have been implemented in many ways, and one significant feature has been the sharp retraction – and continued disinvestment – in civic infrastructures. Ranging from local government to third sector and local communities, in many ways these infrastructures have operated as an intermediary through which families and communities have been hit indirectly. This can be seen in the loss of public spaces and services, such as libraries, children's centres and youth clubs (Horton 2016; Jupp 2013; Penny 2019). Employees, volunteers and users alike have witnessed the effects of austerity measures on their communities, compounding policies levelled in other areas such as welfare, health care and social care. These measures, as noted earlier, have also tended to hit the same groups of people, time and again.

Moreover, understanding the changes that austerity and economic crises have made to collective infrastructures is also key in highlighting the spectrum of emplaced effects. Often, social spaces in communities, funded by local government, offer 'the place and structures and buildings or clubs that enable people to get together, meet, socialise, volunteer, and co-operate' (Gregory 2018, p. 11). The loss of these spaces also means the loss of a whole set of informal activities and interactions that uphold civic relations: sharing economies, care work, volunteering, and more. For Berlant (2016, p. 393), these spaces are also a form of commons: 'the living mediation of what organizes life: the lifeworld of structure. Roads, bridges, schools, food chains, finance systems, prisons, families, districts, norms'. There are, therefore, deep and widely felt reverberations of the erosion of civic spaces and practices, which have a significant role in how austerity is experienced on the ground.

In Chapter 11, Irene Hardill and Roger O'Sullivan explore the role of e-government in a time of austerity, with some governments aiming to deliver more of their public services online. Findings from the Northern Ireland and the Republic of Ireland reveal how such changes can enhance digital and social divides, with older people in particular being excluded from access and engagement with state infrastructure. The chapter presents an important critique of what seems to be the normalising of austerity through e-government and digital platforms, which also has the effect of compounding already existing inequalities. With a focus on labour practices, in Chapter 12 Daniel Škobla and Richard Filčák consider the everyday experience of unemployed and poverty-stricken Roma in Slovakia. Using the framework of 'labour activism', they provide a critique of various activities that have become normalised in years of austerity that are deployed by the state as motivations and incentives for these groups to become job ready and ultimately secure employment. One key and significant outcome of these programmes, they find, is that they have a punitive effect on local Roma communities and as a result serve to widen deep-rooted social inequalities.

Governing urban marginality and outmigration in Hungary forms the focus of Chapter 13 by Cecília Kovai and Tünde Virág. In the context of social fragmentation, economic downturn and growing unemployment, they examine the role of local government in managing these processes and tensions. As their findings from the town of Kallóbánya illustrate, long-term economic crises and austerity can significantly shape relationships between local institutional state powers and marginalised groups, particularly where such groups become more visible as a result of changing population demographics. Closing the collection is Chapter 14 by Eleanor Jupp, with reflections on anti-austerity activism in the UK. Connecting to earlier discussed themes, her contribution draws on research concerning closures of Sure Start Children's Centres, and what she terms 'acts of citizenship' as a form of resistance to austerity cuts. Using detailed participant vignettes, she illustrates how 'story-telling' can be a powerful tool for offering ways to resist austerity cuts to public and community services.

Arranged around these three cross-cutting themes, the book draws together new and emerging multidisciplinary research exploring everyday life in Europe during a time of austerity and economic crisis. With a focus on the quotidian, the collection explores how austerity is lived and experienced, often at the same time as other significant social, political and personal change. Alongside this, we examine how austerity is entrenched in past, present and future experiences and inequalities across Europe. Evidencing the inequalities produced and provoked by these processes, while witnessing how individuals, families and communities 'get by', the collection also envisages potential hopeful, affirmative socio-political futures in the midst of profoundly troubling, uncertain times.

References

Arampatzi, A. (2017) 'The spatiality of counter-austerity politics in Athens, Greece: Emergent "urban solidarity spaces"', *Urban Studies*, 54(9): 2155–2171.

Bassel, L. and Emejulu, A. (2017) *Minority women and austerity: Survival and resistance in France and Britain*, Bristol: Policy Press.

Berlant, L. (2016) 'The commons: Infrastructures for troubling times', *Environment and Planning D: Society and Space*, 34(3): 393–419.

Burrell, K. and Schweyher, M. (2019) 'Conditional citizens and hostile environments: Polish migrants in pre-Brexit Britain', *Geoforum*, 106: 193–201.

Carastathis, A. (2015) 'The politics of austerity and the affective economy of hostility: Racialised gendered violence and crises of belonging in Greece', *Feminist Review*, 109(1): 73–95.

Christophers, B. (2018) 'Intergenerational inequality? Labour, capital, and housing through the ages', *Antipode*, 50(1): 101–121.

Dyck, I. (2005) 'Feminist geography, the "everyday", and local-global relations: Hidden spaces of place-making', *Canadian Geographer*, 49: 233–245.

Edwards, R. and Ribbens, J. (1991) 'Meanderings around 'strategy: A research note on the strategic discourse in the lives of women', *Sociology*, 25(3): 477–489.

Eurofound (2017) *European quality of life survey 2016: Quality of life, quality of public services, and quality of society*, Luxembourg: Publications Office of the European Union.

Eurofound (2019) *Quality of life: Household composition and wellbeing*, Luxembourg: Publications Office of the European Union.

Farnsworth, K. and Irving, Z. (2012) 'Varieties of crisis, varieties of austerity: Social policy in challenging times', *Journal of Poverty and Social Justice*, 20(2): 133–147.

Flesher Fominaya, C. (2020) 'How austerity measures hurt the Covid-19 response', Oxford University Blog, https://blog.oup.com/2020/04/how-austerity-measures-hurt-the-covid-19-response/, accessed 28 April 2020.

García-Lamarca, M. and Kaika, M. (2016) '"Mortgaged lives": The biopolitics of debt and housing financialisation', *Transactions of the Institute of British Geographers*, 41: 313–327.

Garthwaite, K. (2016a) *Hunger pains: Life inside foodbank Britain*, Bristol: Policy Press.

Garthwaite, K. (2016b) 'Stigma, shame and "people like us": An ethnographic study of foodbank use in the UK', *Journal of Poverty and Social Justice*, 24(3): 277–289.

Ginn, J. (2013) 'Austerity and inequality: Exploring the impact of cuts in the UK by gender and age', *Research on Ageing and Social Policy*, 1(1): 28–53.

Greer-Murphy, A. (2017) 'Austerity in the United Kingdom: The intersections of spatial and gendered inequalities', *Area*, 49(1): 122–124.

Gregory, D. (2018) *Skittled out? The collapse and revival of England's social infrastructure*, London: Local Trust.

Hall, S.M. (2019) *Everyday life in austerity: Family, friends and intimate relations*, Basingstoke: Palgrave Macmillan.

Hall, S.M. and Ince, A. (2018) 'Introduction: Sharing economies in times of crisis', in A. Ince and S.M. Hall (Eds.), *Sharing economies in times of crisis: Practices, politics and possibilities*, London: Routledge.

Harrison, E. (2013) 'Bouncing back? Recession, resilience and everyday lives', *Critical Social Policy*, 33(1): 97–113.

Heath, S. and Calvert, E. (2013) 'Gifts, loans and intergenerational support for young adults', *Sociology*, 47: 1120–1135.

Hitchen, E. (2016) 'Living and feeling the austere', *New Formations*, 87: 102–118.

Holdsworth, C. (2017) 'The cult of experience: Standing out from the crowd in an era of austerity', *Area*, 49(3): 296–302.

Holloway, S. and Pimlott-Wilson, H. (2016) 'New economy, neoliberal state and professionalized parenting: Mothers' labour market engagement and state support for social reproduction in class-differentiated Britain', *Transactions of the Institute of British Geographers*, 41(4): 376–388.

Hopkins, P. and Pain, R. (2007) 'Geographies of age: Thinking relationally', *Area*, 39(3): 287–294.

Hörschelmann, K. (2011) 'Theorising life transitions: Geographical perspectives', *Area*, 43(4): 378–383.

Horton, J. (2016) 'Anticipating service withdrawal: Young people in spaces of neoliberalisation, austerity and economic crisis', *Transactions of the Institute of British Geographers*, 41(4): 349–362.

Horton, J. and Kraftl, P. (2012) 'Clearing out a cupboard: Memory, materiality and transitions', in O. Jones & J. Garde-Hansen (Eds.), *Geography and memory: Explorations in identity, place and becoming*, Basingstoke: Palgrave Macmillan, pp. 25–44.

Horton, J., Pimlott-Wilson, H. and Hall, S.M. (in press) *Growing up and getting by: International perspectives on childhood and youth in hard times*, Bristol: Policy Press.

Jupp, E. (2013) 'Enacting parenting policy? The hybrid spaces of Sure Start Children's Centres', *Children's Geographies*, 11(2): 173–187.

Jupp, E., Bowlby, S., Franklin, J. and Hall, S.M. (2019) *The new politics of home: Housing, gender and care in times of crisis*, Bristol: Policy Press.

Knight, D.M. and Stewart, C. (2016) 'Ethnographies of austerity: Temporality, crisis and affect in Southern Europe', *History and Anthropology*, 27(1): 1–18.

Kretsos, L. (2014) 'Youth policy in austerity Europe: The case of Greece', *International Journal of Adolescence and Youth*, 19(1): 35–47.

MacLeavy, J. (2011) 'A "new" politics of austerity, workfare and gender? The UK coalition government's welfare reform proposals', *Cambridge Journal of Regions, Economy & Society*, 4: 355–367.

MacLeavy, J. and Manley, D. (2018) 'Rediscovering the lost middle: Intergenerational inheritances and economic inequality in urban and regional research', *Regional Studies*, 52(10): 1435–1446.

Matsaganis, M. and Leventi, C. (2014) 'The distributional impact of austerity and the recession in Southern Europe', *South European Society and Politics*, 19(3): 393–412.

McCrone, D. (1994) 'Getting by and making out in Kirkcaldy', in M. Anderson, F. Bechhofer and J. Gershuny (Eds.), *The social and political economy of the household*, Oxford: Oxford University Press, pp. 68–99.

McDowell, L. (2012) 'Post-crisis, post-Ford and post-gender? Youth identities in an era of austerity', *Journal of Youth Studies*, 15(5): 573–590.

Moore, P. and Forkert, K. (2014) 'Class and panic in British immigration', *Capital and Class*, 38(3): 497–505.

Morgan, D.H. (1989) 'Strategies and sociologists: A comment on crow', *Sociology*, 23(1): 25–29.

ONS (2014) 'Young adults living with their parents', www.ons.gov.uk/peoplepopulation andcommunity/birthsdeathsandmarriages/families/datasets/youngadultslivingwiththeir-parents, accessed 14 December 2019.

Oswin, N. and Olund, E. (2010) 'Governing intimacy', *Environment and Planning D: Society and Space*, 28(1): 60–67.

Pearson, R. and Elson, D. (2015) 'Transcending the impact of the financial crisis in the United Kingdom: Towards Plan F – a feminist economic strategy', *Feminist Review*, 109: 8–30.

Penny, J. (2019) '"Defend the ten": Everyday dissensus against the slow spoiling of Lambeth's libraries', *Environment and Planning D: Society and Space*. https://doi.org/10.1177/0263775819893685

Pimlott-Wilson, H. (2017) 'Individualising the future: The emotional geographies of neoliberal governance in young people's aspirations', *Area*, 49(3): 288–295.

Pimlott-Wilson, H. and Hall, S.M. (2017) 'Everyday experiences of economic change: Repositioning geographies of children, youth and families', *Area*, 49(3): 258–265.

Power, A. and Hall, E. (2018) 'Placing care in times of austerity', *Social & Cultural Geography*, 19(3): 303–313.

Raynor, R. (2018) 'Intervention – Changing the question from "the end of austerity" to "what ends in austerity?"', *Antipode Foundation*, https://antipodefoundation.org/2018/11/19/what-ends-in-austerity/, accessed 19 December 2018.

Stenning, A. (2020) 'Feeling the squeeze: Towards a psychosocial geography of austerity in low-to-middle income families', *Geoforum*, 110: 200–210.

Tarrant, A. (2013) 'Grandfathering as spatio-temporal practice: Conceptualizing performances of ageing masculinities in contemporary familial carescapes', *Social & Cultural Geography*, 14(2): 192–210.

Tarrant, A. (2018) 'Care in an age of austerity: Men's care responsibilities in low-income families', *Ethics and Social Welfare*, 12(1): 34–48.

Team Future, Pottinger, L. and Hall, S.M. (2017) '"Have you heard that young people are RECLAIMing their future?": Towards a bold, ethical and hopeful politics of Brexit and beyond', *Local Economy*, 32(3): 257–263.

The Guardian (2014a) 'Young adults living at home: Has your bedroom changed?' www.theguardian.com/money/2014/jan/21/young-adults-living-at-home-has-your-bedroom-changed, accessed 14 December 2019.

The Guardian (2014b) 'Young adults living at home: Your pictures and stories', www.theguardian.com/money/guardianwitness-blog/gallery/2014/jan/23/young-adults-living-at-home-your-pictures-and-stories, accessed 14 December 2019.

Valentine, G. and Harris, C. (2014) 'Strivers vs skivers: Class prejudice and the demonization of dependency in everyday life', *Geoforum*, 53(May): 84–92.

Vanderbeck, R.M. (2007) 'Intergenerational geographies: Age relations, segregation and re-engagements', *Geography Compass*, 1(2): 200–221.

Wilkinson, E. and Ortega-Alcázar, I. (2017) 'A home of one's own? Housing welfare for 'young adults' in times of austerity', *Critical Social Policy*, 37(3): 1–19.

Part I

Intergenerational relations and exchanges

2 Eating out, sharing food and social exclusion

Young people in low-income families in the UK and Norway

Rebecca O'Connell, Abigail Knight, Julia Brannen and Silje Elisabeth Skuland

In the wake of the global recession of 2008 and so-called austerity measures implemented in some European countries, levels of relative and absolute poverty have risen among families with children (Gaisbauer et al., 2019). However poverty is defined, access to decent food is at its heart (Dowler and O'Connor, 2012: 45). While much research on food poverty has focused on compromises made in food quantity and quality, to be excluded from customary practices of sociability, including those related to food, is a dimension of relative poverty (Townsend, 1979; Leather, 1996; Lang, 1997; Dowler and Leather, 2000; Healy, 2019; O'Connell; Owen, Padley et al., 2019). Since eating the same food as others is 'a basic mark of belonging' (Stone, 1988: 71), being unable to participate in customary food-related activities, such as showing hospitality or accepting invitations to eat out, may result in feelings of shame (Walker, 2014). In order to avoid these, people may engage in strategies such as 'saving face' (Goffman, 1967) or withdrawing from social life.

The practice of eating, and 'eating out' in particular, arguably falls between conspicuous and inconspicuous consumption (Veblen, 1899; Evans, 2018). While much eating may be quotidian, unremarkable and mundane, eating out is in many countries a commercialised, hence market-mediated, experience. While, in the UK at least, eating out has become more ordinary (Paddock et al., 2017), modes of eating out may still be an important form of class distinction, including for families (e.g. Wills et al., 2011). Food also acts as a cultural symbol of belonging and marker of identity for children and young people, as they engage with food to forge and reject social relations with family and peers (James, 1979; James et al., 2009; Brembeck, 2009). Food may 'other' some children, for example, in the UK through the stigma that is attached to 'free school meals' (Gill and Sharma, 2004; Farthing, 2012; O'Connell; Knight and Brannen et al., 2019). However, their parents and carers go to great lengths to avoid children being seen as 'different' (Pugh, 2009; Martens, 2018). As children grow older and gain more autonomy, they eat in an increasing range of contexts, depending on finances and where they live. Such activities involving 'commensality', that is eating with other people (Sobal and Nelson, 2003), may be important in establishing and cementing their social networks (Backett-Milburn et al., 2011).

While sociological studies of consumption have often emphasised its role in hierarchies of 'distinction' (Bourdieu, 1984), sociologists of childhood note how children, particularly in low-income families, often look to consumer culture to establish a sense of belonging (Pugh, 2009). However, while some research has explored the impact of consumerism on children across national contexts (e.g. Nairn/IPSOS MORI, 2011), less is known about this in relation to food and eating. Indeed, studies of young people's consumption patterns have instead tended to focus on 'clothes, music, film, games, dance, alcohol, drugs and so on' (Bugge, 2015: 71). Yet both childhood and eating are 'deeply steeped in the consumer culture of our time' (Ridge, 2002:37). While there is evidence that people have reduced their expectations about being able to eat out in times of recession and austerity (sometimes termed 'adapted preferences') (Gordon et al., 2013), consensual approaches to defining living standards suggest being able to meet friends for a drink or a bite to eat from time to time is still considered important (Davis et al., 2012).

This chapter draws on the qualitative research from a mixed-methods European Research Council–funded study, Families and Food in Hard Times (grant number 337977).[1] It will examine the degree to which children and young people aged 11–15 years in low-income families participate in, or are excluded from, eating out with friends and how they manage this in two European countries: the UK and Norway.

The countries were selected to provide for 'a contrast of contexts' (Kohn, 1987) in relation to the presence or absence of austerity policies. Prior to the 2008 financial crisis, the UK was already a very unequal country in terms of the distribution of household income. Since 2010, successive governments have cut benefits and funding to local authorities to spend on public services. These have hit many British people hard, particularly those already on low incomes including large and lone parent families. Norway, by contrast, is a very prosperous and egalitarian society (Walker, 2014: 177), with a sovereign wealth fund and generous welfare system, that was barely affected by the financial crisis. The Nordic model includes a comprehensive welfare state and multi-level collective bargaining, with a high percentage of the workforce unionised. However, it is also the case that the tradition of full employment and universal welfare provision has 'relegated social assistance to the margins of social programmes' (Gough, 1996: 12; Lødemel, 1992; Lødemel and Schulte, 1992), and policies concerning labour market activation are central in ensuring entitlement to benefits, ideas that gained ground in the 1990s (Richards et al., 2016). Those most reliant on benefits in Norway account for families in the lowest income group and disproportionately represent ethnic minorities, many of whom entered Norway under its refugee quota system (Statistics Norway, 2019). Meanwhile, poverty is also associated with one-parent households. In 2017, 30.1% of one-parent households belonged to the low-income group compared to 8.8% of dual-parent households (Statistics Norway, 2018).

The discursive contexts of the countries are also different. In Britain, a neoliberal regime, the dominant discourse that 'justifies' austerity measures is that people living in poverty are to blame for their plight, and that many are 'scroungers', 'sponging' off the state, 'frauds', unwilling to work and making the 'wrong choices' (Knight et al., 2018: 207). In Norway, Walker and Chase (2014: 11) found that the use of stigmatising language to describe those on low incomes was 'more muted' compared to other countries, although criticism existed of the 'work shy' who were seen to exploit 'the generous benefit system to support an alternative lifestyle'.

The social and economic contexts of the two countries relate to patterns of eating out. In order to understand the social exclusion of consumers it is necessary to assess what constitutes 'normal' consumption for a particular society and social group. While there are differences in how 'eating out' is defined (Lund et al., 2017: 24) and a lack of up-to-date research that compares the level of commercialisation of eating across the two contexts, there is some evidence that the countries differ, with less (although increasing) time spent eating out in Norway than in the UK (Warde et al., 2007; Lund et al., 2017). More recently, European statistics on the consumption expenditure of private households (Household Budget Survey [HBS]) suggest that the proportion of household expenditure on 'restaurants and hotels' in 2017 is higher in the UK at 9.6% (9.2% in 2007) than in Norway, where it is around 7% (5.9% in 2007).

However, there is less evidence about children's eating-out behaviour or expenditure in the age group (11–15 years) in which we are interested. In the UK, unpublished analysis of the National Diet and Nutrition Survey (Hamilton, forthcoming) suggests that being able to eat out occasionally is a norm for the majority of young people (aged 11–16 years) but that income plays a part in their participation. In Norway, Sletten et al. (2004: 65) note that young people in poor households spend 20% less money than average, but not significantly less on cafés and fast food. Furthermore, in the UK (Warde and Martens, 1997) as well as in Norway (Bugge, 2015; Lund et al., 2017), 'youth' are said to eat out more often than the adult population, albeit this group is older than the age group we are interested in here.

It is also the case that urban environments 'offer much easier access to a varied set of cafes and restaurants' and that 'life-styles in big cities are likely therefore to differ from those in less urbanized areas' (Lund et al., 2017: 31). Hence an 'urbanisation effect' is likely to exist in both countries (Bell and Valentine, 1997), so that availability of cafés and restaurants and shops – hence opportunities for and, possibly, expectations of, eating out – are reduced outside the city.

Following a brief outline of the study and its research methods, the chapter analyses the reports of children in low-income families concerning eating out with friends: the types of activities they engage in and foods they eat, and how they manage taking part in, and being excluded from, eating activities in the context of a lack of family income in these two contrasting countries. It seeks to understand their similar and divergent experiences in relation to the contexts in which they are living.

The study

Families and Food in Hard Times is a comparative study in the sense that it applied the same research methods in different national contexts (Hantrais, 2009:

15). Qualitative interviews were carried out with children and young people, predominantly aged 11–15[2] years, and their parents or carers in families that were on low incomes and struggling to 'make ends meet': 45 families (51 children) in the UK and 43 families (48 children) in Norway.[3] Around two-thirds of the families lived in the capital cities while a third was drawn from contrasting, less urbanised areas marked by social deprivation. In the UK, 30 families lived in an inner London borough (36 children) and 15 families in a coastal town of South East England. In Norway, the sample included 28 families from different urban areas in Oslo (29 children) and 15 families (19 children) from rural areas in non-urban eastern Norway.

Interviews asked participants to recall the last school and non-school day, and the foods eaten during these days. Follow-up questions were around a number of themes, including 'eating with others and socialising – exclusion/inclusion'. With some children we also used a vignette to prompt/elicit talk about being left out of eating with friends due to a lack of money. Other sections of the interview asked, inter alia, about resources (money of their own) and shopping. Interviews were, in nearly all cases and with permission, recorded and transcribed into English or Norwegian. Excerpts were written up in (or translated into) English, along with researchers' field notes, into 'case summaries' using standardised templates that included thematic headings for the family (parent) and child. The case summaries formed the raw data upon which the comparative analysis is based.

The samples in each country included a range of ethnicities and family types (lone vs couple). Slightly more boys than girls took part: UK, 21 girls and 30 boys; Norway, 20 girls and 24 boys. The sample was skewed towards the older age range (31/51 age 13+ years in the UK and 27/48 in Norway).

Eating out and types of food

Despite their low incomes, most of the parents gave their children some pocket money and, in both countries, it was more common for children to have some money, if only irregularly, than none. However, except for one case, none of the young people in Norway was paid as much as the national average, which in 2013 was 127 kroner per week (DNB, 2018). Around a third of children in the UK and about a quarter of children in Norway did not have access to any money. In the UK, children in the sample were therefore worse off than nationally, where less than a fifth of children do not receive pocket money (Main and Bradshaw, 2014).

In both countries, those who did have access to money used at least some – and sometimes all – of it to engage in eating out with friends as part, or the focus, of their activities. We distinguished between buying 'snacks', which included cold foods such as sweets, chocolate and crisps, and 'eating out', which included food consumed in cafés, restaurants and hot food eaten 'outside', on the street, such as buying chicken and chips or a kebab (Table 2.1). A clear, though not unexpected finding is that young people in both countries were much more likely to engage in eating-out activities in the urban compared to the non-urban areas. The problems of expensive transport and lack of local opportunities were mentioned by a number of children in both countries (Tisdall et al., 2006). In Norway, one two-parent family living in the rural area was on a relatively low income because the mother was on work assessment benefits and the father was in insecure employment, as a carpenter. Last year, the family almost halved their food budget when the father was temporarily laid off from work. Of the three children interviewed, only the eldest, 14-year-old Frida, was allowed to go to the local youth club as there was a 50 mph zone and no pavements between their home and 2.5 miles to the venue. In the coastal area in the UK, Callum, age 12, lived with his mother who was caring for two younger children and described herself as 'on the breadline'. Their home was in an area of the coastal town that was very isolated and his mother said was home to lots of 'wannabe gangsters'. They could not afford bus fares (there were no concessions for children during the rush hour) and Callum walked over a mile to school. He had few friends locally and his mother said she struggled to 'get him out'. In contrast, those children who lived in London and qualified for free bus travel often had more freedom to travel than their parents (O'Connell; Knight and Brannen et al., 2019).

But there were also stark differences between the countries. Surprisingly, given what parents said they spent on eating out, Table 2.1 shows that it was young people in Norway, particularly in Oslo, who most often said they did so. More young people in Norway ate out with friends (snacks purchased have been excluded here) than did those in the UK (26/48 compared to 17/51). Furthermore, fewer young people in Norway compared to those in the UK did not socialise around food at all (eat out or buy snacks with friends): 24/51 young people in the UK sample and 8/48 young people in the Norwegian sample. As Bugge (2015: 71) notes, 'fast food has been a particularly successful innovation in post war Norwegian cuisine. Young Norwegians eat considerably more fast food than the adult population'.

Table 2.1 Proportions in urban and non-urban areas in the UK and Norway who eat out with friends[4]

	UK		Norway	
	Urban	*Non-urban*	*Urban*	*Non-urban*
Eat out with friends (sit down and take-away, incl. chicken and chips)	15/36 (42%)	2/15 (13%)	22/29 (76%)	4/19 (21%)
Buy snacks only (biscuits, sweets, crisps, drink)	8/36 (22%)	2/15 (13%)	2/29 (7%)	2/19 (11%)
Do not socialise at all with food	13/36 (36%)	11/15 (73%)	3/29 (10%)	5/19 (26%)
Missing data	0	0	2/29 (7%)	8/19 (42%)
Totals	36	15	29	19
	51		48	

In terms of what they ate in the different places, generally (but not exclusively) the foods eaten by young people comprised snacks like biscuits, crisps, and cakes and sweets as well as 'fast' foods from globalised brands such as McDonald's and TGI Friday's and generic 'American' style foods – such as burgers, fries (or chips) and pizzas. But there were also differences between the countries. In Norway, kebabs were mentioned more often, and in the UK, chicken and chips.

When they ate out, children did so in a variety of places, including on the way to and from school, youth clubs (more prevalent in Norway than the UK and more popular among boys than girls), cafes, fast-food establishments and 'proper' restaurants. Notably the local garage (gas/petrol station) was mentioned a few times in the non-urban areas of both Norway and the UK. In both countries, children mentioned buying foods at school on some days and in shops and cafes adjacent to school, suggesting the importance of the commercialisation of the eating environments surrounding schools (Wills et al., 2018).

Overall, the finding that young people in low-income families in Norway are eating out more often than those in the UK is surprising, given what is known about the frequency with which adults report eating out in the two countries. However, it may reflect the depth of poverty among the UK families in the context of economic retrenchment that is reflected in the finding that around a third of the young people had no access to any money of their own. While in both countries parents placed importance on providing for children's social needs, even at the expense of their own material ones, young people's greater access to money and eating out may reflect an emphasis in Norway on the importance of social participation in general and on social activities for low-income children in particular (Fløtten, 2019). In Norway, sharing a meal or a snack with friends is emphasised as important for children, and this aspect of children's acculturation is prioritised by migrant parents (Skuland, 2019).

Socialising with less money – sharing and reciprocity

Young people in both countries described the ways they managed to socialise with food on a low income. These included 'planning ahead', 'saving' and 'juggling' money given for school lunches and transport, and using vouchers, special offers and ordering children's-sized meals.

In London, Maddy, age 16, who lived with her unemployed grandmother, was given £2 per day that was meant to supplement her school meals. However, she said she often saved it and used it to go out with friends as socialising was important to her. 'I can honestly say that most of my money goes on food'. She and her friends go to global eating outlets like McDonald's, Subway and Nando's, 'not fancy restaurants'.

In Norway, Ketil, a 13-year-old ethnic Norwegian boy, lives with his lone mother who has been unemployed for the last five years. They depend on the support and reciprocity of a strong friendship network but have also resorted to a foodbank (called the 'Poor House'). Ketil says that he sometimes goes to McDonald's. He and his friends use it as a kind of 'third place' (Oldenberg and Brissett,

1982). They go there not only to buy food but 'sometimes we go and sit in the far back, where the people there don't see us, just to relax a bit'. On his phone, Ketil also has apps that give him food/drinks at reduced prices. The Narvesen[5] app encourages you 'to buy three small chocolate to the price of one. Get three buns at the price of one and stuff like that'.

In both countries, a number of children talked about the importance of sharing and reciprocity. Charlie, for example, age 15, lives in a flat with his mother in inner London. Since his mother lost her job they have struggled financially, living on a low level of benefit, and have used a foodbank. Both mother and son go without enough decent food and are sometimes hungry. Charlie regularly goes to the local skate park with his friends but cannot usually eat with them because he lacks the money.

Charlie says his friends buy him food like 'chicken 'n' chips', or a snack, such as crisps, or a drink. However, their generosity has limits, '[they buy things] but not all the time, they don't just like blow out all their money . . . they ask, "do I like want anything?" or I ask them and "I'll pay you back"'. He says he repays them 'eventually, yeah'. His friends, who tend to be older and earn some money, are understanding of his predicament, 'they know they're like . . . they just tell me pay it back when you can . . . cos they know that I don't have a lot of money so . . .'.

In Central Eastern Oslo, another skater, Nils, age 12, is an ethnic Norwegian boy who also lives with his lone mother and no siblings. His mother, registered as 85% disabled, was dependent on benefits. Mentioning that he and his friends have eaten kebab together several times, usually in the summer time when they are out all day, Nils was asked if all his friends have money for kebabs and what they do if one of them cannot afford them. He said, 'they [who cannot afford it] are usually not coming, because first we meet at the skateboard park, right, and then after we ask like "are you joining to buy kebab", right, "wanna come buy kebab" and stuff and then only the ones who have money join'. He says that 'real friends' are the ones who share: 'You can do it [buy kebab for someone else] but then you have to be real friends'. He says that with 'real friends', 'it's who you have spent a lot of time with, it's a bit different'. He explains further that 'if I buy you a kebab then maybe he buys me one another time, that's how I use to do it'. Other children also said they had generous friends paying for meals or snacks seemingly without expecting any form of repayment.

Saving face

Young people also engaged in practices of 'saving face' (Goffman, 1967; Butler, 2017), that is they concealed the reasons they could not eat out from the interviewer and from their friends. In the UK, Danisha, a black British girl aged 11 years, lives in London with her mother and two siblings, both of whom have disabilities, and she helps look after. Her mother is unemployed as she cares for the younger children and is reliant on benefits. Danisha had been invited to a friend's house for a party on two occasions and also to the cinema. On each occasion, she says she 'forgot' to go. Similarly, Faith, a West African girl aged 15 years, lived with her lone father, who works for the National Health Service on a low wage; his tax credits were recently reduced significantly as part of benefit cuts. Faith was sometimes invited out with friends, but usually declined, because, she said, 'I don't really have enough money'. However, like many of the other young people we spoke to, Faith wanted to keep this to herself: 'I don't want to show them that, no, I don't have enough money. I say to them "no, I don't really want to come"'. When asked why she says this, she replies: 'Because I don't want them to see me as this person that is poor. And I say like I'm not poor, just like . . . for this time I don't have money to go out'.

Some young people argued that the food on offer was 'unhealthy' (Bugge, 2015). This may, of course, be an honest assessment. At the same time, some children who gave this reason also lacked the money to do otherwise. For example, 14-year-old Tavio, whose mother grew up in Norway, excused himself on health grounds. He lived in the rural area, with his mother and sister; another brother lived with the father because she could not afford to look after him. She had become unemployed after having been on sick leave for a year without recovering, and she avoids seeking additional help from the social security office to avoid shame. Instead she and Tavio both cut back on food at times. Asked about eating out with friends, he said, 'I don't like to walk into those kebab outlets because the only thing I smell is like food that's being fried and stuff like that. And I think it is nice to smell it and I want to eat it, but it is not healthy for you'. However, he also revealed that another reason for not wanting to go was that 'they'll feel sorry for me' and this is something he wants to avoid.

Despite significant differences between the two countries, then, in terms of social and economic context, the strategy employed by young people for avoiding shame is strikingly similar. As Walker et al. (2013) argue, research across diverse countries suggests that while it is culturally and socially nuanced, shame lies at the core of poverty, and concealment is a common way in which people seek to avoid revealing their situations to others.

Social exclusion

Lack of money to take part in social activities with friends had consequences for making friends, for sustaining friendships and for young people's self-esteem and sense of belonging.

Few of the children in Norway said explicitly that lacking money to eat out put a strain on friendship ties. However, as in the UK, social exclusion was discussed in relation to school lunches (Skuland, 2019; O'Connell; Knight and Brannen et al., 2019). Viviana, age 16, had recently moved to Central Eastern Oslo with her mother and siblings and had changed school. Her unemployed mother, a migrant, was struggling with expensive rent and with debt repayments from her previous marriage. Food was available for purchase at the school canteen, and her classmates also go to a grocery shop and kebab and sushi outlets nearby. 'In school, people go and buy food every day', Viviana says. However, she brings a packed lunch 'so that the money can go to something else'. While she does not articulate a link with her low income, she says 'it is hard to find good friends in a year'.

It was only in the UK that young people talked directly about feeling excluded. Bryony, a white British girl aged 13 years who lives with her brother and lone mother in the coastal area, is acutely aware of the differences between her access to money and that of some of her friends. She sometimes meets her friends at places like McDonald's but she rarely has the money to buy her own food; she says her mother gives her money 'whenever she can', but this is difficult as her mother is living on benefits and has experienced delays in their receipt. Bryony confesses that 'sometimes it's hard' not having the money to join in with her friends, and she goes on to suggest, without quite saying it, that she feels left out:

> It's . . . I don't know really, to be fair it's . . . don't know . . . I mean it's like they get all that and I have to be, like, there while they eat all their food or they get what they want. And . . . I don't know.

Shola, age 14, lives in the inner London area with her mother, a migrant, and a sibling. The family has no recourse to public funds (NRPF) as her mother's legal status is under review; they live on money, food and clothes given to them by the church, friends and charities. She is aware of young people from affluent homes who frequent expensive restaurants. This makes her feel 'different':

> I do have quite a few friends like that. They'll tell me about it and I'd feel left out a bit. So I just like nod and smile, probably walk away or something . . . it makes me feel different.

Shola describes how being poor makes you grow up fast, in particular how to handle money:

> You've just got to learn to be careful. It's like you've got to grow up a bit too fast . . . so you've got to learn to take care of yourself, learn where to go, where not to go, learn how to manage money and where to buy food and stuff like that. And to learn to keep yourself to yourself.

According to Shola, to avoid the shame of not having enough money it is important to learn not to reveal too much about your situation to others. As Goffman (1974: 122) suggests, by 'avoiding overtures of intimacy the individual can avoid the consequent obligation to divulge information'. Children often seek to hide their situations from others, since 'the personal and relational aspects of poverty can bring stigma, shame, sadness and the fear of being identified or isolated for being different' (Ridge, 2011: 82). Indeed, the partial or complete withdrawal from social life is a common strategy across different contexts for reducing the likelihood of experiencing shame (Walker et al., 2013: 228). While shame is individually felt, it is socially constructed and has social implications.

Conclusions

In both countries, children described ways they managed to 'join in' with social activities involving food despite their families' low incomes, for instance by sharing food and pooling resources. Young people also engaged in practices of saving face, through concealing the reasons they could not participate, including suggesting it was their 'choice'. They made excuses and some argued that it was unhealthy to engage in practices such as eating fast food. This likely reflects common strategies for avoiding shame, particularly in Norway and the UK where the experience of shame is shaped by the perceived views of salient others (Walker, 2014).

It was only in the UK, however, that children explicitly mentioned social exclusion in relation to 'eating out'. Given the flexible use of the interview schedule and the need to compress the transcribed material into a case summary, together with the different interests of the partners in each country, it is possible that social exclusion in relation to the school lunch was emphasised more clearly among the young people in Norway. Yet it has also been suggested that income inequality (in the UK) creates status anxiety and, where this is coupled with high levels of consumerism, the market plays an important role in mediating a sense of self-worth and belonging (Bauman, 2006; Wilkinson and Pickett, 2017). Hence the finding is perhaps not surprising.

The research therefore highlights the complex interplay between the extent to which eating is commercialised, the effects of austerity measures, and the customs of eating out for young people as a means of social participation. These factors, as well as the prevailing dominant discourses about poverty in each country, shape young people's social lives and the extent to which they are, or feel, included or excluded from customary practices of sociability related to food.

Notes

1 The research leading to these results has received funding from the European Research Council under the European Union's Seventh Framework Programme (FP7/2007–2013), ERC grant agreement number 337977. The authors wish to thank the funders, the international research team and, most importantly, the children and families who took part in the study.
2 A few children were just outside this age range at interview.
3 The study also included Portugal (45 families with 46 children), though this is not the focus of the analysis in this chapter.
4 While total numbers are small, proportions are given as percentages to aid comparison.
5 A chain of small general shops.

References

Backett-Milburn, K., Wills, W. J., Roberts, M. and Lawton, J. (2011). Food and family practices: Teenagers, eating and domestic life in differing socio-economic circumstances. In S. Punch (ed.), *Children, Food and Institutions*. Abingdon: Routledge.

Bauman, Z. (2006). Children make you happier . . . and poorer. *International Journal of Children's Spirituality,* 11(1): 5–10.

Bell, D. and Valentine, G. (1997). *Consuming Geographies: We Are Where We Eat*. London: Routledge.

Bourdieu, P. (1984). *Distinction: A Social Critique of the Judgement of Taste*. Cambridge, MA: Harvard University Press.

Brembeck, H. (2009). Children's agency in frontiering foodscapes. Pp. 130–148 in A. James, A. Kjørholt and V. Tingstad (eds.), *Children, Food and Identity in Everyday Life*. London: Palgrave MacMillan.

Bugge, A. (2015). Lovin' it? A study of youth and the culture of fast food. *Food, Culture and Society*, 14(1): 71–89.

Butler, R. (2017). Children making sense of economic insecurity: Facework, fairness and belonging. *Journal of Sociology*, 53(1): 94–109.

Davis, A., Hirsch, D., Smith, N., Beckhelling, J. and Padley, M. (2012). *A Minimum Income Standard for the UK in 2012: Keeping Up in Hard Times*. York: Joseph Rowntree Foundation.

DNB (2018). *Seks av ti barn får lommepenger: Her er beløpene foreldrene gir*. Available at: www.dnbnyheter.no/privatokonomi/lommepenger/ [accessed 12 April 2019].

Dowler, E.A. and Leather, S. (2000). 'Spare some change for a bite to eat?' From primary poverty to social exclusion: The role of nutrition and food. Pp. 200–2018 in J. Bradshaw and R. Sainsbury (eds.), *Experiencing Poverty*. Aldershot: Ashgate.

Dowler, E.A. and O'Connor, D. (2012). Rights based approaches to addressing food poverty and food insecurity in Ireland and UK. *Social Science and Medicine*, 74(1): 44–51.

Evans, D. (2018). What is consumption, where has it been going, and does it still matter? *Sociological Review 2019*, 67(3): 499–517.

Farthing, R. (2012). *Going Hungry? Young People's Experiences of Free School Meals*. London: Child Poverty Action Group and British Youth Council.

Fløtten, T. (2019). Poor, but included? Pp. 222–245 in M. Langford, M. Skivenes and K.H. Søvig (eds.), *Children's Rights in Norway*. Oslo: Universitetsforlaget.

Gaisbauer, H., Gottlieb, S. and Sedmark, C. 2019. (eds.) Absolute poverty in Europe: Interdisciplinary perspectives on a hidden phenomenon, Bristol: Policy Press.

Gill, O. and Sharma, N. (2004). *Food Poverty in the School Holidays*. Barnardos.

Goffman, E. (1967). *Interaction Ritual: Essays in Face to Face Behaviour*. New Brunswick, NJ: Transaction.

Goffman, E. (1974). *Stigma: Notes on the Management of Spoiled Identity*. Harmondsworth: Penguin Books.

Gordon, J., Mack, S., Lansley, S., Main, G., Nandy, S., Patsios, D. and Pomati, M. (2013). *The Impoverishment of the UK. Poverty and Social Exclusion UK First Results. Living Standards* [Project Report]. Milton Keynes: Open University.

Gough, I. (1996). Social assistance in Southern Europe. *South European Society & Politics*, 1(1): 1–23.

Hamilton, L. (forthcoming). *Young People's Food and Eating Practices: A Comparison of Higher and Lower Income Households*. PhD thesis, University College London.

Hantrais, L. (2009). *International Comparative Research: Theory, Methods and Practice*. London: Palgrave Macmillan.

Healy, A. (2019). Measuring food poverty in Ireland: The importance of including exclusion. *Irish Journal of Sociology*, 27(2): 105–127.

Household Budget Survey (HBS). *Eurostat*. Available at: https://ec.europa.eu/eurostat/web/household-budget-surveys

James, A. (1979). Confections, concoctions and conceptions. *Journal of the Anthropological Society of Oxford*, 10: 83–95.

James, A., Khorholt, A. and Tingstad, V. (eds.). (2009). *Children, Food and Identity in Everyday Life*. Basingstoke: Palgrave Macmillan.

Knight, A., Brannen, J., Hamilton, L. and O'Connell, R. (2018). How do children and their families experience food poverty according to UK newspaper media 2006–15? *Journal of Poverty and Social Justice*, 26(2): 207–223.

Kohn, M. L. (1987). Cross-national research as an analytic strategy: American sociological association, 1987 presidential address. *American Sociological Review*, 52(6) (December): 713–731.

Lang, T. (1997). Dividing up the cake: Food as social exclusion. Pp. 213–228 in A. Walker and C. Walker (eds.), *Britain Divided: The Growth of Social Exclusion in the 1980s and 1990s*. London: Child Poverty Action Group.

Leather, S. (1996). *The Making of Modern Malnutrition*. London: The Caroline Walker Trust.

Lødemel, I. (1992). *European Poverty Regimes*. Paper presented at the International Research Conference on Poverty and Distribution, Oslo.

Lødemel, I. and Schulte, B. (1992). *Social Assistance: A Part of Social Security or the Poor Law in New Disguise?* Paper presented at the SPRU Conference ('Social Security 50 Years after Beveridge'), York, 27–30 September.

Lund, T., Kjaernes, U. and Holm, L. (2017). Eating out in four Nordic countries: National patterns and social stratification. *Appetite*, 119: 23–33.

Main, G. and Bradshaw, J. (2014). *Child Poverty and Social Exclusion: Final Report of 2012*. PSE study, Poverty and Social Exclusion in the UK.

Martens, L. (2018). *Childhood and Markets: Infants, Parents and the Business of Child Caring*. London: Palgrave Macmillan.

Nairn, A. and IPSOS MORI (2011). *Children's Well-being in UK, Sweden and Spain: The Role of Inequality and Materialism: A Qualitative Study*. London: IPSOS MORI.

O'Connell, R. and Brannen, J. (2016). *Food, Families and Work*. London: Bloomsbury.

O'Connell, R., Knight, A. and Brannen, J. (2019). *Living Hand to Mouth: Children and Food in Low-income Families*. London: Child Poverty Action Group.

O'Connell, R., Padley, M., Owen, C., Simon, A. and Brannen, J. (2019). Which types of family are at risk of food poverty in the UK? A relative deprivation approach. *Social Policy and Society*, 18(1): 1–18.

Oldenberg, R. and Brissett, D. (1982). The third place. *Qualitative Sociology*, 5(4): 265–284.

Paddock, J., Warde, A. and Whillans, J. (2017). The changing meaning of eating out in three English cities 1995–2015. *Appetite*, 119: 5–13.

Pugh, A. (2009). *Longing and Belonging Parents Children and Consumer Culture*. Berkeley: University of California Press.

Richards, C., Kjaernes, U. and Vik, J. (2016). Food security in welfare capitalism: Comparing social entitlements to food in Australia and Norway. *Journal of Rural Studies*, 43: 61–70.

Ridge, T. (2002). *Childhood Poverty and Social Exclusion: From a Child's Perspective*. Bristol: Policy Press.

Ridge, T. (2011). The everyday costs of poverty in childhood: A review of qualitative research exploring the lives and experiences of low-income children in the UK. *Children & Society*, 25: 73–84.

Skuland, S. E. (2019). Packed lunch poverty: Immigrant families' struggles to include themselves in Norwegian food culture. Pp. 135–153 in A. Borch, I. Harsløf, I. G. Klepp and K. Laitala (eds.), *Inclusive Consumption. Immigrants' Access to and Use of Public and Private Goods and Services.* Oslo: Universitetsforlaget.

Sletten, M.A. et al. (2004). Vennskapets pris – fattigdom og sosial isolasjon i ungdomstida. *Tidsskrift for ungdomsforskning*, 4(2): 55–76.

Sobal, J. and Nelson, M. (2003). Commensal eating patterns: A community study. *Appetite*, 41(2): 181–190.

Statistics Norway (2018). *Table: 12599: Personer i husholdninger med lavinntekt, etter gruppe, populasjon, statistikkvariabel og år.* Available at: www.ssb.no/statbank/table/12599/tableViewLayout1/

Statistics Norway (2019). *Flere barn med vedvarende lave husholdningsinntekter.* Available at: www.ssb.no/inntekt-og-forbruk/artikler-og-publikasjoner/flere-barn-med-vedvarende-lave-husholdningsinntekter

Stone, D. 1988. Policy Paradox and Political Reason. Glenview, IL: Scott Foresman and Company.

Tisdall, K., Davis, J., Hill, M. and Prout, A. (eds.). (2006). *Children, Young People and Social Inclusion: Participation for What?* Bristol: Policy Press.

Townsend, P. 1979. Poverty in the United Kingdom: A survey of household resources and standards of living, Harmondsworth: Penguin.

Veblen, T. (1899). *Conspicuous Consumption.* London: Penguin Books.

Walker, R. (2014). *The Shame of Poverty.* Oxford: Oxford University Press.

Walker, R. and Chase, E. (2014). Adding to the shame of poverty: The public, politicians and the media. *Poverty: Journal of the Child Poverty Action Group*, 148: 9–13.

Walker, R., Kyomuhendo, G., Chase, E., Choudry, S., Gubrium, E., Nicola, J., Lødemel, I., Matthew, L., Mwiine, A., Pellissery, S. and Ming, Y. (2013). Poverty in global perspective: Is shame a common denominator? *Journal of Social Policy*, 42(2): 215–233.

Warde, A., Cheng, S., Olsen, W. and Southerton, D. (2007). Changes in the practice of eating: A comparative analysis of time-use. *Acta Sociologica*, 50(4): 363–385.

Warde, A. and Martens, L. (1997). Eating out and the commercialisation of mental life. *British Food Journal*, 100(3): 147–153.

Wilkinson, R. and Pickett, K. (2017). The enemy between us: The psychological and social costs of inequality. *European Journal of Social Psychology*, 47: 11–24.

Wills, W., Backett-Milburn, K., Roberts, M. and Lawton, J. (2011). The framing of social class distinctions through family food and eating practices. *Sociological Review*, 59(4): 725–740.

Wills, W., Danesi, G., Kapetanaki, A. and Hamilton, L. (2018). The socio-economic boundaries shaping young people's lunchtime food practices on a school day. *Children and Society*, 32(3): 195–206.

3 'I feel like it's just going to get worse'

Young people, marginality and neoliberal personhoods in austere times

Daniela Sime and Rebecca Reynolds

Introduction

Austerity has had a disproportionate impact on young people across Europe. Youth poverty is now acute, especially since the economic recession began in 2008. Young people are especially disadvantaged, compared to other age groups (Fahmy, 2015). In the UK, welfare reforms and cuts to service provision (Ortiz et al., 2011; Hopwood et al., 2012), alongside high levels of youth unemployment and insecure work (Boyd, 2014), combine to make young lives precarious, particularly for those growing up in deprived neighbourhoods, which have been the hardest hit (Beatty and Fothergill, 2013). There has been limited research on how young people experience poverty and associated stigma in austerity (Blackman and Rogers, 2017), especially in the new context of increasing neoliberal governance which emphasises the role of employment and puts the main responsibility on young people as the makers of their own success. The ideal neoliberal subject is thus the 'enterprising self' (Kelly, 2006), who can easily adapt to the needs of an unstable labour market and require little or no support from the state. Like in the past, young people are expected to move into adulthood and secure qualifications, employment and housing; however, with an increasing rollback of services and cuts to welfare, pathways are not linear anymore. The transitions that young people are engaged in as they move to adulthood are marked by new risks and uncertainties, framed over the last two decades by ongoing reforms implemented under the pretext of austerity. The social problems are re-positioned beyond a liberal welfare governmentality where the enterprising self is presented as the solution to the risks associated with industrial modernity.

This chapter discusses the particularities of young people's lived experience of austerity in deprived neighbourhoods in Glasgow, the city with the highest rates of deprivation in Scotland. Drawing on data from focus groups with 38 young people aged 14–23 living in some of these areas, we explore young people's positioning as an underclass (Standing, 2011) who experience everyday humiliations and degradations through austerity policies targeting them and the areas in which they live. We argue that young people are integrating aspects of an austerity 'logic' into their sense of self, taking responsibility for their own actions and role as citizens, and this comes with a heavy emotional load and impact on their well-being. However, they are also aware that disinvestment in their local surroundings and themselves as individuals are clear signs of a neoliberal approach which reduces opportunities and deepens inequalities. In closely attending to the lived experience of young people in disadvantaged neighbourhoods, we show how their experience of austerity is mediated through their relationship to place, as well as new forms of neoliberal personhood.

Austerity, poor places and young people

Austerity urbanism (Peck, 2012: 627) comes as a result of 'falling revenues and increasing need': cities have their revenue-raising powers and their budgets restricted. Services are being reorganised or cut and the public workforce is being reduced. Cities are places particularly reliant on services and are home to populations most vulnerable to political vilification, such as minorities and people experiencing poverty. As a result, they are experiencing austerity at its most extreme. The unintended consequences of austerity-driven service changes and cuts are impacting on poorer places and certain groups of people disproportionately (Hastings et al., 2015). This happens not only because of increased levels of need but also because the impacts of service reductions accumulate more quickly in poorer areas and better-off service users have a greater capacity to insulate themselves.

More recent engagements with the importance of place in experiences of poverty (Mckenzie, 2015; Crossley, 2017) highlight how it is essential to understand the wider social contexts which create and reinforce spatial inequalities, while at the same time seeking to understand the experience of living in disadvantaged places. For this reason, it is important to investigate how austerity measures are impacting disadvantaged places, and why and how this may be driven by discursive practices which stigmatise certain places and groups. Lombard (2015: 649) notes that, with austerity policies, there has been a 'hardening of attitudes towards urban poverty and its spatial manifestations'. Clearly, it is not just disproportionate economic impacts of austerity on poor places and their residents but also the increasing stigma to which both are subjected. Austerity policies have come with changing public attitudes towards poverty and 'poor' places. In critiquing the neighbourhood effects thesis, these authors focus overwhelmingly on how discourses reflect and reproduce marginalisation. Less attention is paid to the ways in which space and place are contested, lived and variably experienced by different people (Massey, 1994). This chapter draws on recent empirical evidence produced with young people living in some of these stigmatised neighbourhoods to explore the impacts of structural, economic and political changes under austerity on young people and the neighbourhoods in which they live. In this way, we hope to highlight how structural factors underpin many of the difficulties which people living in so-called poor places face, and which are being exacerbated by current austerity measures.

The ongoing period of austerity has seen increasing numbers of young people entering insecure work through the gig economy and 'zero-hour' contracts, as well as low-paid work. In 2018, youth unemployment was at 9%, the 7th lowest in the EU, and lower than 11.5% for the UK overall and over 15% for Europe. The level of youth unemployment has reduced from 52,000 in 2014 to 28,000 in 2018, a substantial decrease of 46% over the four years. Behind headline falls in youth unemployment rates, low-paid precarious employment proliferates and there is a marked increase in welfare conditionality, with a push to get people into insecure forms of work, which makes it difficult for young people to claim benefits. Youth employment suffers thus from many of the problems associated with insecure, low-paid work. Austerity has seen 'the rapid embedding of labour market trends which had started to emerge pre-recession such as underemployment, self-employment, youth unemployment and insecure forms of working' (Boyd 2014: 1). While young people may be involved in the labour market, the jobs young people do are increasingly typified by irregular and insecure contracts, including 'zero-hour' contracts, part-time work with two or more employers or self-employment. Youth underemployment is also a result of a systematic shift in constructing graduate routes as main indicators of transitional success (Macdonald, 2011) and a reduction over the last decade of apprenticeships and vocational routes available, leading to an oversupply of qualified workers. Achieving the markers of successful transitions to the labour market becomes thus increasingly illusive – with extended periods of poorly paid, precarious work for many.

Neoliberal personhoods and the enterprising selves

Neoliberalism is often defined as a radical form of capitalism which aims to restrict state interventions and mechanisms of support focusing on structural inequalities and aims instead to promote market values. Hilgers (2011: 352) argues that neoliberalism puts 'an extreme emphasis on individual responsibility, flexibility, a belief that growth leads to development, and a promotion of freedom as a means to self-realisation'. However, this projected freedom for self-realisation ignores the economic and social conditions which make some individuals better placed than others to succeed. Consequently, neoliberalism has given rise to the discourse of the 'enterprising self' (Rose, 1998) and the focus on the technologies of self-government, whereby individuals are expected to 'try harder', 'work smarter' and be 'more agile' and adaptable. These new subjectivities expected in marketised societies centre on responsibilisation (Garthwaite, 2017) and 'individualising the future' (Pimlott-Wilson, 2017), where young people are directed to view themselves as 'entrepreneurs' of their own lives, makers of their own success. They must propel themselves through continuous re-skilling and re-training, ongoing personal and professional development, lifestyle and consumer choices (Holdsworth, 2015). In this context, young people are encouraged to see themselves as their own investors – a 'collection of assets' which must be nurtured, trained and promoted by oneself. When plans fail, young people are encouraged to internalise blame for any failures (educational, work-related, personal) rather than examine inherent inequalities and social structures which may lead to their exclusion.

Linked to the shift towards neoliberal personhoods and enterprising selves, young people are shamed and stigmatised publicly if they fail to comply to state-endorsed expectations of success. Media portrayals of young people as 'feral', 'scroungers', 'chavs', 'criminals' or 'welfare cheats' help perpetuate this symbolic and institutional violence which target the youth. This stigma is often generated from the top, by political classes, and used to justify austerity measures, such as cuts to welfare provision, housing and in-work and out-of-work benefits. The language of austerity often presents cuts to welfare services and support as unavoidable, necessary and equally distributed. In reality, young people are most likely to be disproportionately impacted, especially when they find themselves on the margins due to a combination of factors, such as class, ethnicity, gender and migrant/non-migrant status.

Methodology

Getting By was a study carried out by the authors between April and October 2017 in the city of Glasgow. The city has some of the highest levels of poverty in Scotland, with almost half of its people living in the 15% most deprived areas in Scotland, according to the Scottish Index of Multiple Deprivation (SIMD). SIMD ranks small areas (called 'data zones') from most deprived (ranked 1) to least deprived (ranked 6,976) (Scottish Government, 2019). At the time of the study, youth unemployment rates were at 16.6%, with about 27,000 unemployed young people in the city. We carried out six focus groups with young people identified through local organisations. In total, we spoke to 38 young people. Young people were aged 15–23 and included 18 female and 20 male participants. Of these, some were still in education, while others had left school and were looking for work or working. Among our participants, we had young people who lived in state care, asylum-seeking and refugees, and some who were supported by organisations because of their difficult socio-economic circumstances. We recognised these groups were more likely to experience austerity and purposefully sought their participation. In the meetings, we asked young people about their experiences of the places they lived in; their understandings of and feelings regarding austerity and how it impacted them; and explored their barriers to accessing local services.

We used visual mapping to stimulate discussions about place, asking young people to map their local area, identifying places that were important to them and places they were they felt safe/unsafe, and to make comparisons to other locations. The focus groups took place within organisations we recruited for the project, to ensure young people could talk at ease. All young people were recruited through an ethical process of offering information about the project and asking them to opt in, if they wished. To supplement data from the young people, we also interviewed employees of local services and support organisations working with young people. We spoke to six service managers, representing youth support organisations, a youth theatre, sports and music clubs. These interviews are not drawn upon in this chapter but provided useful contextual information. Pseudonyms are used throughout, to protect the participants' privacy.

Young people's experiences of austerity

Everyday poverty struggles and the enterprising self

The economic challenges facing the communities in Glasgow had disrupted traditional pathways to employment for young people leaving school, which had clearly created new everyday risks for this group (Blackman and Rogers, 2017). They described everyday struggles, from having to borrow money or lend to others, to going without essential items, while also seeing other people suffer around them:

> Like, me and my wee brother, we kind of had to fend for ourselves and I was, like, 3 years old and I was going into shops and I was trying to steal, like, food and sweets and that.
>
> (John, 16)

> My neighbour, always asking if I can spare anything, even if it's just bread.
>
> (Shaun, 22)

Participants had all been affected by the economic recession and the decades of disinvestment in apprenticeships, local jobs and public services. Many commented on the difficulties of finding jobs when fewer jobs were available and the challenge of securing jobs with no work experience:

> You can't get a job without experience of working in that kind of place, but how are we supposed to get experience if we can't get a job?
>
> (Mark, 18)

> With this lack of money, it'd be harder to find a job. Like when you are looking for a job, you are asked 'what have you been doing . . . all year?', you need to say 'I've been doing this stuff, this stuff', so it [is] harder.
>
> (Myriam, 22)

For those who did not manage to secure work, the stigma of being unemployed and depending on welfare loomed over them, combined with a sense of feeling worthless. Many commented on the risk of being seen as 'workshy' or relying on benefits, which meant that some chose to not claim benefits they were entitled to. The experience of not finding paid work or being 'stuck' in poor-quality jobs left young people frustrated and pessimistic about their options in future. For Mohammed, working was not a choice but a necessity, as he felt his family could not survive without his income:

> I'm the oldest in the house, other than my mum. And so I have to kind of work enough that I can pay for like half . . . half the rent, half the food, that kind of thing. . . . So, basically if I was to move out like next week, it would

be hard. I reckon I'll stay there until I'm, like, either getting married or something. Probably something like that.

(Mohammed, 20)

While Mohammed felt stuck, Dylan was living with his parents and a younger brother and felt the pressure of having to move out and live independently:

My mum and dad are nagging and stuff. But it's made me aware of what I need to do, like get jobs. Like, I need to step up in work, to get a job, to get a house, to pay for things.

(Dylan, 22)

While the two accounts express different reasons for engaging in employment in terms of necessity and obligation (Mohammed) versus expectations of growing up (Dylan), both have a sense of transitioning and moving on to adulthood, where roles change and so do aspirations and plans for desirable versus possible transitions (Brown, 2011). The pressure of having to provide for the family meant that many of the young people had abandoned education early or delayed education plans. While Mohammed was juggling work and studying for a law degree hoping to become a solicitor, others talked about higher education as the 'back-up' plan, which will potentially always remain an option.

Richard had left a place at college where he was studying architecture and design to take up a full-time job. He went on to explain how one needs to take a job if available, as having a degree does not guarantee career success and he had the immediate pressure of having to contribute to household costs:

Education is always a backup plan. Just in case what you've went for didn't work. That's how I see education. As in, for some people it can take you up to three or four jobs to get your real, actual job that you wanted for your life. So I think life is not about waiting for the right time 'cause you would be sitting there, waiting for the job, but you won't get it. It's always about trying different things. Whatever you feel happy with, and you should do something you like.

Common in young people's narratives was the normalising of everyday struggle on a low income and the emergence of the enterprising self-narrative (Kelly, 2006; Garthwaite, 2017). Young people often said that it was up to them to 'try harder', do more, become better citizens and be more agile in their education, work and personal life. Although many acknowledged that austerity had hit the areas where they lived harder, there was an implicit belief that it was up to individuals to navigate an austere job market and strive for personal success. Ideals of success become thus aligned with employment, shaped also by government narratives of employment as desirable and expected, a sign of successful citizenship and responsibility (Raco, 2009).

Austerity and stigmatised places

Young people had strong views on their local areas, the range of services they accessed, and wider issues associated with local poverty, disadvantage and stigma. When it came to austerity as an overarching policy context, however, they hesitated to make the link between local poverty issues and wider austerity measures. While at times they were critical of disinvestment in areas and dilapidated public places, at other times they blamed the local gangs for vandalising places and not showing any concern for neighbourhoods. Yet others, like Caitlin, explained how persistent disadvantage can push young people into crime and mental ill health:

> I lived on my own when I had my flat, but [the area] was like full of, like, poverty and crime and dodgy people. There's a lot of people, like people my age that are involved in selling drugs and like crime and stealing things, and it's because they all get sanctioned on their benefits when they're late for meetings ... or have mental health problems and no one to help. . . . So none of them have any money..
>
> (Caitlin, 23)

Cuts to local services meant that young people struggled to find safe public parks or youth clubs. Access to support services, such as unemployment support and mental health counsellors, was delayed by complicated appointment systems and waiting lists. As discussed earlier, a stigmatising discourse of austerity in the media and increasingly hardened attitudes towards 'poor people' and 'poor places' (Lombard, 2015) have emerged at the same time as the political project of restructuring the state.

Young people were not immune to these discursive constructions. They were aware of the spoilt identities of the places they lived in and the likely associations people would make between criminality, dilapidation and their areas.

R1: It's embarrassing, people think that you might be one of them [vandals]. It has a huge impact, especially on like friendships as well, 'cause your girlfriend can be like 'Oh, I've been there, so ok, so much violence'.
I: Right. Ok. So it can make you feel uncomfortable about.
R1: Yes.
R2: And some people are gonna be rude . . . saying 'you live in a bad area', so they say something bad because you live like with drunk people.
R3: And other people don't want to come and see you, because they are afraid.

Young people's accounts often started from considering their areas of bad fame and reputation and impact on individuals' chances of success in the job market, due to the postcode stigma or speaking with a local accent, to talking about local crime and addiction problems brought about by the recent welfare reforms and benefit cuts, which had disproportionately impacted young people.

No one wants to employ someone with a really strong accent from a bad background, from a poor area, so it's harder to get jobs.

(Mary, 19)

In Mary's account, speaking with a strong local accent may immediately associate one with poor education, criminality or poor taste, further markers of an underclass struggling with unemployment and area-based stigma. These classed perceptions of marginalisation were informed by individual experiences of exclusion, constantly applying and being rejected for jobs or simply not hearing back from potential employers.

Young people also said they had given up on job centres which were supposed to help because often they felt mistreated by staff in these places. Care-experienced young people discussed how there is a 'bigger picture' whereby young people are pushed into poverty by their families struggling and austerity measures, then they lack timely support and a vicious circle commences:

It's all connected, because I think the benefits system is causing mental health problems. In people and families that wouldn't have had mental health problems . . . in mothers that wouldn't have to struggle every day to feed their kids, kids that had to look after themselves . . . because their parents have turned to drugs and alcohol because they can't cope. In people who are not fit to work, but they're being declared fit to work so they're going to commit suicide. And it's like a vicious circle.

(Caitlin, 23)

The effects of austerity appear thus to be widespread. Austerity creates further stigmatisation of neighbourhoods which have continued to suffer from underinvestment. It impacts young people's families and friends in terms of wellbeing and leads to fractured relationships. Yet while problems impact entire systems, solutions are presented as individualised, whereby young people are expected to find employment in a precarious market, live on very little and maintain healthy relationships and lifestyles. As we have seen, young people are sometimes infused by a sense of personal failure as a result, yet at times they see the structural inequalities and call the government to account.

Impact of poverty on relationships and the self

The experience of growing up in poverty and trying to get by on an everyday basis by juggling money, jobs and living places made young people feel that their family relationships and friendships were severely impacted by their sense of personal failure. The young people who were care-experienced often said that poverty was the root cause of them ending up in care, which then led to an ongoing struggle. Ronnie explained how his family fell apart after his dad became unemployed due to the closure of a local factory and got involved in selling drugs, while Sandra ended up in care when her single mum was struggling to make ends meet:

> My Dad was too busy going and selling his drugs and my Mum just couldn't cope, like, she could barely look after herself let alone 5 kids. So it was my sister, me and Leigh, that pulled together to look after the three younger ones.
>
> (Ronnie, 14)

> My mum was, like, living on the poverty belt and struggling to pay the rent and the bills and, like, put food on the table. So I was being neglected.
>
> (Sandra, 19)

Poverty is stressful, and this stress transfers to individuals' relationships. Young people talked about breaking up with partners as they could not afford a home together and debt put unmanageable pressure on couples. Some were becoming angry at their powerlessness and engaging in arguments or fights with their closest ones over money. Delaying moving in with a partner was common, due to lack of income to secure a place or being unable to cover the associated costs, such as bills.

One of the groups significantly affected were those whose rents were put up by unscrupulous landlords or local authorities applying the Bedroom Tax rule:

> They cut discretionary housing benefit when I lived there, because of the bedroom tax. So they basically, they changed the criteria so that discretionary housing benefit prioritised all the disabled people with extra rooms. And I was in a 2 bedroom flat, which I hadn't asked for, so they started charging me £70 a week for that room. I then lost my discretionary housing benefit so my rent jumped up from £240 to £360, plus £70 a week for a room. And I was only making about £700 a month, so I couldn't, so I'm still paying off debt for that. I'm so angry.
>
> (Caitlin, 23)

These negative emotions and tense relationships brought by poverty were in addition to the diminishing hope and increasing feelings of desperation and low self-esteem. Young people talked about the humiliations they had to suffer and how these impacted on their sense of agency and self:

> I'm pretty sure that most of my generation, especially the ones that are in care, are pretty angry about the way that they're treated and the way that the whole system's dehumanised them.
>
> (Claudia, 22)

The emotional burden of poverty and the impact on their mental health were a constant in young people's accounts. Some commented how difficult it was to keep in touch with friends living in other areas if they could not afford to keep in touch, and how friends would stop visiting. Many said they lost friends as a result:

> It affects your friendships, you can't go out, can't text, can't be anywhere. So you end up not seeing them, then they give up on you.

(Myriam, 22)

Family relationships were strained, friends and partners left and moved on, services of support were not available or when available, they often mistrusted young people and were telling them to 'try harder'. This raises a serious issue in relation to the long-term impacts of youth marginality and the continual perception of young people as deficient and unable to become successful at the making of their own pathways. The emotional labour of having to cope with family relationships and friendships under the added pressure of poverty left young people insecure about their ability to ever re-balance their mental and emotional states and move forward. For many, the hope of support for themselves or those like themselves was gone and the future looked bleak:

> I feel like it's just going to get worse. The thing they're doing now with tax credits, I think that's going to mean that the people that are going to suffer most are innocent children that are going to go hungry because their parents don't know how to manage that they don't have enough money.

(Caitlin, 23)

The evidence shows that attempts to responsibilise individuals have ripple effects, as they also impact young people's familial and friendship networks. Young people felt marginalised and humiliated by practices of individualisation but also isolated from friends and family members as a result of decisions they had no control over, such as housing and the areas they lived in. They also felt angry at the effect their economic situation had on their relationships and mental health, which made it difficult for them to imagine a better future.

Conclusion

The implementation of neoliberal values by the major UK political parties since the 1990s and the expansion of neoliberal approaches to service delivery and welfare reforms have had a profound effect on the most vulnerable and marginalised groups. Increasingly, structural inequalities and government problems are re-framed as residing in the willingness and capacity of several actors and authorities to emphasise the entrepreneurial self. Individuals are encouraged to think of themselves as being their own project, which can only be accomplished by individual strive and effort. Societal problems are thus reframed as pushed on to the individual to solve. The limitation associated with the emphasis on the enterprising self has been critiqued by Stuart Hall (1988), who argues that the Thatcherist attempts to reposition the government's role were quite obviously focused on 'restoring the prerogatives of ownership and profitability' and create the 'political conditions for capital to operate more effectively' (p. 4). Equally, research on austerity has tended to focus on its economic impacts, ignoring the everyday experiences of individuals who suffer its damaging consequences. Following others (Hall, 2019), we have shown that only by examining in depth individuals' everyday experiences of austerity can we see a clearer picture of the devastating effects neoliberal austerity measures are having on individuals, their families and communities.

We have shown that young people are aware that they cannot be made responsible for the lack of good-quality jobs or them being 'stuck' instead of transitioning to desirable and expected roles. Yet, the responsibilisation agenda has infused their narratives, and the evidence presented shows how young people internalise the narrative of the entrepreneurial self and see themselves as either successful or less successful investors in the business of life. Dunn (2004) has argued that the successful adoption of a market economy 'requires changing the very foundation of what it means to be a person' (2004: 6). In the neoliberal governmentality, individuals are made to feel responsible for managing risks associated with precarious jobs, education pathways, health and wellbeing, housing, family and peer relationships. For young people who are not able to enterprise themselves, a range of services are on 'standby' to intervene and encourage and support them to engineer their selves in ways which become aligned with a market-driven economy and state expectations. Rather than helping young people who are disadvantaged by the neoliberal models, targeted interventions often compound their disadvantage, pushing them into more debt, poverty, stress and helplessness. Austerity and cuts have had an impact on communities and the effects trickle down through bedroom taxes, stress, unemployment and being in care, and with few services available and no safety nets, young people feel increasingly frustrated and marginalised. The intersections of place-based disadvantage, group marginalisation, class and individual challenging circumstances place young people in an impossible position in terms of their ability to have a meaningful and fulfilling life. As financial decisions continue to be made under the umbrella of austerity, the costs of the 2020 pandemic and Brexit and cuts to services and job losses continue to bite, without a substantial change in welfare policies and investment in tackling the root of social problems like poverty. This makes it likely that young people will remain increasingly vulnerable and at the mercy of the market-driven values and expectations.

Acknowledgement

We acknowledge funding received from the British Academy for the project which informed this chapter: Getting By: Young People's Experiences of Poverty at the Intersection of Ethnicity, Class and Gender (Ref: MD160010). We are also grateful for the time given to the project by the partner organisations and all the young people who shared their experiences so openly and generously. Special thanks to Helena Pimlott-Wilson and the editorial team for useful suggestions on an earlier draft.

References

Beatty, C. and Fothergill, S. (2013) *Hitting the poorest places hardest: The local and regional impact of welfare reform,* Sheffield: Centre for Regional Economic and Social Research.

Blackman, S. and Rogers, R. (2017) *Youth marginality in Britain: Contemporary studies of austerity,* Bristol: Policy Press.

Boyd, S. (2014) Labour market changes and implications for policy and labour market information (LMI) in Scotland, *Fraser of Allander Economic Commentary,* 38(2), 63–80.

Brown, G. (2011) Emotional geographies of young people's aspirations for adult life, *Children's Geographies,* 1, 7–22.

Crossley, S. (2017) *In their place: The imagined geographies of poverty,* London: Pluto.

Dunn, E. (2004) *Privatizing Poland: Baby food, big business and the remaking of labour,* Ithaca, NY: Cornell University Press.

Fahmy, E. (2015) On the frontline: The growth of youth deprivation in Britain, 1990–2012, *Discover Society,* 20.

Garthwaite, K. (2017) 'I feel I'm giving something back to society': Constructing the 'active citizen' and responsibilising foodbank use, *Social Policy and Society,* 16(2), 283–292.

Hall, S. (1988) 'Introduction: Thatcherism and the crisis of the Left', in S.Hall, *The Hard Road to Renewal: Thatcherism and the Crisis of the Left,* London: Verso.

Hall, S.M. (2019) Everyday austerity: Towards relational geographies of family, friendships and intimacy, *Progress in Human Geography,* 43(5), 769–789.

Hastings, N., Bramley, G., Gannon, M. and Watkins, D. (2015) *The cost of the cuts: The impact on local government and poorer communities,* York: Joseph Rowntree Foundation.

Hilgers, M. (2011) The three anthropological approaches to neoliberalism, *International Social Science Journal,* 61, 351–364.

Holdsworth, C. (2015) The cult of experience: Standing out from the crowd in an era of austerity, *Area,* 49(3), 296–302.

Hopwood, O., Pharoah, R. and Hannon, C. (2012) *Families on the front line: Local spending on children's services in austerity,* London: Family and Parenting Institute.

Kelly, P. (2006) The entrepreneurial self and 'youth at-risk': Exploring the horizons of identity in the twenty-first century, *Journal of Youth Studies,* 9(1), 17–32.

Lombard, M. (2015) Discursive constructions of low income neighbourhood, *Geography Compass,* 9(12), 648–659.

Macdonald, R. (2011) Youth, transitions and un(der)employment: *Plus ça change, plus c'est la même chose? Journal of Sociology,* 47, 427–444.

Massey, D. (1994) *Space, place and power,* Cambridge: Polity Press.

Mckenzie, L. (2015) *Getting by: Estates, class and culture in austerity Britain,* Bristol: Policy Press.

Ortiz, I., Chai, J. and Cummins, M. (2011) *Austerity measures threaten children and poor households: Recent evidence in public expenditures from 128 developing countries,* New York: UNICEF.

Peck, J. (2012) Austerity urbanism: American cities under extreme economy, *City,* 16(6), 626–655.

Pimlott-Wilson, H. (2017) Individualising the future: The emotional geographies of neoliberal governance in young people's aspirations, *Area,* 49(3), 288–295.

Raco, M. (2009) From expectations to aspirations: State modernisation, urban policy, and the existential politics of welfare in the UK, *Political Geography*, 28, 436–444.

Rose, N. (1998) *Inventing ourselves: Psychology, power and personhood,* Cambridge: Cambridge University Press.

Scottish Government (2019) *Scottish index of multiple deprivation*, available online at: https://www2.gov.scot/Topics/Statistics/SIMD

Standing, G. (2011) *The precariat: The new dangerous class*, London: Bloomsbury.

4 Austerity, youth and the city

Experiences of austerity and place by disadvantaged urban youth in Ireland

Sander van Lanen

Introduction

As austerity became the de facto shared European policy response in the aftermath of the 2008 financial crisis, its effects on urban areas have been widely studied (Kitson, Martin and Tyler, 2011; Donald et al., 2014; Holgersen, 2015; Hinkley, 2017). Initially, such investigations were predominantly of a quantitative, anecdotal or policy-focused nature. Increasingly, in-depth qualitative engagement with populations living and working under an austerity regime is emerging (Horton, 2016; Cloke, May and Williams, 2017; Raynor, 2017; Hall, 2018; Hitchen, 2019). However, these examples predominantly focus on the United Kingdom. Widening the focus to include contexts such as Ireland, which has implemented a fierce austerity programme and paid a high price for the economic crisis, is therefore useful (Fraser, Murphy and Kelly, 2013; Taft, 2013). Although official narratives portray Ireland as the poster child of austerity, which successfully exited the Troika[1] bailout programme, returned to market-borrowing, and experienced an economic recovery (Roche, O'Connell and Prothero, 2017), experiences on the ground provide a radically different reality (Fraser, Murphy and Kelly, 2013; Hardiman and Regan, 2013; van Lanen, 2017c).

This chapter focuses on the everyday experiences of austerity by disadvantaged urban youth in Dublin and Cork. Such everyday narratives of crisis conceptualise austerity as more than a fiscal policy and includes the mundane and intimate ways in which it affects the everyday spaces of urban life (Hitchen, 2019). Thus, centring austerity experience rather than nationwide or regional economic figures sketches a more complicated picture of such 'everyday austerity' (Hall, 2018). The combined effects of crisis, recession and austerity resulted in rising levels of deprivation (CSO, 2016). In-depth qualitative research can provide eloquent, subtle and complicated insights into the everyday realities of austerity (Horton, 2016), and reveal the 'politics of everyday austerity at the street level, where the effects of public-service cut-backs, job losses and increased exposure to socio-economic risks are experienced in daily life' (Peck, 2012, p. 632). In this chapter, I focus on the everyday austerity experiences of youth from neighbourhoods of concentrated deprivation in Ireland to argue that austerity urbanism interacts with social and spatial characteristics to assemble locally specific austerity emergences and forms of social exclusion.

Austerity urbanism and social exclusion

Urban austerity, as a neoliberal response to a neoliberal crisis (Aalbers, 2013), is more than a repeated round of 'roll-back, roll-out' neoliberalism as it affects an already neoliberalised urban territory (Peck and Tickell, 2002; Peck, 2012). Formed as crisis management, Peck (2012) identified three dimensions of austerity urbanism. First, 'destructive creativity' delineates the intensified destruction of the social state as austerity reaches into 'hard to reform' spheres and re-targets outcomes of previous rounds of neoliberalisation. Second, 'deficit politics' entails the privileging of financial order through privatisation of public assets, infrastructure development and social services over sustainable social and physical investments. Third, 'devolved risk' refers to the 'downloading' of responsibilities and management of budget cuts through fee-based services, entrepreneurial management and private sector involvement to externalise public risk. Through these mechanisms, austerity affects both the management of urban space and the lives lived under urban austerity.

This chapter aims to evaluate how austerity affects urban life for disadvantaged urban youth in Ireland, and especially how processes of 'destructive creativity', 'deficit politics' and 'devolved risk' shape their social exclusion. I employ Schuyt's (2006; see also Aalbers, 2010) three causes of social exclusion: not being allowed to, not able to belong and not willing to belong. 'Not being allowed to' refers to intentional exclusion of individuals, for example 'illegal' immigrants legally prohibited to work or receive social benefits. Those 'not able to belong' are not formally excluded but are for various reasons not fully able to participate, for example individuals with a disability or who are unable to consistently hold a stable job. Responsibility for being unable to participate is thus placed on those excluded. 'Not willing to belong' often follows consistent experiences of rejection by moral gatekeepers or exclusion by the majority, and is thus both a result of and factor in social exclusion.

To connect the regulatory framework of austerity urbanism to the individual and collective experiences of austerity and social exclusion, I apply the concept of assemblage to the lifeworld (McFarlane, 2011; Anderson et al., 2012). According to Buttimer (1976) and Seamon (1979), the lifeworld constitutes the spatio-temporal horizon of everyday life. The lifeworld is conceptualised as an assemblage containing and connecting various entities and their relations, which are both potentially affected by austerity. Austerity itself is not necessarily part of the lifeworld assemblage but an atmospheric and affective phenomenon which encapsulates this assemblage (Hitchen, 2016). As such, austerity permeates the relations between the individual and material, institutional and social entities and affects the assembling of austerity lifeworlds. Austerity manifests itself in individual lifeworlds through changing relations and entities. These austerity manifestations can be conceptualised as a reconstitution of the lifeworld assemblage. This reconstitution is always relational to its previous formation, making the assembling of austerity lifeworlds path-dependent as austerity arrives in a context established by contemporary relations and past transformations. A lifeworld assemblage approach is used here to assess the role of space, class and age in the reshaping of everyday life for youth from Knocknaheeny and Ballymun, Ireland.

Disadvantaged urban youth

Young people are considered especially vulnerable to the adverse effects of crisis, recession and austerity (Verick, 2009; Murphy, 2014). For example, they are more likely to lose employment and have fewer resources and networks to fall back on (Verick, 2009). The open Irish economy was vulnerable to economic shocks, and state responses created a fiscal crisis ultimately serviced by outside assistance, in the form of a Troika bailout, under conditions of austerity (Fraser, Murphy and Kelly, 2013). In Ireland, this vulnerability was exacerbated by the direct targeting of young people under 25 by several austerity measures – for example by the introduction of lower Jobseeker's Allowance rates and intensified activation measures for under-25s. Particularly relevant for feelings of social exclusion, contemporary Irish youth, growing up during the Celtic Tiger period of neoliberal prosperity (O'Riain, 2014; van Lanen, 2017a), is the first generation growing up under neoliberalism to come of age in crisis conditions (McGuigan, 2016). Furthermore, more recent portrayals of Ireland as the poster child of austerity (Kinsella, 2012, 2014) potentially feeds perceived exclusion, as urban youth do not necessarily profit from the national economic recovery. Austerity thus potentially separates young people from their self-identified markers of inclusion. As the negative effects of austerity are aggravated for the urban poor (Peck, 2012), it can be argued that disadvantaged youth from Dublin and Cork are hardest hit by austerity and recession in Ireland.

It is for these vulnerabilities that the experiences of disadvantaged urban youth can offer an especially pertinent insight into Irish everyday austerities and the transformations its implementation brings to everyday experiences. I draw upon interviews conducted with 33 young adults, ages varying from 18 to 25 years old, who lived in two of Ireland's most deprived urban neighbourhoods in its two major cities – Dublin (Ballymun) and Cork (Knocknaheeny). These interviews, revealing disadvantaged urban youth's austerity experiences, are employed to illustrate how individual and collective austerity experiences are shaped by intersections of space, class and age. A comparative approach enables an examination of commonalities and differences between the two Irish neighbourhoods and cities and is thus attentive to the specific role of urban geographies in austerity experiences. As such, this chapter moves beyond a single case study to analyse the commonalities and variations of austerity experiences and the role of space and place in their urban formation.

Local institutional landscapes and costs of living

Space, class and age cannot be completely separated from one another or from further factors affecting austerity manifestations in everyday life. Taking this multiplicity of influences on everyday austerity into account, I analyse the influence of these specific factors on austerity experiences of youth from Ballymun and Knocknaheeny. Spatial variation in austerity vulnerability has been widely established from the international to the local scale (Aalbers, 2009; Kitson, Martin and Tyler, 2011; O'Callaghan et al., 2015; Crescenzi, Luca and Milio, 2016). This chapter moves beyond spatially variegated consequences of austerity to focus specifically on what shapes locally specific austerity emergences and their impacts on everyday life in Ireland. It thus extends analysis beyond austerity outcomes to include the processes of assembling local austerity lifeworlds and how destructive creativity, deficit politics and devolved risk settle down in a neighbourhood.

Local austerity manifestations are path-dependent and respond to actually existing histories of neighbourhood neoliberalisation (Peck and Tickell, 2002; Bathelt and Glückler, 2003). Although austerity affects all of Ireland, youth had different austerity experiences in Knocknaheeny and Ballymun. In Knocknaheeny, participants predominantly experienced austerity through employment loss or the inability to find employment. Although unemployment experiences existed in Ballymun, comparable levels of unemployment and employment loss existed in both neighbourhoods (Haase and Pratschke, 2012), and austerity in Ballymun was largely experienced elsewhere. Ballymun's larger population, in combination with programmes implemented as part of the Ballymun regeneration and its local history of community activism (Boyle, 2005), provided a deeper institutional penetration which delivered employment, education and training programmes. Among others, Ballymun was served by the Ballymun Job Centre, a significantly larger YouthReach facility offering second change education, several youth clubs and other support services for its 'customer base'.

> I made CVs up in the Job Centre, the Ballymun Job Centre, and I went around shops . . . so I went to the Job Centre, and they helped with a mock interview and stuff, gave me tips and stuff.
>
> (Donna, Ballymun, 23)

Destructive creativity responds to historical, social and political neighbourhood constellations and is thus path-dependent. Through these institutional presences, unemployed Ballymun youth, such as Donna, were more often absorbed in training or employment programmes than youth from Knocknaheeny. Participation in such programmes was sometimes funded or programme participants were provided modest social welfare top-ups, and their presence and capacity mitigated the experience of austerity through unemployment. As such, extended access to training and participation enabled Ballymun youth to participate and relatively mediated their exclusion from professional development.

Nonetheless, Ballymun young people were affected by austerity through devolved risk. In Ballymun, austerity predominantly emerged through financial management of the household (van Lanen, 2018). Sometimes participants shared responsibility for household finances, were contributors to household income or felt the consequences of lower household income. By offloading responsibility of care to families and communities (Fraser, 2016), financial risk was devolved to and experienced in the household, as was the case for Tara (below). The insufficiency of household income relates to Ballymun's local circumstances. In Dublin, including Ballymun, rents and the general cost of living were higher than in Cork and Knocknaheeny (Numbeo, 2016). A larger share of household income had to be reserved for such costs, limiting what disposable income was left after rent and paying for necessities, if these necessities could even be covered.

> There was times when it did get hard, like, with me mom's hours being cut, and losing her job, and a lot going on at home, . . . it was kind of hard for my mom to . . . financially support three kids and a grandchild, . . . herself, and a fiancé.
>
> (Tara, Ballymun, 18)

As the costs of social reproduction are often managed on the household level, and participants often contributed to household expenses, everyday austerity manifested in the household as stress over bills, eviction notices, lack of food or the discontinuation of long-running activities. Devolved risk to the household thus hampered the ability of households and individuals to participate in society, either through lack of money or experienced stress. The introduction and emergence of austerity in the lifeworld, and its impact on social exclusion, is thus shaped by geographies of institutional penetration and cost of living. Local assemblages of social reproduction shaped the varying austerity experiences of participants in Knocknaheeny and Ballymun.

However, neighbourhoods are not completely locked in by previous institutional arrangements and local histories. Both neighbourhoods were undergoing regeneration projects during and after the crisis. The Ballymun regeneration project, predominantly funded by public-private partnerships, collapsed when private partners pulled out or went into receivership. In Knocknaheeny, however, the recession caused only a slight delay and newly developed housing and services were delivered at the time of research. As a result, the regeneration and public space itself hardly emerged as manifestation of austerity in Knocknaheeny.

In Ballymun, on the contrary, the consequences of the interrupted regeneration were among the most prominent narratives of crisis, recession and austerity. Through the private organisation of Ballymun Regeneration Limited and its funding as a public-private partnership (Power, 2008), the Ballymun regeneration was directly exposed to financial and economic risk. This form of devolved risk proved catastrophic. Ballymun's landscape contained empty meadows, an abandoned shopping centre, and less housing than initially promised. Apart from substandard housing and public space, this landscape provides a constant visible reminder of austerity and recession (Storm, 2014). The vacated shopping centre in particular, located at the heart of the neighbourhood, was a constant sign of loss and broken promises. This simultaneous disruption of the built environment and the socio-economic reality of participants, austerity and recession became embedded in the physical locality of Ballymun itself.

The spatial contexts in which youth reside thus shape austerity encounters in the everyday lifeworld. Geographies of institutional presence, cost of living, and the vulnerability of regeneration projects to crisis and recession mediate experiences of Irish austerity by youth in Ballymun and Knocknaheeny. The spatial characteristics of Ballymun affect how financial risk is devolved, through combined effects on household income rather than through immediate exclusion from professional activity. Space, both in its physical and qualitative sense, is part of the lifeworld assemblage and thereby affects its reconstitution under the influence of austerity. This results in a geography of austerity that is shaped beyond geographies of differently affected populations; space itself plays a vital role in the everyday manifestation of austerity and the forms of exclusion it creates. Nonetheless, the influence of space and place interacts with other characteristics of groups and individuals to shape personalised austerity experiences.

Age and access to housing

Among the characteristics mediating austerity experiences in place is the age of young people. Age played a role in several ways. First, several Irish austerity measures were directly directed at young people. For example, since 2008, rates of Jobseeker's Allowance are differentiated by age for young adults under 26 (Figure 4.1). Between 2008 and 2014, a common rate of €197.80 per week was reduced to weekly rates of €100 for those aged 18–24, €144 for 25-year-olds, and €188 for those over 25. In 2013, then Minister for Public Expenditure and Reform Brendan Howlin presented these differentiations as incentives towards employment and training (Howlin, 2013). Furthermore, several labour market activation processes, such as Youth Guarantee and the Employment and Youth Activation Charter, specifically addressed unemployed youth.

Representing a form of destructive creativity (Peck, 2012), these measures reveal novel regulations and standards to implement further reductions in welfare spending. Furthermore, youth was often mobilised in legitimising narratives of austerity, which was presented as a strategy to safeguard the wellbeing of future generations (Horton, 2016). Beyond these measures, the implementation of age-neutral policy differentially impacts on different age groups. Here, I explore this dynamic through the sphere of housing availability for youth from Ballymun and Knocknaheeny.

Generally, three forms of housing are available in Ireland for independent living: owner-occupancy, private rental accommodation, and social housing. Although private rents initially declined after the 2008 crash, rents have since been spiralling out of control to reach record heights in Ireland's urban centres (Daft.ie, 2019). Kapila (2016) calculated that to live affordably in the Dublin

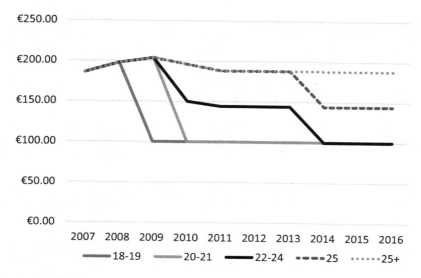

Figure 4.1 Jobseeker's Allowance weekly rates per age

region, which contains Ballymun, required an hourly income more than twice the minimum wage on a 36 hour/week job. Simultaneous transformations in the labour market resulted in increased precarity, low wages and unemployment, to which young people are extremely vulnerable (Verick, 2009; Murphy and Loftus, 2015).

Together with disinvestment in social housing (Hearne, Kitchin and O'Callaghan, 2014), the responsibilities and risks of housing are devolved from national and local authorities to individuals. Although unemployment has been falling in recent years, the national rise in working poverty and prevalence of people working involuntary part-time (Murphy and Loftus, 2015) eroded income and thus ability to pay rent, and therefore the ability to access affordable and decent housing for disadvantaged youth. Young people's heightened vulnerability to labour market volatilities thus presents a barrier into affordable housing for disadvantaged urban youth and limits their ability to participate and belong in society (Schuyt, 2006).

Similar developments prevent especially disadvantaged youth, with lesser access to parental wealth support (Carney et al., 2014; Arundel and Hochsten-bach, 2018) and access to owner-occupancy, and thus the ability to secure housing through home ownership. Furthermore, in response to the financial crisis and the collapse of the preceding property bubble, heightened deposit requirements for mortgages were introduced in Ireland. These reduce mortgage accessibility and practically exclude youth from Ballymun and Knocknaheeny from owner-occupancy.

The remaining option is social housing, which traditionally served as accommodation for those who were unable to afford owner-occupancy or private rental accommodation. Upward pressure on private rents and households falling into mortgage arrears increased the pressure on social housing waiting lists in Ireland. Together with disinvestment in social housing during the crisis years, this resulted in a 60% increase of households on the social housing waiting list between 2008 and 2013 (O'Connor and Staunton, 2015).

> There's a waiting list of 8 to 10 years, even more. Especially I'm single, so, and I'm young. . . . But I'm homeless, yeah, that will get me up the list a bit.
>
> (Simon, Knocknaheeny, 24)

By their age, youth are lacking the long waiting time required to access social housing, to which only the most severe priority conditions, such as prolonged homelessness in the case of Simon, can provide increased access. Beyond mere waiting time, young people are at a disadvantage for social housing as the Irish social housing stock is mostly unsuitable for young people and singles, and housing is thus prioritised for families (Threshold, 2010). This creates a situation where single or small-family youth are not allowed access to a part of the social housing stock and not able to access more suitable accommodation due to its relative absence. Increased investment in social housing seems unlikely (Hearne, Kitchin and O'Callaghan, 2014), and new initiatives to provide affordable housing provide expensive and ineffective rental support to private landlords (Hearne and Murphy, 2017). Although this does not result in reduction of state expenses, it strengthens the normative status of market-based housing provision through 'creative destruction' of social housing provision.

Age thus affects the ability for youth to gain access to affordable housing provisions. Young people's access to affordable housing, and thus independent living, is severely constrained or even prevented under conditions of austerity and recession. The interactions of such exclusion with spatial characteristics is clear in Ballymun, where the regeneration project resulted in a significant reduction of social housing in the neighbourhood (Haase and Pratschke, 2012). Although youth are not formally disabled to enter into the various forms of housing, localised consequences of destructive creativity and devolved risk make them unable to access housing. Being unable to belong, to participate in independent lives, is one aspect of social exclusion (Schuyt, 2006; Aalbers, 2010) that disadvantaged urban youth experience in Ireland under austerity.

Class, austerity and access to services

Because of segregation, space and class are highly related in disadvantaged urban neighbourhoods. This concentration of poor working-class populations is often a reason they are labelled and stigmatised as disadvantaged (Wacquant, 2007). In both Ballymun and Knocknaheeny, unemployment rose quickly in the post-crisis period (Haase and Pratschke, 2012, 2016), which added to already existing financial insecurities. The inflating property bubble and corresponding collapse of the Irish construction sector affected large groups of lower-educated workers who were previously absorbed in building-related activities (Storey, 2011; Bobek and Wickham, 2015).

Especially in Ballymun, the combination of falling employment and social welfare rates led to the retreat of private facilities following falling overall disposable income.

> There was a café down there, there were shops, but again, recession hit and this place is basically desolate, there is, we've lost . . . the café, . . . religious shops, . . . basically the place is empty, there is no shops left.
>
> (Hannah, Ballymun, 19)

Reduced spending power created a neighbourhood devoid of private amenities and employment opportunities as expressed by Hannah. Simultaneously, harsh funding reductions for the community and voluntary sector resulted in service decline and closure (Harvey, 2012). Deficit politics, which prioritise fiscal consolidation over service provision, thus lead to service decline while destructive creativity affected the operations of available services through increasingly competitive funding structures. Remaining community services experienced staff pressure or had to refocus towards labour activation programmes. Overall, neighbourhoods like Ballymun and Knocknaheeny run the risk of becoming spaces deserted of opportunities and facilities as public service provision declines and inhabitants are not able to acquire similar private services. Nonetheless, as discussed before, local histories and context affect the intensity with which these neighbourhoods lose their services and amenities. Overall, the classed nature of these neighbourhoods, with high unemployment and low-paying or irregular work arrangements, affects the spatial qualities available to disadvantaged urban youth under austerity. It thus reinforces the extent to which disadvantaged urban youth are allowed and able to participate in society. The classed nature of austerity and its deficit politics (Peck, 2012; Fraser, Murphy and Kelly, 2013) not only manifests through affected individuals but also through its concentrated consequences among the classed spatialities of deprived urban neighbourhoods.

Although class is not necessarily an entity in the lifeworld assemblage, it is a mediator of the relationships between various entities and the classed subject at the centre of the lifeworld. In particular, it affects the real and potential relations of individuals to income and employment, which in turn affect the monetary availability of opportunities, goods and services. The dynamics of austerity urbanism thus shape how youths are able and allowed to participate in paid work, education, housing and other elements of urban life. During times of austerity and recession, these relationships suffer from ongoing precarisation, which in an increasingly commodified and marketised urban space affects access to the opportunities and possibilities offered by urban space. The combined consequences of falling disposable income through labour market developments and austerity results in 'time-space expansion': the spatio-temporal separation from services, facilities and needs which predominantly affects lower-class individuals and groups (Katz, 2004; van Lanen, 2017b).

The urban nature of Ireland's economic recovery and consequent concentration of employment in cities (O'Callaghan et al., 2015) might increase urban access to employment for youth, especially in Ballymun. However, this also created a severe housing affordability crisis (Hearne and Murphy, 2017), which traps youth in their parental home and thus the neighbourhood. Austerity shapes places of exclusion, both reducing services in areas of concentrated deprivation and preventing affordable access to better serviced neighbourhoods. Combined with territorial stigmatisation (Wacquant, 2007), spatial consequences and sources of social exclusion intensify under austerity urbanism. Crisis and recession create new urban spaces, and space and place play a crucial role in the experiences of austerity by disadvantaged urban youth. Furthermore, the economic recovery risks consolidating such spaces of exclusion if it is not carefully managed.

Conclusion

This chapter illuminated how age, space and class mediated the austerity experiences of youth from areas of concentrated deprivation by eliciting the austerity experiences of young adults from Ballymun in Dublin and Knocknaheeny in Cork, Ireland. Comparing youthful austerity experiences in two urban contexts provided the opportunity to place gendered and classed experiences of austerity in their geographical context. Therefore, it facilitated an explicit attention to the role of space and place in the experiences of austerity. Starting from a conceptualisation of austerity urbanism as constituted by destructive creativity, deficit politics and devolved risk (Peck, 2012) and social exclusion as constituted by the abilities, allowances, and willingness to participate and belong (Schuyt, 2006; Aalbers, 2010), it traced how austerity affected the abilities to be professionally, residentially and personally active in urban Ireland. By thinking of the lifeworld as an assemblage, it becomes possible to see factors such as space, age and class as mediating actors governing the capabilities and relations that shape localised austerity experiences.

Through this framework, it was shown how the local context shaped the pathways through which risk is devolved and as such influences capabilities to belong and not-belong through geographies of institutional presence and costs of living. Access to affordable housing, and thus to secure independent living, was restrained by an interaction of effects related to participants' young age. Destructive creativity, which reduced unemployed income for young adults, and the devolving of the responsibility to acquire housing to the household level decreased youth's ability of urban independent living. Finally, the classed nature of disadvantaged urban spaces and austerity made Ballymun and Knocknaheeny vulnerable to service decline, as deficit politics reduced funding for social and community services while falling rates of disposable income reduced the presence of private services and amenities. As space, age and class shape austerity experiences of disadvantaged urban youth in Ireland, youth's exclusion from housing, professional opportunities and urban amenities is not formally imposed by austerity, but various factors create an assemblage in which the possibility to belong and participate in 'normal life' is seriously reduced.

The reality of austerity is complex and messy, and its experiences vary tremendously among individuals and places. Nonetheless, delving into the interferences of austerity, space, age and class provide insight into the conditions and interactions of such factors to shape localised austerity lifeworlds and the emergence of austerity within socio-spatial contexts. Together, this provides an important insight into the assemblage of contemporary social exclusion under austerity that produces disadvantaged urban youth as one of the groups most negatively affected by austerity.

Note

1 The tripartite committee of the International Monetary Fund, the European Central Bank and the European Commission.

Bibliography

Aalbers, M. B. (2009) 'Geographies of the financial crisis', *Area*, 41(1), pp. 34–42.

Aalbers, M. B. (2010) 'Social exclusion', in Hutchison, R. (ed.) *Encyclopedia of urban studies*. Thousand Oaks, CA: Sage, pp. 731–735.

Aalbers, M. B. (2013) 'Neoliberalism is dead . . . Long live neoliberalism!', *International Journal of Urban and Regional Research*, 37(3), pp. 1083–1090.

Anderson, B. et al. (2012) 'On assemblages and geography', *Dialogues in Human Geography*, 2(2), pp. 171–189.

Arundel, R. and Hochstenbach, C. (2018) *The spatial polarization of housing markets and wealth accumulation*. Working Paper Series No 32. Amsterdam: Centre for Urban Studies.

Bathelt, H. and Glückler, J. (2003) 'Toward a relational economic geography', *Journal of Economic Geography*, 3(2), pp. 117–144.

Bobek, A. and Wickham, J. (2015) *Employment in the Irish construction sector: A preliminary background report*. Dublin: TASC – Think-tank for Action on Social Change.

Boyle, M. (2005) 'Sartre's circular dialectic and the empires of abstract space: A history of space and place in Ballymun, Dublin', *Annals of the Association of American Geographers*, 95(1), pp. 181–201.

Buttimer, A. (1976) 'Grasping the dynamism of lifeworld', *Annals of the Association of American Geographers*, 66(2), pp. 277–292.

Carney, G. M. et al. (2014) '"Blessed are the young, for they shall inherit the national debt": Solidarity between generations in the Irish crisis', *Critical Social Policy*, 34(3), pp. 312–332.

Cloke, P., May, J. and Williams, A. (2017) 'The geographies of food banks in the meantime', *Progress in Human Geography*, 41(6), pp. 703–726.

Crescenzi, R., Luca, D. and Milio, S. (2016) 'The geography of the economic crisis in Europe: National macroeconomic conditions, regional structural factors and short-term economic performance', *Cambridge Journal of Regions, Economy and Society*, 9(1), pp. 13–32.

CSO (2016) *Survey on income and living conditions (SILC)*. Dublin: CSO.

Daft.ie (2019) *The Daft.ie rental price report: An analysis of recent trends in the Irish rental market 2018 Q4 year in review*. Dublin: Daft.ie.

Donald, B. et al. (2014) 'Austerity in the city: Economic crisis and urban service decline?' *Cambridge Journal of Regions, Economy and Society*, 7(1), pp. 3–15.

Fraser, A., Murphy, E. and Kelly, S. (2013) 'Deepening neoliberalism via austerity and "reform": The CASE of Ireland', *Human Geography*, 6(2), pp. 38–53.

Fraser, N. (2016) 'Contradictions of capital and care', *New Left Review*, 100, pp. 99–117.

Haase, T. and Pratschke, J. (2012) *Pobal HP deprivation index for small areas: Datasets electoral divisions*. Dublin: Pobal. Available at: www.pobal.ie/Pages/New-Measures.aspx

Haase, T. and Pratschke, J. (2016) *The Pobal HP deprivation index: 2016 deprivation index by local electoral area*. Dublin: Pobal. Available at: www.pobal.ie/Pages/New-Measures.aspx

Hall, S. M. (2018) 'Everyday austerity: Towards relational geographies of family, friendship and intimacy', *Progress in Human Geography*, 43(5), pp. 769–789.

Hardiman, N. and Regan, A. (2013) 'The politics of austerity in Ireland', *Intereconomics*, 45(1), pp. 4–32.

Harvey, B. (2012) *Downsizing the community sector: Changes in employment and services in the voluntary and community sector in Ireland, 2008–2012*. Dublin: Irish Congress of Trade Unions Community Sector Committee.

Hearne, R., Kitchin, R. and O'Callaghan, C. (2014) 'Spatial justice and housing in Ireland', in Kearns, G., Meredith, D., and Morrissey, J. (eds.) *Spatial justice and the Irish crisis*. Dublin: Royal Irish Academy, pp. 57–77.

Hearne, R. and Murphy, M. P. (2017) *Investing in the right to a home: Housing, HAPs and hubs*. Kildare: Maynooth University.

Hinkley, S. (2017) 'Structurally adjusting: Narratives of fiscal crisis in four US cities', *Urban Studies*, 54(9), pp. 2123–2138.

Hitchen, E. (2016) 'Living and feeling the austere', *New Formations*, 87, pp. 102–118.

Hitchen, E. (2019) 'The affective life of austerity: Uncanny atmospheres and paranoid temporalities paranoid temporalities', in *Social & cultural geography*. London: Routledge.

Holgersen, S. (2015) 'Economic crisis, (creative) destruction, and the current urban condition', *Antipode*, 47(3), pp. 689–707.

Horton, J. (2016) 'Anticipating service withdrawal: Young people in spaces of neoliberalisation, austerity and economic crisis', *Transactions of the Institute of British Geographers*, 41(4), pp. 349–362.

Howlin, B. (2013) *Address to Dáil Éireann on expenditure estimates 2014*. Dublin: Government of Ireland.

Kapila, L. (2016) 'How much should you earn to live in different parts of Dublin?' *Dublin Inquirer*. Available at: http://dublininquirer.com/2016/02/23/mapped-how-much-should-you-earn-to-live-in-different-parts-of-dublin/ (Accessed: 22 February 2019).

Katz, C. (2004) *Growing up global: Economic restructuring and children's everyday lives*. Minneapolis: University of Minnesota Press.

Kinsella, S. (2012) 'Is Ireland really the role model for austerity?' *Cambridge Journal of Economics*, 36(1), pp. 223–235.

Kinsella, S. (2014) 'Post-bailout Ireland as the poster child for austerity', *CESifo Forum*, 15(2), pp. 20–25.

Kitson, M., Martin, R. and Tyler, P. (2011) 'The geographies of austerity', *Cambridge Journal of Regions, Economy and Society*, 4(3), pp. 289–302.

McFarlane, C. (2011) 'The city as assemblage: Dwelling and urban space', *Environment and Planning D: Society and Space*, 29(4), pp. 649–671.

McGuigan, J. (2016) *Neoliberal culture*. Basingstoke: Palgrave Macmillan.

Murphy, M. (2014) 'Ireland's youth – paying the price for their elders' crisis', *Policy Network*. Available at: www.policy-network.net/pno_detail.aspx?ID=4574&title=Irelands-youth---paying-the-price-for-their-elders-crisis (Accessed: 21 January 2016).

Murphy, M. and Loftus, C. (2015) 'A precarious future: An Irish example of flex-insecurity', in Riain, S. Ó. et al. (eds.) *The changing worlds and workplaces of capitalism*. London: Palgrave Macmillan, pp. 98–117.

Numbeo (2016) *Cost of living comparison between Cork and Dublin*. Available at: www.numbeo.com/cost-of-living/compare_cities.jsp?country1=Ireland&city1=Cork&country2=Ireland&city2=Dublin (Accessed: 16 June 2016).

O'Callaghan, C. et al. (2015) 'Topologies and topographies of Ireland's neoliberal crisis', *Space and Polity*, 19(1), pp. 31–46.

O'Connor, N. and Staunton, C. (2015) *Cherishing all equally: Economic inequality in Ireland*. Dublin: TASC.

O'Riain, S. (2014) *The rise and fall of Ireland's Celtic tiger: Liberalism, boom and bust*. Cambridge: Cambridge University Press.

Peck, J. (2012) 'Austerity urbanism; American cities under extreme economy', *City: Analysis of Urban Trends, Culture, Theory, Policy, Action*, 16(6), pp. 626–655.

Peck, J. and Tickell, A. (2002) 'Neoliberalizing space', *Antipode*, 34(3), pp. 380–404.

Power, A. (2008) 'Rebuilding Ballymun: Stepping into the future', in McCrann, A. (ed.) *Memories, milestones and new horizons: Reflections on the regeneration of Ballymun*. Belfast: Blackstaff Press, pp. 27–43.

Raynor, R. (2017) 'Dramatising austerity: Holding a story together (and why it falls apart. . .)', *Cultural Geographies*, 24(2), pp. 193–212.

Roche, W. K., O'Connell, P. J. and Prothero, A. (2017) *Austerity & recovery in Ireland: Europe's poster child and the great recession*. Edited by W. K. Roche, P. J. O'Connell, and A. Prothero. Oxford: Oxford University Press.

Schuyt, K. (2006) *Steunberen van de Samenleving*. Amsterdam: Amsterdam University Press.

Seamon, D. (1979) *A geography of the lifeworld: Movement, rest and encounter*. New York: St. Martin's Press.

Storey, A. (2011) *Ireland's debt crisis: Roots and reactions, Irish new left review*. Available at: www.irishleftreview.org/2011/11/21/irelands-debt-crisis-roots-reactions/ (Accessed: 22 February 2019).

Storm, A. (2014) *Post-industrial landscape scars*. London: Palgrave Macmillan.

Taft, M. (2013) *A really really special case requires a really really special solution, unite's notes on the front*. Available at: http://notesonthefront.typepad.com/politicaleconomy/2013/01/with-considerable-speculation-about-an-impending-deal-on-bank-debt-with-the-taoiseach-and-the-german-chancellor-jointly-sta.html (Accessed: 22 February 2019).

Threshold (2010) *Access to housing for one-person households in Ireland*. Dublin: Threshold.

van Lanen, S. (2017a) 'Austerity beyond the budget cut: Experiences of austerity urbanism by disadvantaged urban youth', *Lo Squaderno*, 47, pp. 49–53.

van Lanen, S. (2017b) 'Living austerity urbanism: Space – time expansion and deepening socio-spatial inequalities for disadvantaged urban youth in Ireland', *Urban Geography*, 38(10), pp. 1603–1613.

van Lanen, S. (2017c) *Youth and austerity in the city: Geographies of precarity in disadvantaged urban areas in Ireland*. University College Cork.

van Lanen, S. (2018) 'Encountering austerity in deprived urban neighbourhoods: Local geographies and the emergence of austerity in the lifeworld of urban youth', *Geoforum*, 110, pp. 220–231.

Verick, S. (2009) *Who is hit hardest during a financial crisis? The vulnerability of young men and women to unemployment in an economic downturn, IZA discussion paper*. 4359. Bonn: SSRN.

Wacquant, L. (2007) *Urban outcasts: A comparative sociology of advanced marginality*. Cambridge: Polity.

5   Children and families coping with austerity in Catalonia

*Maria Prats Ferret, Mireia Baylina and
Anna Ortiz Guitart*

Introduction: ten years of recession in children's daily lives

The 2008 economic crisis has had particularly negative effects on labour market outcomes in Southern Europe. In 2011, Spain, Italy and Greece had unemployment rates of 25%–30% (Instituto Nacional de Estadística, 2019). Spain's economic and financial crisis has deeply affected the labour market, triggering a loss of jobs and rising unemployment. The most immediate consequences have been increased poverty, social exclusion of the population (Navarro & Clua-Losada, 2012; Méndez, 2014) and reduced wellbeing and quality of life that has, to a greater or lesser extent, made lives more vulnerable (Pitarch Garrido, 2014). The medium-term consequences of this situation could have implications for top-level priorities like health and education, highlighting the importance of social reproduction, understood as 'the material and social practices through which society is reproduced day by day, generation after generation' (Katz, 2001, p. 711).

This financial and economic crisis has given rise to an international debate where policies proposed, which are more or less interventionist, gave strong financial support to banks and private companies (Albertos Puebla & Sánchez Hernández, 2014). However, despite the harshness of the crisis there are limited responses which identify the links to problems within the structure of the capitalist economic system in which the responsibility for the living conditions of the population becomes an externality (Carrasco, 2009).

The financial crisis has thrown light on the conflict between capital and social reproduction. As Pérez Orozco has pointed out (2010, p. 35), the collective mechanisms for guaranteeing access to dignified living conditions, in terms of universality and equality, are tending to disappear, while those mechanisms that collectivise the creation of sufficient profit levels for capital are being strengthened. Thus, the effort to re-establish the initial order and create wellbeing on a daily basis is being increasingly left in the hands of families. In their analysis of the impact of the crisis on families and children, Navarro and Clua-Losada (2012) point out that the situation in Spain, prior to the crisis, was already characterised by a higher risk of poverty than other countries in the European Union, due to a lower level of social protection in the face of unemployment.

It is indeed the case that unemployment and an unstable and precarious labour market have triggered a situation of economic and social vulnerability in families in Spain. Households are therefore left with little or no social assistance, as access to resources is privatised and there is a loss of adequate and stable sources of income. The crisis has highlighted the fragility of a market-based system that overlooks or disparages the sustainability of life. Only the enormous amount of domestic and care work that is being done, mainly by women, makes it possible for the economic system to continue functioning. In terms of feminist economics, this has been analysed as a crisis of civilisation (Carrasco, 2001, 2009; Pérez Orozco, 2010) that needs to be tackled from multiple viewpoints as part of an all-embracing reformulation of the system of production and reproduction.

It is true that during the neoliberal era, women have become important players in the global economy, gender issues have become prominent and many indicators of gender inequality have improved in Spain (Benería, 2014). Nevertheless, the deterioration of social conditions is reversing the progress made so far. Women are affected as workers (in a still gender-segmented and segregated labour market), as mothers, as caregivers or as monoparental heads of families. The role of families as a system of social reproduction makes visible how crisis is also lived intergenerationally, so that many actors intervene as victims and/or active agents in coping with the problem depending on their position in the life cycle. For instance, senior citizens provide pensions that help precarious household budgets, underlying the solidarity between generations, the role of the extended family and the shrinkage of the Spanish and Catalan welfare state. Over a decade after the start of the crisis, the recession has worsened the situation for families and introduced new elements into the analysis. The crisis has had a significant impact on the economic wellbeing of many children in Spain (Caparrós & Gelabert, 2015; Ayllón, 2017), one of the few countries in Europe that still lacks a universal child benefit.

The longevity of the recession and the severity of its impact have given rise to a great deal of in-depth analysis in Catalonia, Spain and Europe that has unravelled specific features: the increased feminisation of poverty (Fuente, 2017); the situation of risk for children who live in large or single-parent families, as well as those considered as standard (two adults and two children); and the recognition that young people aged between 14 and 17 are the most heavily affected (Ayllón, 2017). This focus on the adolescent age group highlights the conditions in which they are passing to adulthood, in terms of educational opportunities and physical and mental health. It reveals their perspective on issues like the housing crisis, evictions and changes of residence (Valiño, 2015); the migration of young people to other countries to find work (Allen, 2016; Van Mol, 2016); the construction of gender in relation to work, in a crucial stage of the formation of identity (McDowell, 2012); and the loss of educational opportunities and subsequent lowering of aspirations for the future. These situations highlight still further the need for a critical, gender-based perspective that shows how female poverty is the result of a model of social organisation that not only privileges fields dominated by men but also has further repercussions involving multiple generations of the family. Women, children and grandparents are all affected by the effects of financial crisis, adding to the gendered dimension of the crisis the intersection with the age or the generational dimension.

This chapter explores the analysis of the impact of the economic crisis on children in our region, Catalonia, from its origins, via reports from non-governmental organisations and governmental institutions. This analysis is complemented by interviews with experts from Catalonia, mainly drawn from the field of education in a broad sense, since in times of crisis educational institutions and actors are taking on an enlarged role in relation to social reproduction. A critical reading has been undertaken to detect the unequal effects of the crisis in the child population, with a particular emphasis on the role played by gender in this process.

A cross-sectional examination of the crisis with a gender and age perspective

Reports from four public and private bodies providing data have been analysed to ascertain the impact of the crisis on children in Catalonia. This analysis has taken a gender perspective to focus on the key issue of the impact of austerity on children and families, and it has been limited to the central years of the crisis, from 2012 to 2016. There are seven reports analysed in all, produced by UNICEF (2012a, 2012b, 2014, 2016), the Catalan Ombudsman (Síndic de Greuges, 2012), the Red Cross (Creu Roja, 2013) and the DESC Observatory (Valiño, 2015). In this review we include the majority of existing available reports on this issue published during these years.

UNICEF has analysed the situation of children in Spain in four reports. The first, *Childhood in Spain 2012–13. The Impact of the Crisis on Children* (2012a), showed that children suffer directly from the crisis when their fathers and mothers are without a job or income, or when they are evicted from their home. Children's diet becomes impoverished and they suffer from a deterioration of their home environment and a lack of resources for medical treatment. The child population is also affected indirectly by cuts to public spending on welfare benefits, grants, school meals and books. UNICEF observed a general increase in poverty and analysed its impact on children's lives, the poorest age group because they lacked a system of protection (such as that available to old-age pensioners).

In this context, UNICEF mentioned changes of residence imposed by the financial situation, the impossibility of paying for school meals and buying clothes and an increased dependency on social organisations. There was also evidence of reductions in the quality of children's nutrition and living conditions as well as in the quality of domestic coexistence. Reductions in income affected spending on education, extracurricular activities and clothes for school and sport. Changes were also detected in families' strategies for saving money: fewer leisure activities and holidays, greater control of energy consumption and changes in diet. Evictions trigger changes of residence, to another city, region or country, and sometimes changes in the people who look after children, as well as increased overcrowding and degradation of the environment. It is worth noting that this first UNICEF report included children's own opinions about the crisis, which come from a survey with 6,000 students aged 11–12. The results indicate that children notice and suffer from the stress of the adult population, they feel guilty, and this situation instils fear and insecurity in them.

Also in 2012, UNICEF presented the report *Childhood Wellbeing as Seen by Children* (UNICEF, 2012b), which summarises a study of quality of life and subjective wellbeing for children aged 11–12 in Spain. It shows that levels of wellbeing depend on several factors – geography, gender, context and use of time, characteristics of the population – as well as children's own perceptions and concerns. The study identifies the 'happiest children' and those 'on the fringes' of or 'excluded' from high levels of wellbeing. The children also made a subjective analysis of various fields, such as their household, material goods, interpersonal relationships, residential area, health, organisation of time, school or college and personal satisfaction.

As regards gender differences, the girls gave higher scores for aspects of their wellbeing associated with material goods, interpersonal relationships, residential area and school. The boys give higher scores to personal satisfaction and organisation of time. Girls are also more satisfied than boys with respect to services (such as libraries or public transportation), school and pocket money. In contrast, boys are more satisfied with themselves, their freedom and their appearance. The report concludes by highlighting the main results and the fact that when adolescents are questioned about their rights, they demonstrate high levels of subjective wellbeing.

Two years later, in 2014, UNICEF produced the report *Childhood in Spain 2014. The Social Value of Children: Towards a Cross-Party Consensus on Childhood* (UNICEF, 2014). It starts from the premise that the situation of children has grown worse: there is an increased risk of poverty, unemployment has risen, the data on domestic material deprivation have grown worse, austerity policies and spending cuts have become more severe and there has been a reduction in the birth rate. The report also provides data that highlight worrying structural deficiencies, such as the high levels of school failure and cuts in educational investment. The 2014 report demonstrates differences in the impact of the crisis on children according to their ethnicity, national origin, family formation, parents' work situation or disability, but no differences are recorded with respect to gender.

The 2016 UNICEF report, *Equity for Children: The Case of Spain*, traces Spain's alarming journey through the crisis. Of all the richest countries in Europe, Spain has one of the most unequal distributions of income. In recent years, Spain has sharply declined in two notable indicators of equality: income and life satisfaction. Gender differences are mentioned twice in this report: girls present worse indicators of health in every country and the life satisfaction of girls, especially those of immigrant origin, is lower than that of boys. This is particularly troubling because inequality in these levels of satisfaction is associated with the development of risk situations such as smoking, harassment and violence. In conclusion, the 2016 UNICEF report shows how the years of crisis have been marked by stagnation or even a deterioration in the relative position of boys and girls in the lower levels of income and wellbeing.

The report on child poverty in Catalonia drawn up by the Catalan Ombudsman (Síndic de Greuges, 2012) provides an exhaustive analysis of children's living conditions and public social policies. In the underage population, it is the adolescent population, aged from 14 to 17, that is at the greatest risk of poverty. Next come children living in large families; in third place, children of adolescent mothers (aged between 13 and 19); and in fourth place, children who live with only one parent. What is particularly worrying about these results is that Catalonia suffers from more child poverty than most European countries and that there is more poverty in children than in the population as a whole (Síndic de Greuges, 2012). From a gender-based viewpoint, the study demonstrates how the increase in the rate of female employment activity compared to previous decades does not correspond to a situation of equality with men as regards working conditions, which are still worse for women. This inequality affects children's wellbeing in all families, particularly when mothers are the main or the only adult family providers, especially when there are lone young mother families.

As regards the report by the Red Cross (2013), the impact of the crisis on children in Catalonia is growing and their situation is becoming increasingly precarious. The report provides detailed and highly relevant information about the cost involved for families with children at school (books, school meals, clothes, shoes, activities and transport) and about the ways in which families organise themselves to obtain the resources needed. The report concludes that school should be a promoter of social equality in a context in which a growing number of families are unable to take on the expenses of schooling and receive insufficient welfare benefits to help them do so. The report also presents nutritional problems and shows that school can be the only guarantor of a healthy and varied daily meal.

The Red Cross report is particularly scrupulous in its use of non-sexist language, but it projects an image of women that heightens their profile as victims or passive beneficiaries or receivers of the organisation's aid policies. At the same time, women are depicted as the ones in charge of social reproduction and this role is even reinforced in times of crisis. This is clearly exemplified by the fact that, of the nine testimonies presented, only one comes from a man (a professional), whereas the eight testimonies from women come from three professionals, one volunteer and four receivers of aid. There has clearly been a move towards feminisation, but it would be desirable to see profiles that help break down gender stereotypes and dualisms without ignoring women's role and responsibilities in social reproduction.

Another noteworthy report was later published by the DESC Observatory (Economic, Social and Cultural Rights) (Valiño, 2015), which examines the effects of the housing crisis in Catalonia on the physical and mental health of the people affected, paying special attention to the situation of children. Changing schools for financial reasons, like eviction, is one of the less visible phenomena affecting children's wellbeing. The report points out that difficulties in meeting household expenses can also trigger a change of both residence and school, as well as the renunciation of leisure activities, with an accompanying danger of a loss of social capital and difficulties in forging links with the new neighbourhood.

All these reports describe how this period of austerity has affected the daily life of children and young people in Catalonia. They make it clear that not just adults suffer from the consequences of economic crisis. Families as a whole, comprising adult(s), children and young people, are obliged to cope with the effect of crises, and through this process gender differences appear both among children and among parents. Intergenerational relationships and ties emerged as fundamental in ameliorating the negative impacts of crisis. Schools and educators also contribute to smooth the process, going beyond their educational role to a social service support role. This expansion of the role of schools is not sufficiently recognised or supported, as we will see in the following section.

Experts as committed social agents in difficult times

To complete this approach to the subject under study, short interviews with experts were also undertaken. These were mainly professionals in the educational field whose work involves direct contact with children, young people and families. From 2013 to 2017, interviews were conducted with 36 professionals (30 women and 6 men) from various medium-size Catalan cities. Twenty-four of the interviewees were teachers in primary or secondary education or other branches of education, in both public and private educational establishments, and two people who care for young people and families. The interviewees formed part of the researchers' professional and social circle. Gender differences among the teachers considered are in line with the feminisation of the preschool and primary education in Catalonia due to cultural reasons of role identification (Institut Català de les Dones, 2018). Child education has always been associated with the care of children and it is a role still attributed to women. Moreover, since a preschool and primary education teacher is the least paid education stage of all, this work may also be discouraging for the male gender due to breadwinning stereotypes.

The questions formulated were as follows: (1) What are the social and economic characteristics of the workplace (school, primary school, etc.)? (2) Have you noticed the economic crisis in your workplace? (3) How does the economic crisis affect your workplace and your work? (4) How does the economic crisis affect your students? The interviews were conducted orally (two thirds) or by e-mail (one third). Furthermore, in order to complement these opinions and appraisals, five technicians from the local authorities working in the fields of education, childhood, youth, gender equity and social work were interviewed, along with the president of the Catalan Federation of Parents' Associations (FAPAC)[1] at the time and two young people who run a children's leisure association. The president of the FAPAC noted that the circumstances of poverty have diversified with the crisis and increasingly affect the middle-class swathe of today's population. For instance, the crisis has affected families in which both parents have lost their job, exhausted their unemployment benefit and entered a dynamic of poverty, especially when there are debts or mortgages to pay.

In the preschool and primary education stage: meeting basic needs

The compulsory school system in Catalonia begins at the age of 6 with primary education (6 to 12 years old) and continues with secondary education (12 to 16 years old). Before that, children can attend preschools (prior to 6 years old) to be prepared for the following school stage or to allow parents to work a full day. Childcare at preschools is undeniably expensive, more so in the private than in the public sector. In the preschool and primary education stages, the most tangible repercussions of the crisis include reductions in permanent staff, drops in teachers' salaries, salary cuts in the event of illness, problems in covering leave with substitutions, lower budgets for the maintenance of buildings and facilities and the purchase of materials, as well as reductions in teacher-training sessions. During the first decade of the 21st century, when there was a period of relatively stable birth rates, public preschools (managed by the local or regional government) were full; they now have empty places, and some of the filled places are taken by families that can no longer assume the cost, which is then subsidised by the public authorities. Town halls and county councils grant scholarships from their social services resources to cover the preschool fees, meals or both to the families that need them. Often the scholarships do not cover all the expenses but they are distributed among more children. 'The goal of the local administration is that no one is left without schooling or food and the resources are awarded until the budget is exhausted' (local education technician). These institutions also look for volunteer families to pay for a child's scholarship. This is an extra source of resources to reach everyone's needs.

It is apparent, according to one of the local education technicians, that 'many children have their only good meal of the day' in their preschool, and generally speaking, local authorities are witnessing an increased need to cover basic needs such as this. It is also noticeable that, among the families that can still afford the school or preschool fee, they do not use the school meal service anymore, or only do so from time to time.

The same dynamic is seen in childcare before and after school hours. This seems to be a direct consequence of families having more time, due to lack of jobs, and less available resources. It has also been noted that some families find it difficult to pay for school outings. In many cases, teachers have decided to reduce the number of outings on offer, although sometimes the local authorities allocate resources to schools to guarantee one outing per level per year or to maintain at least one leisure activity. As regards extracurricular activities, a lower rate of participation has been observed: 'I don't do extracurricular activities because we can't afford them' is one of the reasons given by younger children to their teachers. This under-scheduled activity reveals inequalities in children's landscapes of play and informal education in times of austerity, as observed in other contexts (Holloway & Pimlott-Wilson, 2018).

Female primary school teachers suggest that the school offers a lower quality of education than before the start of the crisis, which affects the most vulnerable students, especially those who have learning difficulties or newcomers from other countries. They refer to fewer specialised teachers for children with special needs, less individualised attention and the absence of 'welcome classrooms' (small classrooms for foreign children who arrive once the term has started), among others. This is not expressed by men interviewed, being evidence of how the dominant female experience continues to give priority to care for others, both in the private and the public sphere (England, 2010; Le Petitcorps, 2019), which leads to an identification of the needs of the domestic or community group. Certainly, 'poverty makes people move' (female local technician in education), and it also implies that some foreign families have returned to their country of origin and that others have changed neighbourhoods in search of more affordable housing.

These new dynamics reveal a context of change and uncertainty that has repercussions on children's everyday lives. Giamello and Castro (2017), for example, have observed how some children have become isolated due to their parents' lack of time, another crisis effect when parents have to work multiple jobs to make ends meet, and their lack of social networks and financial resources. The press refers to these children as the 'latchkey generation' because there is nobody in when they get back home.

Economically speaking, some schools have endeavoured to make themselves as aware as possible of the impact of the economic difficulties affecting families in order to facilitate payments and reschedule outings so that pupils can take part in them. One teacher commented that the town hall subsidised outings for pupils with greater difficulties and, as a result, more pupils have been able to take part in them in the last two academic years. This same teacher highlighted the fact that the disappearance of grants for textbooks and school materials has made families reuse them. The Parents' Association in some schools has set up an anti-cuts and anti-crisis committee to put forward proposals and initiatives for obtaining economic resources, among them to develop a stock of items to be given to those in need and to create a solidarity subsidy (through the fees of the Parent's Association) to address the non-payment of school materials and school outings or to assist with declining school budgets.

In the secondary education stage: effects of the internalisation of shortcomings

Adolescence seems to be a more complicated period in times of economic crisis. Children up to the age of 12 are more protected in terms of basic needs and attention to infant poverty, whereas the period from ages 12 to 18 gives rise to new personal challenges in fields such as leisure, health, work and sexuality. We shall now examine the respective impact of the crisis on pupils, families, teachers and schools.

The secondary school teachers interviewed noted that some students' academic performance was affected by being unable to complete their assigned tasks due to lack of materials, while others could not take part in extracurricular activities or outings due to their cost. In the light of these circumstances, textbooks, clothes and materials are shared, recycled and used to greater advantage and outings are refocused and reorganised.

Teachers reported a lack of motivation when it comes to studying due to the lack of any expectations of finding future employment. A male secondary school teacher expressed that 'at their age we knew that we would work when adults. Can you imagine what it must be like to grow up knowing that you will not work?' Economic hardship experienced in families also was raised as impacting on pupils' emotional situation: 'We feel that the level of anxiety or uneasiness felt by some pupils is due to economic problems experienced at home' (female secondary school teacher). Educators and technicians agree that there is a situation of adolescents' emotional distancing within families, since 'families in severe crisis situation have adult references who are always distressed by other things and there's a lot of tension in the home' (local social worker). In these situations, schools are important sites to deal collectively with issues that concern young people. Again, teachers act as more than educators when discussing private matters with adolescents, especially family problems.

As it has been mentioned in the previous section by a local technician on education, the teachers interviewed also noted significant changes with regard to the working situation of their parents, with extreme situations in which both the father and mother are without work or in which one of them has to emigrate to another country in search of work: 'Some [immigrant] families have returned to their countries and the same reason was given when informing the school, "we have to leave, we cannot find any work here" ' (female secondary school teacher). At this stage of education, women teachers observe that some families do whatever they can so that their sons and daughters do not notice the decrease in income, or they realise how some parents do not reveal to the school that one of the parents has lost his/her job.

A higher number of families encounter problems in paying for registration fees, materials, outings and so forth as they cannot afford gas and electricity at home. Consequently, they face greater difficulties in providing their children with extra tuition, speech therapy, psychology and so on. This is expressed thus by the following interviewee, who also brings up the matter of cuts in public health: 'Particularly in situations in which a student needs external assistance from a professional they cannot pay for it and, via the public route, they spend months awaiting their turn' (female secondary school teacher).

Despite teachers' 'endeavour to offset shortcomings imaginatively', as a female secondary school teacher states, most of the teachers interviewed consider that the decrease in resources received by the secondary school affects the service that can be given to pupils. Both local authorities and families fall behind in the payments needed for the smooth running of schools. The following opinion reveals some of the actions undertaken to reduce expenses in the schools where these interviewees work:

We have rationed the photocopies given to pupils substantially. Repairs cannot be undertaken, nor can maintenance, because the resources are not being received. We had to ration the school's heating and cleaning. Recreational outings cease to be undertaken and very few field trips are organised.

(female secondary school teacher)

This professional collective has experienced important grievances such as drops in teachers' salaries, loss of pupil classroom hours, increases in the number of pupils per class and a reduction in time to dedicate to individual pupils, especially those with learning difficulties. Expressions such as 'the increase in hours and cuts have undoubtedly reduced the quality of classes' (male secondary school teacher), 'substitutions of colleagues who are on leave are not covered' or 'teachers on leave do not earn what corresponds to them' (female secondary school teacher) provide the context of demotivation driven by the economic and social crisis which has led some professionals to protest – without success. Objecting to going on outings as a means of protesting against the cuts made to civil servants has been one of their reactions.

Concluding discussion

In Catalonia we find ourselves in a doubly unfavourable context: on the one hand, the context of greater poverty and social exclusion found in most countries in the European Union, combined with a reduced quality of life and social welfare; on the other hand, the context of recession and economic crisis, reflected in policies of cuts in social spending, particularly as regards attention to families and childhood.

This is the context of the issue under analysis: the impact of the crisis on children in Catalonia. None of the sources consulted suggested children are cushioned from the impact of the economic crisis; on the contrary, they all recognised that children constitute one of the affected collectives. It is also apparent that, over the long duration of the crisis, many children's situations have grown progressively worse, both in strictly financial terms and in terms of their perception of satisfaction with their lives.

The impact of the economic crisis on children has increased and deepened, while the lack of government financial resources has led to more cuts in social support for children and families. The reports and statistics analysed emphasised and denounced this trend, and experts started to talk about the 'recession generation' (Funes, 2016) or 'children of recession' (Escolán, 2014) to refer to those children who have lived much of their lives under austerity.

Gender has also had an impact on levels of social vulnerability. Women (with children) were at greater risk of poverty. This was confirmed by the existence of many single-parent families headed by women who cannot singlehandedly buffer the family against welfare and budgetary cuts. Rather, the effects of austerity trickle through families, with different generations and genders experiencing cuts in a variety of ways and then supported by the people who make up social institutions, namely the schools. Unemployment and reduced income, evictions and consequent changes of residence, reduced social spending and difficulties in buying children's clothes, materials and food are just a few examples of this scenario of deprivation. UNICEF (2016) identifies childhood as a social seismograph, as a lighthouse warning of problems ahead. The consequences of this situation accumulate and become evident in schools. These increasing difficulties have to be tackled by fewer staff and fewer resources; there are more requests than ever for grants or subsidies for school meals, but fewer of these are available. Children's academic performance is also negatively affected by hardships and lack of motivation.

This agreement about the diagnosis means that there is also a consensus about the crucial need to strengthen the social protection of children and young people. Various institutions have pointed out that this very necessary attention does not only benefit the children themselves. They freely recognise that neglect of children in a context of financial crisis leads, in the long run, to greater social costs for society as a whole.

All the sources analysed herein expressed themselves in terms of the family and referred more to the sphere of reproduction than to that of production, yet the government policy focuses on the individual adult while effects are family-wide. The reports emphasise the diversity of family types and stress the negative aspects: less logistical support in everyday life, fewer economic resources, more expenses when new members join the family circle. And if families are of foreign origin, a higher risk of vulnerability is detected.

In short, going beyond poor families (of whatever type), any families that stray from the traditional nuclear model are considered one of the 'new risks' of modern society in times of recession. It is very surprising that there is not more reference to women, who have been and continue to be the basic pillar of reproduction (see Hall et al., 2017) Moreover, if the effects of unemployment have upset gender relations in the family unit, it would also have been interesting to delve into how these traditional relations are being redrawn, into whether new masculinities and femininities are being constructed, and into the extent to which new gender contracts can be found in family units.

As regards the experts, they also express concerns about working conditions and the difficulties in achieving professional fulfilment at a time when pupils' and families' demands are more numerous and intense. However, this group is the most proactive in the sense of pointing out and positively appraising responses to the crisis, through reorganising, reformulating or creating new mechanisms that strengthen the resilience of these professionals, of schools and of families and children. Teachers are working through adverse conditions themselves as wages and security decrease, yet they work in the interests of families. Educationalists are tackling the effects of crisis through schools.

One noteworthy gap in the analysed reports is the gender dimension of the crisis and its possible differential impact on girls and boys. In this regard, it is paradoxical that, while there are studies that show how, from the process of primary socialisation, the family context has a direct impact on the emergence and consolidation of gender stereotypes (Mosteiro, 2010; Barberá, 2005), the impact of the lack of resources and support for girls and boys has not been analysed on a differentiated basis. However, what has been noted is that the largely invisible adolescent group (Cahill, 2000; Weller, 2006) bears the brunt of the risk of poverty. It would be interesting to delve into the specific needs of this group to thrash out these data qualitatively. Analysing the crisis from the perspective of children sheds light on the most vulnerable group, placing a major reproduction crisis and the role of women in childcare at the core of the issue, and revealing the need to dig deeper into the differences between boys and girls according to their identities. A gender perspective would pave the way for future research that sets these findings – that educationalists are tackling the effects of crisis through schools – out in detail and defines the proposals for improvement more specifically.

Note

1 This can be understood as the equivalent of a federation of parent-teacher associations (PTA) in English-speaking contexts.

References

Albertos Puebla, J.M. and Sánchez Hernández, J.M., eds. (2014). *Geografía de la crisis económica en España*. Valencia: Universitat de València.

Allen, K. (2016). Top girls navigating austere times: Interrogating youth transitions since the 'crisis'. *Journal of Youth Studies*, 19(6), pp. 805–820.

Ayllón, S. (2017). Growing up in poverty: Children and the great recession in Spain. In: Cantillón, B., Chzhen, Y., Handa, S. and Nolan, B., eds., *Children of austerity. Impact of the great recession on child poverty in rich countries*. New York: UNICEF and Oxford University Press, pp. 219–241.

Barberá, E. (2005). *Psicología y género*. Madrid: Prentice Hall.

Benería, L. (2014). Neoliberalism and the global economic crisis: A viewpoint from feminist economics. In: Verschuur, C., Guérin, I. and Guétat-Bernard, H., eds., *Under development: Gender*. London: Palgrave Macmillan, pp. 257–285.

Cahill, C. (2000) Street literacy: Urban teenagers' strategies for negotiating their neighbourhood. *Journal of Youth Studies*, 3(3), pp. 251–277.

Caparrós, F. and Gelabert, M. (2015). Pobreza y vulneración de los derechos en la infancia. *RES, Revista de Educación Social*, 20, pp. 1–7.

Carrasco, C. (2001). La sostenibilidad de la vida. *Mientras Tanto*, 82, pp. 43–70.

Carrasco, C. (2009). Women, sustainability and social debt. *Revista de Educación, número extraordinario 2009*, pp. 169–191.

Creu Roja (2013). *L'impacte de la crisi en la infància i l'entorn escolar*. Barcelona: Creu Roja.

England, K. (2010). Home, work and the shifting geographies of care. *Ethics, Place and Environment*, 13(2), pp. 131–150.

Escolán, E. (2014). La pobresa vista amb ulls d'infant. *Ara*, 8 November.

Fuente, M. de la (2017). Crisi, austeritat i pobresa amb perspectiva de gènere. *Barcelona Societat: revista de coneixement i anàlisi social*, 21, pp. 10–20.

Funes, J. (2016). Vingui demà, quan sigui gran. *Ara*, 12 January.

Giamello, C. and Castro, G. de, eds. (2017). *Nativos de la crisis: los niños de la llave*. Barcelona: Educo.

Hall, S. M., McIntosh, K., Neitzert, E., Pottinger, L., Sandhu, K., Stephenson, M-A., Reed, H. and Taylor, L. (2017). *Intersecting inequalities: The impact of austerity on Black and minority ethnic women in the UK.* London: Runnymede and Women's Budget Group. www.intersecting-inequalities.com

Holloway, S. and Pimlott-Wilson, H. (2018). Reconceptualising play: Balancing childcare, extra-curricular activities and free play in contemporary childhoods. *Transactions of the Institute of British Geographers,* 43(3), pp. 420–434.

Institut Català de les Dones (2018). *Les dones a Catalunya, 2018. Dades elaborades per l'Observatori per a la Igualtat de Gènere.* Barcelona: Generalitat de Catalunya.

Instituto Nacional de Estadística (INE). 2019. *Encuesta de Población Activa (EPA).* Madrid: INE. www.ine.es

Katz, C. (2001). Vagabond capitalism and the necessity of social reproduction. *Antipode,* 33(4), pp. 708–727.

Le Petitcorps, C. (2019). Care and domestic work. In: Orum, A., ed., *The Wiley Blackwell Encyclopedia of urban and regional studies.* London: John Wiley & Sons. https://doi. org/10.1002/9781118568446.eurs0038

McDowell, L. (2012). Post-crisis, post-Ford and post-gender? Youth identities in an era of austerity. *Journal of Youth Studies,* 15(5), pp. 573–590.

Méndez, R. (2014). Crisis económica y reconfiguraciones territoriales. In: Albertos Puebla, J. M. and Sánchez Hernández, J. M., eds., *Geografía de la crisis económica en España.* Valencia: Universitat de València, pp. 17–38.

Mosteiro, M.J. (2010). Los estereotipos de género y su transmisión a través del proceso de socialización. In: Radl Phillip, R., ed., *Investigaciones actuales de la mujer y del género.* Santiago de Compostela: Servicio de Publicaciones e Intercambio Científico de la Universidad de Santiago de Compostela, pp. 239–252.

Navarro, V. and Clua-Losada, M. (2012). *El impacto de la crisis en las familias y en la infancia. Observatorio social de España.* Barcelona: Ariel.

Pérez Orozco, A. (2010). Crisis multidimensional y sostenibilidad de la vida. *Investigaciones Feministas,* 1, pp. 29–53.

Pitarch Garrido, M.D. (2014). Desigualdades regionales, pobreza y vulnerabilidad social en España durante la crisis (2017–2013). In: Albertos Puebla, J. M. and Sánchez Hernández, J. M., eds., *Geografía de la crisis económica en España.* Valencia: Universitat de València, pp. 201–229.

Síndic De Greuges De Catalunya (2012). *Informe sobre la pobresa infantil a Catalunya.* Barcelona: Síndic de Greuges de Catalunya.

UNICEF (2012a). *La infancia en España 2012–13. El impacto de la crisis en los niños.* Madrid: UNICEF.

UNICEF (2012b). *El bienestar infantil desde el punto de vista de los niños.* Madrid: UNICEF.

UNICEF (2014). *La infancia en España 2014. El valor social de los niños: hacia un pacto de Estado por la Infancia.* Madrid: UNICEF.

UNICEF (2016). *Equidad para los niños. El caso de España.* Madrid: UNICEF.

Valiño, V., ed. (2015). *Emergència habitacional a Catalunya: Impacte de la crisi hipotecària en el dret a la salut i els drets dels infants.* Barcelona: Observatori DESC.

Van Mol, C. (2016). Migration aspirations of European youth in times of crisis. *Journal of Youth Studies,* 19(10), pp. 1303–1320.

Weller, S. (2006) Situating (young) teenagers in geographies of children and youth. *Children's Geographies,* 4(1), pp. 97–108.

Part II

Ways of coping through crises

6 An informal welfare? Urban resilience and spontaneous solidarity in Naples, Italy, after the Great Recession

Serena Romano

This chapter discusses the results of a study carried out between 2016 and 2017 on spontaneous solidarity in a post-recession context, focusing specifically on the case of the former judicial psychiatric hospital in Naples (OPG): an imposing structure vacated in 2008 and occupied by a group of activists in 2015, when it underwent a major 'spontaneous' renewal inspired by the principles of solidarity and self-help. The former OPG occupies a large building that served as a monastery in the 16th century and later as military barracks. Eventually it became a forensic psychiatric hospital before being shut down and abandoned in 2008. The building is located in Naples, in the Avvocata neighbourhood, one of the city's most densely populated areas and one with the highest presence of migrants (Strozza et al., 2014). The occupation and re-opening of this building in March 2015 did not just radically alter its former intended use. The initiative added new *social life* to the neighbourhood itself. Activists claim that, after initially showing some reluctance, lots of locals now spend time at the OPG. The building's new function, implied in the name the founders gave to the project – 'Je So Pazz', Neapolitan dialect for 'I am crazy' – is to bring freedom to a place that alienated and condemned people suffering from mental disorders while making the structure an intermediary between the population and the institutions, promoting political claims and reforms of urban politics.

This case study illustrates that it is at the city level that we encounter the most evident aspects of public restructuring, including those affecting welfare and social inclusion. This is particularly the case for Italy, where the Great Recession's immediate impact on the already stagnating economy of the country was only minor if compared to (a) the financial outcomes experienced by other nations or (b) to the secondary, much more disruptive effects of austerity packages introduced after the first years of the crisis (Brandolini et al., 2013: 151). Government's adjustments on the public budget have notoriously impacted living standards and income distribution, especially to the detriment of certain categories of citizens (e.g. pensioners and young unemployed), thus amplifying cases of urban 'social suffering', which are still felt in the aftermath of the crisis (Fregolent and Savino, 2014: 15). We are using the city with its transformations as the geographical level at which to analyse processes and effects of austerity. One of the most evident and recurring effects is undoubtedly the growing 'social polarization' (Schönig and Schipper, 2016: 8) between the part of the urban population that depends on local infrastructures and public services and those who can instead rely on private services. Such a phenomenon that spans big economic hubs (Musterd et al., 2016) and the metropolises of the 'periphery' is also encountered in Naples (Morlicchio, 2015; De Rosa and Salvati, 2016), which is my field of analysis.

Furthermore, the focus on the city offers an important insight into the effects of austerity on how the urban population *adapts* to change. The many initiatives of urban solidarity launched by the third sector, activists, and normal citizens testify not only to the existence of an unfulfilled social demand but also to a more general deep transformation of the urban space in the 'post-welfare city' (DeVerteuil, 2017). Neoliberal economic and political reforms have disrupted older urban geographies based on systems of assistance and support of the local population (i.e. the 'welfare city'), creating new urban configurations where spontaneous solidarity is left almost entirely alone to assist the most vulnerable ones (Sotiropoulos and Bourikos, 2014). It remains to be seen, however, whether resorting to informal solidarity actors at times of emergency stands prominently as a *coping strategy* for only these strata of the population or extends to the citizenship as a whole.

The urban perspective on austerity studies is used to examine the effects of 'social resistance' to change triggered by both fiscal restraint and decreasing social and economic rights. While in post-recession times institutional urban public policies seem to veer towards eliminating some social rights, it is interesting to look at examples of social solidarity aimed at advancing innovative practices and collective social claims increasingly filling the gaps left open by public policies. In doing so, the chapter sets off from two fundamental premises. First, institutional *social innovation* practices are not always compatible with *social progress* as an objective (Moulaert et al., 2013), especially when transformation is affected by austerity needs, with fiscal restraint objectives hardly ever meeting those of social justice and inclusion, and in fact leaving a great part of social demand unsatisfied. Second, and in accordance to the relevant recent literature, I believe that austerity processes should always be read against their respective urban 'geographies', rather than national ones, for their 'economic, political, and social implications' to be fully grasped (Donald et al., 2014: 4).

The case study

This chapter draws on insights from a case study conducted on Sant'Eframo OPG in Naples, a 'solidarity lab' offering about 50 different social, political, recreational and sports activities, including laboratories, medical and help centres, here referred to as 'help desks'. The aim of the study was to examine the social function of spontaneous forms of urban solidarity and ascertain whether user participation in such activities should be interpreted as exclusively *instrumental* (i.e. replacing public institutions and services) or as a means of social inclusion and participation in the city's public and political life, aiding a process of *urban resilience* by the population. In order to do so, three main questions were formulated: What *types of users* participate in the OPG services? What types of use are made of the help desks and what are the *modes of participation* to the activities? *Why* do the users visit the help desks?

The fieldwork was divided into three phases. During phase one, I met one of the founders of the project, visited the structure and learnt about its current activities. During the second phase, I met the activists who were responsible for each help desk/laboratory and analysed the roles and organisation of the activities. Finally, I interviewed the users of the help desks and laboratories. Three main methods were used. *Non-participant observation* in the common areas of the structure, during the weekly meetings planned for the various activities and at help desks, was conducted throughout the fieldwork (2016–2017). 'Remote' and passive observation of social encounters and interactions in the structure allowed me to understand and record organisational and behavioural patterns (Sharma, 1997: 159) of both activists and the OPG's users in the structure, as well as the presence of different informal roles and rules put in place in each of the areas of the structure.

Another method used consisted of in-depth interviews with six of the founders of the OPG and activists who manage the help desks to investigate further the overall perceived role of the structure and its intended social role for those who take an active daily part in its organisation. Finally, semi-structured interviews with 10 Italian and 20 foreign users domiciled or resident in Naples and who took part at least once at the time of the interview in the activities taken into consideration. These interviews were conducted between 2016 and 2017 and interviewees were selected via targeted sampling among those who used the following services: popular medical clinic, paediatrics help desk, psychiatric counselling, help desk for nutrition, gynaecology help desk, workers help desk, immigrants' help desk, and Italian language school for foreigners. The interviewed users were mainly young and adult women, aged 24–54, living in the neighbourhood or in the areas surrounding the OPG. The high predominance of women among the interviewees mirrors the actual, mainly female composition of the regular users, which is also due to men's less availability to be interviewed. Moreover, many of the potential interviewees (above all males) claimed that they could not speak Italian, thus declining to be interviewed. Although it was therefore impossible to ask them about their participation in the activities of the structure, this is nonetheless indicative of the fact that most immigrants turning to the OPG's services are of recent immigration or they lack any experience of full integration, even if they have lived in the city for many years. In this respect, we can assume that OPG's activities which attracted them most and in which they participated (e.g. the School of Italian) may be an important means to counter marginality for these groups.

'Je So Pazz': not your typical squat

Conceptually the OPG can be defined as a 'squat', however the structure does differ substantially from a typical one. The social gathering function is certainly there, being one of the project's distinctive features and evident in the spatial organisation of the structure: visitors and users socialise in the indoor lounge area, or the outdoor one, at the bar, or sit in the garden-courtyard. The latter is the main informal gathering space of the OPG, the natural setting for visitors to congregate before their respective activities. However, upon entering the building the visitor immediately perceives that the OPG is more than a squat where people spend time together. This is confirmed not only by notes recorded during my non-participant observation, but also by informational material produced by activists and participants. Help desks' weekly agendas, leaflets on special events, awareness and political campaigns' banners are designed to be informative tools which clarify the intended role and organisation of each of the activities and try to involve participants in the most active manner possible. Visitors are welcomed immediately by the activists and then directed to the person/room that might help them – something one would expect to experience in a public office and which also exemplifies the hybrid nature of the OPG.

The heterogeneous social and demographic nature of users gathering here is another element that marks this structure as an atypical squat. Among those observed, the group of 'regulars' is not only made up of young activists or migrants, although they make up a good part of those who turn to the help desks. Also populating the common areas of the structure on a daily basis are professionals who serve voluntarily at the help desks, children from the neighbourhood who attend the social after-school or sports programs, workers in need of legal assistance (a process requiring multiple visits at the structure in the same week), and Neapolitan and foreign patients waiting for their turn at the medical clinic. Thus, the OPG presents itself as an informal meeting place, where the visitor never feels like he/she is intruding in the lives of the occupants, being rather always encouraged to be part of the community. Most of the regulars that I have interviewed know at least one of the activists who manage the structure, and the latter make a constant effort to get acquainted with everybody who visits, even only occasionally. However, as I now discuss, the help desks and laboratories qualify the OPG as a site that offers reliable 'services' to the population.

Help desks and labs

The School of Italian for foreigners counts about 50 users divided in two classes, based on their level of knowledge of Italian. The school is open twice a week for about two hours and is organised in an informal way, with two or more 'classes' sharing the spaces, according to the level of proficiency attained. The school is a weekly scheduled appointment that the users can rely on, being at the same time informal and flexible. For example, students do not necessarily show up for class all at the same time; some often arrive in the middle or by the end of class, according to their personal and work needs.

The popular medical clinic centre includes the gynaecology, psychiatric and paediatric help desks and is managed by doctors who provide voluntary free assistance twice a week. It is open to anybody looking for medical or bureaucratic information or a physical examination. It often works as the first access point for families with children who reside illegally in the country and who are in need of general information, consulting or paediatric assistance. The popular medical clinic that hosts the help desk operates like a regular medical practice. Informational leaflets and brochures on the clinic, prevention and health issues are available in the waiting room. The management of the patients is generally handled by the doctors, although it is often left to the patients' own sense of self-organisation, informality and mutual respect. For example, patients try to remember the order of arrival and their place in the line, making exceptions for those who report an urgency or need to go back to work. This also seems to attest to the role of these help desks as spaces dominated by a strong sense of community and mutual help. Despite everything being self-organised, I have never observed arguments emerging among the patients in the waiting rooms or complaints concerning its organisation. Most of users are migrants, although some Italians use the help desks too, particularly the recently inaugurated gynaecological one.

The legal help desk for workers operates once a week, providing legal help on work-related issues to Italian and foreign users, with immigrants representing the majority of users. It also educates users on subjects like illegal employment, mobbing, and workers' rights. Its organisation is slightly different from other help desks of the OPG. The order of arrival and the management of the users, although relying on informality and flexibility, are managed by the persons responsible for the lab, who direct users to the desks based on their needs. In most cases, one or more migrants help to handle the users. These are generally persons who have a good knowledge of Italian and can help their fellow countrymen to submit their case to the lawyers.

Similar in its structure to the workers' desk, the immigrant desk is open once a week and mainly assists users in handling administrative and bureaucratic paperwork. As with all the other desks, it is often the first point of contact inside the structure for illegal migrants who want to adjust their status or that of their relatives or other members of the community. In this case, too, users often visit with relatives or friends who already have direct or indirect experience with the help desk and its procedure. This seems to be the most successful program of the OPG, together with the School of Italian, with a large, although occasional, weekly turnout of users.

Four forms of participation

Solidarity is one of the core principles of the OPG's manifesto. According to the activists I interviewed, its philosophy is to be a social and political project. A fundamental aspect emerging clearly from the in-depth interviews that I conducted with some of those in charge of the help desks is that the activists regard their role and that of the project as one of political fight and antagonism aimed at promoting solidarity and self-help. Interviewees insisted that the OPG does not just offer alternative services to the institutional ones. One of them explained that the project's goal 'is not to replace the state and the local institutions, but rather to trigger a process of participation that is open to all the citizens', involving them in the project's political and civic claims. To this end, each of the help desks has been organised so as to be linked to a number of political macro-projects: health, migrants, work and the fight against poverty.

The activity and intentions of the OPG project are of major importance to describe the role played by informal solidarity as actors of social innovation leading to social inclusion. In particular, the main purpose of my fieldwork was to explore the different uses of the 'services' offered and their roles in facilitating social participation and reducing marginality. To this end, the interviews were based on questions around the following themes: the uses of the OPG services; the social relationships with other visitors and the exchange, solidarity and help relationships; relationships with the structure's neighbourhood and its inhabitants; and reasons that led the interviewees to turn to the OPG rather than to private and state institutional services, and their relationship with the latter.

Interviews have been used to 'test' our initial hypothesis that two macro-categories of users populate the desks: *instrumental* users (benefitting from the OPG's solidarity only in cases of an immediate need or problem) and *active* users (militants and activists of the structure, with a strong political motivation and a deep sense of belonging to the project). An added purpose of the interviews was to explore DeVerteuil's idea (2017) that those who turn to informal and self-organised forms of solidarity are above all the most vulnerable subjects, and verify this assumption by considering the reasons that led users to turn to the OPG services. Our initial hypothesis on this matter was that users turned to informal solidarity mostly for lack of alternatives from state institutions, or lack of a solid social network in the city able to function as a 'safety net' (which we predicted for foreigners and in particular those of recent immigration).

Among the diverse results of the research, there is significant evidence concerning precisely our attempted initial subdivision into two categories of users. The field research immediately pointed out that the possibilities of participation to the OPG's initiatives cannot be reduced to the initial binary formulation. In fact, we found at least four different models of participation and interaction with the activities offered by the organisation. The data collected through the interviews is discussed into the following sections. The first one focuses on the respondents' answers concerning (1) the services/help desks/workshops they used, (2) their assiduity as attendees at the OPG and (3) their familiarity with other regular attendees. At a general level, this first section analyses different modes of participation in the OPG's activities. The second section examines the subjective experiences of users and expands on answers concerning the motivations leading the respondents to the structure (rather than to other state or private institutions), their satisfaction with their experience and their opinions on the overall project.

Exploring different modes of participation

Partially in line with the first hypothesis, a large proportion of the interviewees belong to what I have originally defined as the instrumental users category, which includes all those participants who seem to have turned to the help desk only to resolve an immediate need/problem (thus using the OPG mainly in an instrumental manner). However, the interviews showed how instrumental users (as per Table 6.1) can be subdivided into two further categories corresponding respectively to the *instrumental and occasional* participation model (users who use the OPG in an instrumental way and only occasionally, without following up or participating in other activities) and the *instrumental and assiduous* participation model (users who are still using the OPG in an instrumental way for one or more specific objectives, but who report to take part in different activities organised inside the structure).

Only a small number of the interviewees belongs to the group of instrumental and occasional users. This is constituted mainly by immigrants who turn to the legal help desk for work, the immigrant assistance help desk and the popular medical clinic. Respondents of this very small group (two or three of all the interviewees) say they have *never been* in the structure before, that they are not habitual attendees, and they have turned to the structure for a specific problem under a friend or a relative's advice. Except for this mode of access, however, the respondents belonging to the 'instrumental and occasional' model do not seem to have social relationships with other habitual attendees and are not well informed about the different activities going on. Yet, contrary to our initial expectations, users of this category are not of recent immigration. Those who visit the structure for the first time have lived in Italy for many years and have 'landed' on the OPG thanks to their compatriots or employer's advice. While it is true that, among the interviewees, we found only two instrumental *and* occasional users, our initial hypothesis about the predominance of the instrumental model cannot be considered as totally wrong, as the instrumental and assiduous users group is wider than the first one. Users belonging to this category are those who have turned to a help desk or a workshop at least two times in order to complete an individual plan. This applies to many of the attendees of the School of Italian, who turn to OPG up to

Table 6.1 Modes of participation in the OPG's activities

Instrumental and assiduous	*Varied*
Frequent use of services, often linked to the accomplishment of a project (e.g. a cycle of paediatric visits) or a single plan (School of Italian).	Participation in different activities and initiatives.
Instrumental and occasional	*Active*
Seldom use of resources/services as an alternative to those offered by other institutions.	Frequent and varied participation and mutuality, collaboration and identification with the political stance of the project.

Source: Elaboration of personal data.

two times a week, even if only instrumentally, that is, until they are able to attend it or acquire the level of Italian they want to learn.

In this regard, it is interesting to note that the school-workshop is quite often a very fast place of transit for users. Mostly the students of Indian and Ceylonese origin say they have attended the school for some weeks and left it once they have learned the basic rules for communicating in Italian.

> My husband came first [to the school], and then I came too following him after a couple of months, but we did not attend together. He attended the class for a month and learnt some Italian necessary to work and I am going to attend for some other time until I learn more Italian and I can start work too. The only person I know here for now is my husband, who is accompanying me.
>
> K., from Sri Lanka, on her first week at the School of Italian (interview conducted in English)

Then there is another group of instrumental and assiduous users, including some patients of the popular medical clinic, in particular mothers with children needing paediatric care who have repeatedly turned to the help desks for inspection visits or asking assistance for a new health problem. However, users who frequently visit the structure do not necessarily report to have deeper relationships with the OPG community than those of 'occasional' users. As in the previous example, the instrumental but assiduous users' social relationships are generally limited to the person who made the 'connection' (another user or militant met outside the structure) introducing them to the OPG's activities, and to some acquaintance (often compatriots, for immigrants users), without seemingly making friends or having mutual help with other habitual users and activists.

A large part of the interviewed users say that they have participated in the past, as well as in the present, in other activities of the structure. Many of the former or present students of the School of Italian have returned to the structure to ask for legal advice or a consultation at the clinic. This aspect is, in several cases, indicative of the immigrants' gradual integration in the OPG's activities. The School of Italian, the medical clinic and the immigrant assistance help desk can be considered as a first (instrumental) landing for many of the immigrants who start to attend the structure in a more assiduous and varied way.

Yet, the experiences of a varied participation collected in the interviews do not always follow this path. Some users, especially women, who began to attend the OPG in a varied way, participating in events, parties, and other recreational activities, have then made an instrumental use of their different help desks when needed. Generally, this model of participation, which I label 'varied', is different from the instrumental one but it can nonetheless allow users to achieve their objectives or to find a solution to contingent problems. Almost all the interviewed users of this group say they have turned to the OPG services for a specific problem.

However, their participation in the OPG's activities seems to be of a different type than that characterising the instrumental users, both occasional and assiduous. Users of this group, for instance, have a deeper relationship with the activists (whom they know by name and with whom they talk about their problems or needs) and other attendees. Although no one in this users group seems to have had any exchange and help relations in the structure, often the interviewed user says s/he has suggested to a friend or a relative to turn to the structure in order to solve his/her problem. This aspect suggests that the users who participate in a varied way in the structure's activities are also able to develop a trust relationship with volunteers and other members of the community, something which will be discussed further again later.

> One of my compatriots brought me here initially to solve a legal problem with my documents. While I am doing this, I have also started the School of Italian, so I am visiting the structure a couple of times a week now.
> A., from India, first month at the OPG (interview conducted in Italian)

Finally, a minor but still significant part of the respondents fit an 'active' participation model. This group includes people participating in one or more help desks who also participated (or used to participate) in the organisation and managing of the OPG's different activities. This group's most interesting and unexpected aspect is its rather varied composition. It does not include just Neapolitan activists and militants supporting the OPG political project but also foreign users, such as Erasmus students working as teachers in one or more or the language courses offered by the structure, or immigrant workers participating actively in different political and awareness campaigns on black labour and exploitation, sometimes also collaborating to the management of the structure, from cleaning to the help desks' organisation and distribution of information leaflets outside the organisation.

The users' experience: roles and reasons

Looking at the 'open' section of the questionnaire submitted to the interviewees, we can elaborate further on the subjectivity of the users' experience. We expected that most of users turned to the help desks because of their incapability/impossibility to access to local institutional welfare services. At the same time, we expected the people turning to self-organised services to come predominantly from highly marginalised social groups, deprived of a local network of solidarity to turn to for help and support, when necessary. Interviews have partly disproved our hypothesis. The results of the research can be synthesised, again, according to the participation models we have already outlined. The few interviewees belonging to the instrumental and occasional model are all non-Italians and most of them are foreigners of recent immigration, with some exceptions consisting of international students (such as Erasmus students interested in learning and teaching languages) and long-term immigrants. When asked, 'Why have you turned to this desk rather than going to a public or private institution?', most of the times the respondents said their decision was a *forced choice*, dictated by their status as irregulars and that without the necessary documents, there is no alternative in the city for them to resolve the problem or urgency that led them to the OPG.

If, instead, we look at the users that participate in an instrumental-assiduous way, we can make a significant distinction between Neapolitan/Italian and foreign users. Most of the Neapolitan interviewees describe their choice to turn to the OPG (instead of other institutions) in terms of convenience, both geographic (for the inhabitants and workers of the neighbourhood) and organisational (compatibility between life and work times for many women visiting the popular medical clinic), but above all economic. Sometimes the interviewees of this group said they made this choice precisely because they preferred not to depend on either the public services – considered as ineffective and inaccessible due to their long waiting lists – or the expensive private ones.

For many interviewed women visiting the medical clinic, the gynaecological help desk was a valid alternative as it is inexpensive and well organised. This is an important aspect above all for the young women interviewed at the medical clinic who said that they came to the clinic in order to benefit from their 'right to *a really* free health', as one respondent said, in the face of the amount of money they should have paid for the same service in a public structure. It is not uncommon that these respondents spontaneously mention financial cutbacks to public health and social services as one of the main reasons behind their decision to turn to the OPG to solve a medical problem. Sentiments of disillusion towards the financial management of public health and social services are not uncommon among these women, as well as frustration for the implications in terms of economic burden upon the citizens.

However, economic convenience is by no means the sole reason for resorting to the services offered by the OPG. An unexpected element emerging from the interviews with the instrumental and assiduous users concerns the element of *trust*. Non-Italian users, most notably, often tell about their trust relationship with volunteer doctors, saying this was preferable to the doctor-patient relation they had experienced in the public or private structures in the past and appears to be a decisive element for many immigrants who decide to turn to the popular medical clinic again and again. Many among the interviewed said they had turned habitually to other (mostly public) health facilities, and even after they had obtained the required documents, they continued using the clinic to complete their plan or because they feel they have received a better examination than the one offered by a public institution. Italians, too, in a couple of cases, choose the help desks of the OPG over private and public actors because of the sense of trust they have built here, although they mainly mention economic convenience and urgency as the most important factors driving their decision.

> I experienced some personal problem in my family and did not know where to go. I knew M. [one of the activists involved in the desk] from other projects and he suggested that I came here to talk to someone. It was my first time

coming but it worked for me and I am coming often. This is so far the first place that I trust to go and talk about my problem.

C., from Italy, first month at the psychiatric counselling desk (interview conducted in Italian)

Coming back to our initial hypothesis, we expected that most of the OPG's users (that is, its instrumental users) would turn to the organisation's services as an alternative to the inefficiencies of public services and to avoid the high costs of the private services, or in order to receive assistance in the absence of a social solidarity network. It is true that all these aspects are among the reasons that lead the instrumental users to turn to the OPG. However, contrary to expectations, the Neapolitan users are more strictly 'instrumental' than the immigrant ones. Turning to grassroots forms of solidarity merely for convenience or easiness is not a prerogative of most marginalised or vulnerable social groups, as we predicted, but rather of those who are better integrated and familiar with the OPG's community, participating in its different social and recreational activities.

The participation of users involved in the social and political initiatives of the OPG seems often motivated by their support for the social/political cause of the overall project, with particular reference to the collective instances of renewal and change but also because of the element of trust regarding doctors, lawyers and volunteers working there, as mentioned already. If we consider again the initial question in this chapter concerning the social role of informal solidarity activities, an element emerges in particular and rather unexpectedly: as the fieldwork progressed, it became clear that among the interviewed there is a population segment that is not particularly disadvantaged or marginal and who turns to the help desks for practical convenience other than affordability.

We can accept our initial hypothesis according to which for most users, both Neapolitans and foreigners, the help desks are used in a mere instrumental way and with little political and civic involvement. On the other hand, we cannot deny the *inclusive* effects of these forms of solidarity and their role in producing a form of 'resistance' by the local population to the progressive narrowing of the citizens' social and economic rights.

As mentioned already, activists consider the services as *only* the first step towards the users' inclusion in the fight to reform the institutions and fully participate in public life. They believe that the awareness and information campaigns they organise, combined with the lack of services and infrastructure that often forces the population to turn to informal solidarity networks, makes the political nature of their activities immediately visible and leading to action. Whether instrumentally used or not, however, the help desks alone appear important tools of social inclusion.

The School of Italian, for example, stands as the first real possibility for many immigrants of learning and communicating correctly in Italian, and is apparently successful in transitioning many of them from a condition of complete marginality into a path of integration with the labour market, the neighbourhood and the city itself. Going to the popular clinic, at the same time, can be seen as an important act of civic and political awareness, if not resistance, for many women who felt both the public and the private sectors were unfair or inefficient in guaranteeing health care as a right of the citizen.

Even more impressively, the only element shared perhaps by all the different users, instrumental and otherwise, immigrants and otherwise, is a common feeling regarding the lack of alternatives. The users' answers to my final question, 'What would you have done if you hadn't come here, today?', are indicative. Thinking about an alternative was difficult for all the interviewees. For irregular immigrants, the answer was necessarily a total lack of options, as it was for the many users of the legal help desk for work and the immigrant assistance help desk. Many said they had never thought to contact a union and even so considered that to be too dangerous for their status as compared to the legal advice they could get from the OPG. For regular immigrants and Neapolitans, however, the answer was difficult as well. None of the interviewees mentioned the private sector as a possible solution to their problems while many said they prefer to turn to a third actor, which appears to be closer to their needs, other than being really 'public', strictly speaking. This is true for the patients of the popular medical clinic, who would have turned to the hospital, although expressing a deep frustration and scepticism about the possibility to solve their problems.

Conclusions

The case of the OPG is illustrative of a general recurring trend historically observed at times of emergencies, when communities resort to mutual help and informal channels of solidarity. However, the end of the Great Recession did not seem to have reduced this trend. Austerity cutbacks to health care and social services in big cities such as Naples slowly transformed into 'permanent austerity' eras (Pierson, 2002; Pavolini et al., 2016; Schönig and Schipper, 2016), transitioning their populations in a constant state of unfulfilled social demand. Actors of informal solidarity such as non-governmental organisations and the third sector became fundamental pillars of the aforementioned *post-welfare* city with evident implications for their potential growth and success.

However, as the interviews with founders of the OPG have evidenced, the role of these actors cannot be solely that of a state's surrogate, the risk being that informal solidarity can become the established valid arrangement (but by no means a long-term sustainable or desirable solution) to a growing social demand, in the absence of proper political actions to reform the system. As a matter of fact, the main intent of the OPG as a social lab is that of 'shaking' people and triggering a process of urban resistance and reform. The recent political commitment of some of the activists of the OPG, who came together to found the electoral alliance Potere al Popolo ('Power to the People', 2017), is an expression of this trend and of the potential powerful role that informal solidarity can have on restructuring the system.

References

Brandolini, A., D'Amuri, F., & Faiella, I. (2013). Country case study-Italy. The great recession and the distribution of household income. In S. P. Jenkins, A. Brandolini, J. Micklewright, & B. Nolan (a cura di), *The great recession and the distribution of household income* (pp. 130–152). Oxford: Oxford University Press.

De Rosa, S., & Salvati, L. (2016). Beyond a 'side street story'? Naples from spontaneous centrality to entropic polycentricism, towards a 'crisis city'. *Cities*, 51, 74–83.

DeVerteuil, G. (2017). Post-welfare city at the margins: Immigrant precarity and the mediating third sector in London. *Urban Geography*, 38(10), 1–17.

Donald, B., Glasmeier, A., Gray, M., & Lobao, L. (2014). Austerity in the city: Economic crisis and urban service decline? *Cambridge Journal of Regions, Economy and Society*, 7, 3–15.

Fregolent, L., & Savino, M. (a cura di). (2014). *Città e politiche in tempo di crisi*. Milano: FrancoAngeli.

Morlicchio, E. (2015). The roots of social cohesion: Urban spaces, community and neighbourhood in European cities. In S. Romano e G. Punziano (a cura di), *The European social model adrift: Europe, social cohesion and the economic crisis*. Farnham: Ashgate.

Moulaert, F., MacCallum, D., Mehmood, A., & Hamdouch, A. (2013). General introduction: The return of social innovation as a scientific concept and a social practice. In F. Moulaert, D. MacCallum, A. Mehmood, & A. Hamdouch (a cura di), *The international handbook on social innovations*. Cheltenham: Edward Elgar.

Musterd, S., Marcińczak, S., van Ham, M., & Tammaru, T. (2016). Socioeconomic segregation in European capital cities. Increasing separation between poor and rich. *Urban Geography*, 1–22.

Pavolini, E., León, M., Guillén, A. M., & Ascoli, U. (2016). From austerity to permanent strain? The European union and welfare state reform in Italy and Spain. In *The sovereign debt crisis, the EU and welfare state reform* (pp. 131–157). London: Palgrave Macmillan.

Pierson, P. (2002). Coping with permanent austerity: Welfare state restructuring in affluent democracies. *Revue française de sociologie*, 369–406.

Schönig, B., & Schipper, S. (eds.). (2016). *Urban austerity: Impacts of the global financial crisis on cities in Europe*. Berlin: Verlag Theater der Zeit.

Sharma, R. K. (1997). *Sociological methods and techniques*. New Delhi: Atlantic Publishers and Distributors.

Sotiropoulos, D. A., & Bourikos, D. (2014). Economic crisis, social solidarity and the voluntary sector in Greece. *Journal of Power, Politics & Governance*, 2(2), 33–53.

Strozza, S., Cipriani, A., & Forcellati, L. (2014). Caratteristiche e comportamenti demografici dei residenti nei quartieri di Napoli. *Rivista Economica del Mezzogiorno*, 28(1–2), 31–68.

7 Austerity and men's hidden family participation in low-income families in the UK

Anna Tarrant

Introduction

A burgeoning interdisciplinary and largely feminist orientated literature confirms that austerity both in Europe and the UK is a gendered condition (European Women's Lobby, 2012; Hall, 2019, 2020; Karamessini and Rubery, 2014). Research demonstrates that the impacts of austerity policies have had particularly pernicious and disproportionate consequences for women and children (e.g. Hall, 2016, 2017; Jupp, 2017; MacLeavy, 2011; Women's Budget Group, 2018). In the UK, these impacts are directly linked to the response of the Conservative–Liberal Democrat coalition that was formed after the UK economy went into recession from 2008 to 2010 (Ridge, 2013). This government instigated a programme of reforms that fundamentally reduced government spending and borrowing (ibid, 2013), in order to pay back the national debt (Kitchen et al., 2011). Key changes included welfare state withdrawal and reform, unprecedented cuts to social security provision and the retraction of the service sector, which predominantly employs women, causing rising unemployment (Ridge, 2013; McKay et al., 2013).

The decimation of state-supported services has also increasingly required families to take on the greater share of the 'caring burden', namely unpaid care work (Power and Hall, 2017). Unpaid work is not distributed evenly, and evidence across Europe suggests that the allocation of unpaid work to women has increased since the recession (European Women's Lobby, 2012; Mauro et al., 2015; Women's Budget Group, 2018). Discourses of individualisation and self-responsibility, where citizens are increasingly expected to take responsibility for the welfare of others and their own (Jensen and Tyler, 2012; van der Heijden et al., 2016), have also accompanied such changes, supplanting acknowledgement of already existing and 'deeply entrenched structural inequalities and systems of privilege' (Jensen and Tyler, 2012, p. 1).

As well as disproportionate impacts on women, in the UK context, austerity reforms have distinct geographies, with especially regressive effects for ex-industrial areas, cities and London (Hamnett, 2014). Overall, however, austerity policies have had an uneven impact on the poorest in society, meaning that households already at the greatest risk of poverty, such as female-headed or Black, Asian and minority ethnic households, have been profoundly affected (Tucker,

2017; Women's Budget Group, 2018). Women's existing risk to poverty and vulnerability has therefore been exacerbated, particularly as policies have been blind to their gendered effects.

Why consider men?

If women in the majority shoulder the burden of austerity impacts, this begs the question: why consider men's experiences? It is certainly not an intention to obscure the significant emotional, relational and everyday labour that women are required to engage in at times of economic crisis (see also Hall, 2020). Indeed, the interpretations presented in this chapter are feminist in perspective and acknowledge both austerity and caregiving within families as feminist issues (see also Feminist Fightback Collective, 2011). Yet there is evidence to suggest that economic crises also reconfigure gendered identities (McDowell, 2004), affecting relations between men and women as well as practices in the family (Moura et al., 2015), with social and personal impacts that are experienced in everyday life (Hall, 2017, 2019, 2020).

An emerging body of literature has addressed the re-gendering of the caring landscape, linked to processes of recession and austerity. This evidences some change in distributions of labour between men and women (Boyer et al., 2017), demonstrating that men are increasingly engaging in the everyday tasks of social reproduction and care, linked in part to changing expectations of father involvement and increased male unemployment at times of recession and economic crisis (Boyer et al., 2017; Tarrant, 2018). These processes shape new constructions of masculinities (Moura et al., 2015). While the challenge to traditional norms of masculinities such as breadwinning can produce difficulties for some men (Moura et al., 2015), others are optimistic that economic crisis and recession also give rise to new conceptualisations of 'caring masculinities' (Elliott, 2016). At the conceptual level, these are masculine identities that reject domination and aggression and value qualities of interdependence and care (Elliott, 2016).

As I argue elsewhere however, understanding of the contextual conditions that might support such identities to flourish, or of the particularities of the austerity context in either enabling or impeding men's family participation and progress towards gender equality, is lacking (Tarrant, 2018). Furthermore, very little is known about how care is arranged and organised both within and across households, and between men and women of different generations, particularly in low-income families. In addressing these omissions and in recognising that gender is relational, fluid and complex, the current focus of debate might be critically extended via attention to the uneven gendered and classed impacts of austerity in the long term.

This chapter presents men's experiences of low-income family life and the impacts of austerity, beginning with an appraisal of the current state of debate, whereby negative portrayals of low-income fatherhood serve to obscure men's participation in family life. This is followed by discussion of the methodology and methods employed for the Men, Poverty and Lifetimes of Care (MPLC) study, upon which the discussion in this chapter is based. Emerging findings are then presented offering insights into the men's lived experiences of austerity as it impacts on their everyday lives, their care responsibilities and on the resources they have to fulfil those responsibilities. The chapter concludes that in order to extend understanding of the gendered impacts of austerities both in the UK and across Europe, men's family participation and the intergenerational processes that produce it are an essential consideration.

'Dad deprivation?' Appraising the current state of debate

Recent public and policy discourse highlights a disconnect between perceptions of men's roles in low-income family life and how they are lived. In a context where engaged and involved models of fatherhood are a new cultural imperative (Dermott and Gatrell, 2018; Miller, 2018), men in low-income families are often stereotyped as absent, feckless, irresponsible and uncaring. Notably, at various flashpoints and periods of historical significance, particularly pessimistic constructions of fatherhood have gained authority in mainstream and political commentary. Usually directed at marginalised fathers, they reflect a recurring set of anxieties about a 'culture of fatherlessness' (Williams, 1998) linked to a broader crisis of masculinity that ostensibly pervades low-income communities and families via the intergenerational transmission of individual deficiencies.

The urban riots in a number of urban centres in the UK in 2011 saw a revival of the 'crisis of fatherlessness' narrative. This was couched within the new language of 'Broken Britain' that was asserted by then Prime Minister David Cameron to describe and explain social exclusion (see McKenzie, 2010). Across the political spectrum, notions of poor and 'feral' parenting were employed to account for the civil unrest (DeBenedictus, 2012), expressed within a recurrent set of concerns about their belonging to an apparent 'underclass' population (Tyler, 2014). Government intervention was deemed the only route to getting these fatherless, 'ineffectual' families back on track (Harker and Martin, 2012). Single mothers in particular were hyper-visible within these explanations, despite constituting only 10% of the rioting population (Allen and Taylor, 2012). Yet notions of 'dad deprivation' (Ashe, 2014), absent fathers, and a lack of male role models were also regularly referenced to account for the civil disobedience, violence and criminality expressed by the young men involved (see Ashe, 2014; Lammy, 2011; Featherstone et al., 2017). An emphasis on place was also notable, and the absence of fathers from lone-mother-headed households was extended to anxiety about the absence of men from entire neighbourhoods, crassly dubbed 'men deserts' in a press release by the Centre for Social Justice (2013).

This chapter does not seek to unpick the nuances of absent father discourses at any great length; other authors, including those cited, have already done important analysis in this regard (e.g. Mann and Roseneil, 1994; DeBenedictus, 2012; Williams, 1998). However they are a significant component of the gendered 'political register of austerity' (Allen et al., 2014, p. 5) and act as simplistic yet powerful weaponry in an austerity agenda characterising inauspicious and progressively punitive policy approaches (see MacDonald, 2017). They also obscure the varied and dynamic ways in which men in a number of generational positions participate in low-income family life and respond to broader structural change. As a counterpoint, the MPLC study addressed the relative absence of men's accounts of family, poverty and austerity both from academic research and policy discourse.

Men, Poverty and Lifetimes of Care

The main aim of MPLC was to examine men's care responsibilities in low-income families and localities against a backdrop of significant social and economic change, linked to recession and the accompanying politics of austerity in the UK. The study took place in a northern English, post-industrial city. In this city, worklessness, financial exclusion, impacts of poor housing on health, poor educational attainment and reduced life chances are concentrated in particular localities (see White et al., 2016).

The identification of a limited research literature foregrounding the voices of men and fathers in low-income contexts lead to consideration of a more unusual methodological approach involving the exploration of existing qualitative evidence. Qualitative secondary analysis (QSA) of two existing datasets stored in the Timescapes Archive (Neale and Bishop, 2012) was conducted prior to fieldwork and informed the research design for MPLC (see Tarrant, 2016; Tarrant and Hughes, 2019). Following Young Fathers (FYF; Neale et al., 2015) and Intergenerational Exchange (IGE; Emmel and Hughes, 2014) provided initial insights about men's experiences of low-income family life in the city of study from the perspective of young fathers (aged 25 and under) and grandfathers. As well as enabling longitudinal insights into men's experiences of marginalisation and care, the QSA strand also aided identification of significant knowledge gaps that neither the literature nor data could address (see Tarrant, 2016). These gaps were explored for the new empirical data collection phase of the MPLC study (2015–2017) and included structured focus on the circumstances of, and developments in, men's care arrangements and responsibilities, their lived experiences of caring in financially constrained contexts and their experiences of service provision and support.

The fieldwork for MPLC comprised a creative, qualitative mixed-methods approach (Emmel and Clark, 2009) including semi-structured interviews with key informants from the third and voluntary sector, biographical interviews with men identified as living in low-income families, and photovoice and participant observation at a community centre located in a ward whose population is living in the most deprived fifth of the city according to the 2010 Indices of Multiple Deprivation (IMD).

Access to the field was underpinned by engagements with voluntary and third-sector workers whose offer involved support for men experiencing deprivation and oriented in particular to men's identities as fathers or father figures. As key stakeholders, some of these individuals had already been instrumental to the success of identifying participants for IGE and FYF. Following Emmel et al. (2007), building relationships of trust with key local gatekeepers proved to be a successful route to identifying socially excluded and 'hard to reach' individuals and families. Spending time at a community centre where a contact had been established also complemented this approach, and it was also possible to recruit men from there.

Recruitment from the community centre was surprisingly fruitful and unexpected given evidence that men in low-income communities are generally less visible in community spaces where much academic research on poverty and low-income family life often takes place (McKenzie, 2010). McKenzie (2010) identified this in her study of estate life in St Ann's, Nottingham. She argues that while seemingly invisible in spaces of research, the 'missing men' were in fact very present. She located men in 'male spaces' like the gym and the barbershop, and discovered that many communicated via Messenger or spent time in the flats of friends playing Xbox. They also had more transitory lives and identities. Emmel and Hughes (2010) observed similar transitory processes in IGE, their study of a family life on a low-income estate in Northern England. When they interviewed women in their homes, they found that sons and partners often popped in and out of the interviews or withdrew when they began to perceive that the study, which examined grandparental investments in their grandchildren's future aspirations, was not about or for them. The community centre accessed for MPLC was unique in its determined and vocal efforts to support men on low incomes with their mental health in the locality it was based.

In combination, gatekeepers and ethnographic techniques at the community centre produced a diverse sample of men who were fathers or in father-like relationships in low-income families and places. Biographical interviews were conducted with 26 men in different generational positions. The sample comprised six young fathers (aged 25 and under), 12 mid-life fathers (aged 26–55), one grandfather and seven men providing kinship care in a number of generational positions. This included a father with a complex care arrangement, an uncle, four grandfathers, and a great-grandfather. Photovoice was also conducted with some of these men (with limited success but albeit insightful; Tarrant and Hughes, 2020), as well as participant observation in the community centre where insights were gained into men's experiences of deprivation and caregiving in place (see also Wissö, 2018). The final sample comprised men who were in economically precarious positions but also variably marginalised by their age, generational position, gender (in terms of being caregivers as men) and social class, and according to their residence in deprived communities and localities. It is the lived experiences and caregiving responsibilities of these men that this chapter now explores and seeks to render more visible.

Family participation across generations

The majority of the men who contributed to MPLC were highly involved in family life and actively participating in (and in some cases fighting for the ability to) care for children. Engagement with gatekeepers from a range of voluntary and third-sector organisations revealed the diverse ways men are participating in low-income family life not only as fathers but also in father-like roles and in a number of different generational positions. Public and policy responses noticeably dwell on fathers as a particular generational and familial position. This excludes and renders invisible the family participation of older generations of men. As Morrell et al. (2016, p. 82) highlight, for example, as research about fatherhood has expanded, the definition of fathers also increasingly incorporates more than those who are biological fathers. This can include 'a male sibling who is standing in for an absent or a deceased father, a grandfather, an older male family member, or an unrelated man who undertakes childcare'. Yet in general, empirical research on men, families and poverty has focused on younger fathers (e.g. Neale et al., 2015; Weber, 2018). MPLC revealed the importance of men in different generational positions that were filling gaps in care provision in low-income families.

Of particular interest here are the men who are kinship carers. The practice of family and friends care, also known as kinship care, is a largely invisible societal role (Grandparents Plus, 2018). While largely thought to be provided by women, it has become a key placement option for children whose parents are no longer deemed capable or able to provide care for their children. According to McCarton et al. (2018), kinship carers as a population tend to be older, experience poverty and deprivation and suffer from ill health. Kinship placements also tend to support children facing multiple adversities often without receiving adequate resources for their care. The MPLC participants demonstrated many of these factors.

The seven interviewees providing kinship care were either in the process of securing parental responsibility or had already secured formal status at the time of the interview. These men described varied trajectories into kinship care and engagements both with social services and the justice system. Formally, some were identified by social services as appropriate carers, while others had to fight for recognition. Most notably, these men were approached as potential carers when female relatives were either incapacitated due to ill health or had died. More often than not, this was linked to their own experiences of deprivation.

In one especially tragic case, care was required for five children following the premature death of a mother at 32 years old. Her death was caused by cancer that had gone unreported because of her distrust of professionals following multiple ignored claims of abuse by her partner. Pearce's case differed. The decision to become the main carer for two of his grandchildren, aged 5 and 2, was ostensibly a pragmatic one, based around his and his wife's employment circumstances. However, his experience of becoming a primary caregiver demonstrated the valuable insights men gain when engaging in caregiving. Pearce, age 57, says:

> I were having a stressful job. So I just said right, I will jack it in. I'll look after the kids. But it were a massive learning curve because I've never done it before. I mean, when my kids were growing up, I were working on nights for nine years and I went full time on days but I never had to deal with small ones. At the time, my kids were nine and ten when I came off nights. So it were a massive learning curve for me and really, really hard. I can see what women sort of complain about when they've got kids round their feet all day

and it's nice when my wife comes home. We get these to bed and we can talk and I've got adult conversation.

In a follow-up interview, Pearce revealed that he was now searching for employment to fit flexibly around the children's needs. He revealed that finding work at his age, that accommodates the children's schedules, and pays adequately was a particular challenge:

We struggle. This is why I am going back to see them [social services] in September. We get this income support but I can't claim anything. . . . But will they get me a job? And I can't because I have two kids to look after. Have to get this family credit thing: £300 a month. I know I've got a job if I want it. I'm going to try and get a job at a friend's company: delivering beds. I'm hoping that he will let me have all the holidays off or it is no good to me. I cannot afford to put these in full time . . . if they are off for six weeks in holiday, it will cost me more than I can earn. This will be £70 a day. Childcare is £10 per afternoon each. £7.50 per morning: a couple of hundred pound a week; and I am going to earn a hundred pound.

Balancing care responsibilities in the current labour market, where cultural and workplace expectations assert pressures on men to work longer, fixed hours (Norman and Fagan, 2017), were limiting employment opportunities for Pearce. Findings by the Office for National Statistics (2017) suggest that under- and over-employment and a lack of flexible working are key issues in the austerity context, exacerbated by reduced entitlements to social security for the purposes of childcare. Pearce's narrative therefore reveals the value of men's family participation, as well as the ways in which context mitigates against his involvement by producing economic hardship.

Pearce's experience was by no means unique. Sam, age 51, also explained that he had been asked by social services to leave work in order to settle the children and pass assessments, only then to be asked later how he planned to support the children financially once the time-limited financial support attached to the Special Guardianship Order[1] (SGO) they had obtained had ended. He explains:

They asked me to give my job up to look after him [grandson, age 4]. Then they started going into your private life and your finances. One of the questions that came up was – 'How are you going to support him?'

In a later telephone conversation with Sam he said that his status had become confused. He asks; 'am I a worker, job-seeker or government employee?' His question eloquently expresses confusion about kinship carer status and how men are positioned precariously within a broader system of welfare, social support, employment and policy.

Yet as Sam and Pearce acknowledge, economic hardship is a real concern, characterising the everyday lived experience of kinship carers under the conditions of austerity. Experiences of economic hardship linked to caregiving were raised by the majority of the participants and are explored next.

Economic hardship

Recent research by Grandparents Plus (2018) has identified a direct link between kinship care and poverty. Forty-three percent of kinship carers stated that their income was insufficient for meeting the needs of their children, a finding that is consistent with previous studies confirming a longer-term pattern (Nandy and Selwyn, 2013). While the research evidence has linked this to the high prevalence of single, female carers (see MacDonald et al., 2016), the men in MPLC were also notably affected by the financial constraints that taking on unanticipated care of children later in life engendered.

The majority of the men interviewed were protected in part by the secure employment they had had in the past, coupled with the ability to accrue savings (a patriarchal dividend not afforded to most women). Taking on unanticipated care responsibilities, often for multiple children, did however have a marked impact on these men's household finances and incomes. Following the death of his sister, Theo, age 39, was weighing up whether to acquire an SGO for his two young nephews. This was a decision social services were not supporting him with and that he felt were not being transparent about in terms of his entitlements. While decisions were being made, Theo also had to care for two older children and a baby. In all, he calculates that he had only £3.60 a day to provide for three nephews (aged 18, 8 and 6), a niece (age 16) and great niece (age 1).

Many of the participants were also acutely aware that austerity-driven government policy was responsible for the hardships they faced and that these were only likely to intensify. Kinship carer Paul, age 61, a grandfather with an SGO for two of his grandchildren, also reflects:

> It's just a hard life and the government's going to make it harder. . . . I mean financially, you know, to look after a child. This is my view. I mean, I think I get tax credits for [granddaughter]. She isn't my child, if you understand what I mean. This is what I'm saying. If she was plonked in somebody else's house, if you understand what I mean, they get fortunes for them, you know, and I think I get about £30 a week or something like that, to bring a thirteen-year-old child up.

As I argue elsewhere (Tarrant, 2018), participants were forced to ask themselves more limiting questions about how they could manage their circumstances. Rather than focus on what they ought to do, they had to consider what had to be done (see Deacon and Williams, 2004). Where men's involvement as primary caregivers is already precarious through its challenge to established gendered norms, the political conditions of austerity often challenged their efforts.

Conclusion

The MPLC study offers unique insights into the processes that both support and constrain men's participation in family life in low-income families and contexts. Contributing new evidence, this research alerts us to the intensification of need for caregiving by men under the conditions of austerity.

These findings critically challenge stereotypes of men in low-income families and localities as uncaring. Such assumptions stall progress towards gender equality by reinforcing that care is women's labour and excluding men in low-income families from cultural expectations of involved and engaged models of fatherhood. In support of existing research, MPLC confirms that austerity policies are deeply impacting on the everyday lives of families (albeit in uneven and unseen ways), as these men articulate. For kinship carers in particular, family policies are producing hardships and conditions that are quite antithetical to those that broadly enable caring masculinities to flourish. However, looking beyond the father generation, we are able to see how austerity also has distinct intergenerational effects, redistributing care across households and among a wider set of interdependencies. Gendered and classed inequality is therefore felt and experienced beyond the household and transferred across generations, producing alternative exchanges of care.

With regards to gender, new research in direct engagement with policy makers and practitioners must ensure that gender equality is a statutory requirement across the health and social care landscape, both in the UK and internationally. One approach to this is to implement and evaluate more transformative father-inclusive, gender-equal and compassionate policy and practice environments that empower men, of any generation, to meet their expressed desire to 'be there' (e.g. Tarrant and Neale, 2017). This is not to suggest an individualised approach in which individual men (and women) in families bear the continued burden of unpaid labour. Rather, austerity also presents an opportunity to disrupt the ostensible slide towards crisis and instead to harness radical structural transformations across Europe in which men's caring masculinities are supported to prosper.

Note

1 A Special Guardianship Order appoints a 'special guardian' for a child – usually a relative or friend – until they turn 18 (see Grandparents Plus, www.grandparentsplus.org.uk/special-guardianship-orders). Financial support for SGOs is means-tested and discretionary.

References

Allen, K. and Taylor, Y. (2012) Placing parenting, locating unrest: Failed femininities, troubled mothers and riotous subjects, *Studies in the Maternal*, 4 (2).
Allen, K., Tyler, I. and De Benedictis, S. (2014) Thinking with 'White Dee': The gender politics of austerity porn, *Sociological Research Online*, 19 (3): 2, www.socresonline.org.uk/19/3/2.html

Ashe, F. (2014) All about Eve: Mothers, masculinities and the 2011 UK riots, *Political Studies*, 62 (3): 652–668.

Boyer, K., Dermott, E., James, A. and MacLeavy, J. (2017) Regendering care in the aftermath of recession? *Dialogues in Human Geography*, 7 (1): 56–73.

Centre for Social Justice (2013) *Lone parents tally heads for two million as numbers rise 20,000 a year, says CSJ report*, Press Release, www.centreforsocialjustice.org.uk/core/wp-content/uploads/2016/08/CSJ-Press-Release-Lone-Parents.pdf

Deacon, A. and Williams, F. (2004) Introduction: Themed section on care, values and the future of welfare, *Social Policy & Society*, 3 (4): 385–390.

DeBenedictus, S. (2012) 'Feral' parents: Austerity parenting under neoliberalism, *Studies in the Maternal*, 4 (2).

Dermott, E. and Gatrell, C. (2018) *Fathers, families and relationships*, Bristol: Policy Press.

Elliott, K. (2016) Caring masculinities: Theorizing an emerging concept, *Men & Masculinities*, 19 (3): 240–259.

Emmel, N. and Clark, A. (2009) *The methods used in connected lives: Investigating networks, neighbourhoods and communities*, ESRC National Centre for Research Methods NCRM Working Paper Series 06/09.

Emmel, N. and Hughes, K. (2010) 'Recession, it's all the same to us son': The longitudinal experience (1999–2010) of deprivation, *21st Century Society*, 5 (2): 171–181.

Emmel, N. and Hughes, K. (2014) Vulnerability, inter-generational exchange, and the conscience of generations, in: J. Holland and R. Edwards (eds.), *Understanding families over time: Research and policy*, Basingstoke: Palgrave Macmillan.

Emmel, N., Hughes, K., Greenhalgh, J. and Sales, A. (2007) Accessing socially excluded people: Trust and the gatekeeper in the researcher-participant relationship, *Sociological Research Online*, 12 (2).

European Women's Lobby (2012) *The price of austerity – the impact on women's rights and gender equality in Europe*, Report, www.womenlobby.org/IMG/pdf/the_price_of_austerity_-_web_edition.pdf

Featherstone, B., Robb, M., Ruxton, S. and Ward, M.R.M. (2017) 'They are just good people . . . generally good people': Perspectives of young men on relationships with social care workers in the UK, *Children & Society*, 31 (5): 331–341.

Feminist Fightback Collective (2011) Cuts are a feminist issue, *Soundings*, 49: 73–83, www.feministfightback.org.uk/wp-content/uploads/FF-Article-Soundings-12.11.pdf.

Grandparents Plus (2018) *What is kinship care?* www.grandparentsplus.org.uk/what-is-kinship-care

Hall, S.M. (2016) 'Family relations in times of austerity: Reflections from the UK, in: S. Punch, R. Vanderbeck and T. Skelton (eds.), *Families, intergenerationality and peer group relations*, Singapore: Springer.

Hall, S.M. (2017) Personal, relational and intimate geographies of austerity: Ethical and empirical considerations, *Area*, 49 (3): 303–310.

Hall, S.M. (2019) Everyday austerity: Towards relational geographies of family, friendship and intimacy, *Progress in Human Geography*, 43(5): 769–789.

Hall, S.M. (2020) The personal is political: Feminist geographies of/in austerity, *Geoforum*, 110: 242–251.

Hamnett, C. (2014) Shrinking the welfare state: The structure, geography and impact of British government benefit cuts, *Transactions of the Institute of British Geographers*, 39 (4): 490–503.

Harker, C. and Martin, L. (2012) Familial relations: Spaces, subjects, and politics (guest editorial), *Environment and Planning A*, 44 (4): 768–775.

Jensen, T. and Tyler, I. (2012) Austerity parenting: New economies of parent-citizenship, *Studies in the Maternal*, 4 (2): 1.

Jupp, E. (2017) Home space, gender and activism: The visible and the invisible in austere times, *Critical Social Policy*, 37 (3): 348–366.

Karamessini, M. and Rubery, J. (2014) *Women and austerity: The economic crisis and the future for gender equality*, London: Routledge.

Kitchen, M., Martin, R. and Tyler, P. (2011) The geographies of austerity, *Cambridge Journal of Regions, Economy and Society*, 4: 289–302.

Lammy, D. (2011) *Out of the ashes: Britain after the riots*, London: Guardian Books.

MacDonald, M., Hayes, D. and Houston, S. (2016) Understanding informal kinship care: A critical narrative review of theory and research, *Families, Relationships and Societies*, 7 (1): 71–81.

MacDonald, R. (2017) *Voodoo sociology, unemployment and the low-pay, no-pay cycle*, www.the-sarf.org.uk/voodoo-sociology/

MacLeavy, J. (2011) A 'new politics' of austerity, workfare and gender? The UK coalition government's welfare reform proposals, *Cambridge Journal of Regions, Economy and Society*, 4 (3): 335–367.

Mann, K. and Roseneil, S. (1994) 'Some mothers do 'ave 'em': Backlash and the gender politics of the underclass debate, *Journal of Gender Studies*, 3 (3):317–331.

McCarton, C., Bunting, L., Bywaters, P., Davidson, G., Elliott, M. and Hooper, J. (2018) A four-nation comparison of kinship care in the UK: The relationship between formal kinship care and deprivation, *Social Policy and Society*, 17 (4): 619–635.

McDowell, L. (2004) Work, workfare, work/life balance and an ethic of care, *Progress in Human Geography*, 28 (2): 145–163.

McKay, A., Campbell, J., Thomson, E. and Ross, S. (2013) Economic recession and recovery in the UK: What's gender got to do with it? *Feminist Economics*, 19 (3): 108–123.

McKenzie, L. (2010) *Getting by: Estates, class and culture in austerity Britain*, Bristol: Policy Press.

Miller, T. (2018) *Making sense of parenthood: Caring, gender and family lives*, Cambridge: Cambridge University Press.

Morrell, R., Dunkle, K., Ibragimov, U. and Jewkes, R. (2016) Fathers who care and those that don't: Men and childcare in South Africa, *South African Review of Sociology*, 47 (4): 80–105.

Moura, T., Spindler, E. and Taylor, A. (2015) Portugal's masculinities crisis: Gender equality in the era of flagging economies, *Ex aequo*, 32: 87–100.

Nandy, S. and Selwyn, J. (2013) Kinship care and poverty: Using census data to examine the extent and nature of kinship care in the UK, *British Journal of Social Work*, 43 (8): 1649–1666.

Neale, B. and Bishop, L. (2012) The timescapes archive: A stakeholder approach to archiving qualitative longitudinal data, *Qualitative Research*, 12 (2): 53–65.

Neale, B., Lau Clayton, C., Davies, L. and Ladlow, L. (2015) *Researching the lives of young fathers: The 'Following Young Fathers' study and dataset*, Following Young Fathers Briefing Paper Series no. 8, www.followingfathers.leeds.ac.uk.

Norman, H. and Fagan, C. (2017) Why are men working such long hours? *Working Families Blog*, www.workingfamilies.org.uk/workflex-blog/why-are-uk-men working-such-long-hours/.

Office for National Statistics (2017) *EMP16: Underemployment and overemployment*, www.ons.gov.uk/employmentandlabourmarket/peopleinwork/employmentand employeetypes/datasets/underemploymentandoveremploymentemp16

Power, A. and Hall, E. (2017) Placing care in times of austerity, *Social & Cultural Geography*, 19 (3): 303–313.

Ridge, T. (2013) 'We are all in this together'? The hidden costs of poverty, recession and austerity policies on Britain's poorest children, *Children & Society*, 27 (5): 406–417.

Tarrant, A. (2016) Getting out of the swamp': Methodological reflections on using qualitative secondary analysis in research design, *International Journal of Social Research Methodology*, 20 (6): 599–611.

Tarrant, A. (2018) Care in an age of austerity: Men's care responsibilities in low-income families, *Ethics & Social Welfare*, 12 (1): 24–28.

Tarrant, A. and Hughes, K. (2019) Qualitative Secondary Analysis: Building Longitudinal Samples to Understand Men's Generational Identities in Low Income Contexts, *Sociology*, 53 (3): 538–553.

Tarrant, A. and Hughes, K. (2020) The ethics of technology choice: Photovoice methodology with men living in low-income contexts, *Sociological Research Online*.

Tarrant, A. and Neale, B. (2017) *Learning to support young dads,* Responding to Young Fathers in a Different Way: Project Report, http://1v9xdi344dkt24du831vqd38. wpengine.netdna-cdn.com/files/2017/04/SYD-final-report.pdf

Tucker, J. (2017) *The austerity generation: The impact of a decade of cuts on family incomes and child poverty*, Child Poverty Action Group Report, www.cpag.org.uk/sites/ default/files/Austerity%20Generation%20FINAL.pdf

Tyler, I. (2014) The riots of the underclass? Stigmatisation, mediation and the government of poverty and disadvantage in neoliberal Britain, *Sociological Research Online*, 18 (4): 6.

van der Heijden, K., Visse, M., Lensvelt-Mulders, G. and Widdershoven, G. (2016) To care or not to care? A narrative on experiencing caring responsibilities, *Ethics and Social Welfare*, 10 (1): 53–68.

Weber, J.B. (2018) Becoming teen fathers: Stories of teen pregnancy, responsibility, and masculinity, *Men & Masculinities*, 26 (6): 900–921.

White, A., Seims, A. and Newton, R. 2016. *The state of men's health in Leeds: Main report,* Leeds: Leeds Beckett University and Leeds City Council.

Williams, F. (1998) Troubled masculinities in social policy discourses: Fatherhood, in: J. Edwards, J. Hearn and J. Popay (eds.), *Men, gender divisions and welfare*, London: Routledge, pp. 63–100.

Wissö, T. (2018) 'Researching fatherhood and place: Adopting an ethnographic approach', in: E. Dermott and C. Gatrell (eds.), *Fathers, families and relationships*, Bristol: Policy Press.

Women's Budget Group (2018) *The impact of austerity on women in the UK*, www.ohchr. org/Documents/Issues/Development/IEDebt/WomenAusterity/WBG.pdf

8 Austerity, economic crisis and children

The case of Cyprus

Christos Koutsampelas, Sofia N. Andreou,
Evangelia Papaloi and Kostas Dimopoulos

Introduction

The outbreak of the European debt crisis prompted many countries to adopt austerity policies in an effort to stabilise public finances. Austerity in some countries resulted in large reductions in government deficits, thereby implying substantial fiscal effort.[1] However, these fiscal policies came at a cost. They generated social tensions, exacerbated the duration of the recession, damaged enterprises and caused distress to households, especially the more vulnerable.

Cyprus was one of the countries hit hardest by the recession. Gross domestic product (GDP) contracted by about 10% in real terms between 2012 and 2014, a reduction second only to Greece.[2] The first signs of the recession were evident as of 2009, when unemployment started to escalate and economic activity slowed down. This prompted the left-wing government of President Christofias to take pre-emptive austerity measures in an effort to reduce deficits. These measures, which included increases in taxes and social insurance contributions and reductions in benefits, constituted the first wave of austerity in Cyprus. The second came with the collapse of the financial sector in 2013 due to the high exposure of the two biggest Cypriot banks to low-quality housing loans and Greek government bonds (Clerides, 2014). The consequential downgrade of Cypriot government bonds and the inability of the state to finance its public deficit lead to a tripartite international bailout (worth of €10 billion) between the European Commission, the European Central Bank, the International Monetary Fund and the government of Cyprus widely known as the Memorandum of Understanding (MoU). The MoU, agreed on 2 April 2013, saved Cyprus from a total economic breakdown, but it also came with substantial cuts in wages and pensions, new increases in taxes and cuts in benefits. Cyprus's economy contracted significantly for two successive years and returned to some degree of growth in 2015. After 2016, the economy started to recover and in 2017–2018 it recorded robust growth rates.

The aim of this chapter is to provide a narrative of how these economic and fiscal episodes affected families with children. Our focus is on children aged below 12 and especially those more vulnerable to income deprivation. The decision to concentrate this on this demographic group is important for three reasons. First, it is a matter of social concern that 1 out of 4 children in Europe is at risk of poverty or social exclusion. This amounts to 24 million children in EU28 in 2017. In Cyprus the corresponding figure is 44,000 children.[3] Second, the risk of poverty or social exclusion is higher for children than it is for adults (Atkinson and Marlier, 2010), implying that not enough is done at present to protect children in this regard. Finally, there is evidence that persons who experience poverty during their childhood are more likely to face the same risks as adults (Heckman, 2006, 2008).

This means that child poverty has an intergenerational dimension. For those living in poverty, their own children are also likely to struggle against these similar and persistent disadvantages. Recent streams of the literature also demonstrate that inequalities affecting children in early age have lasting personal consequences (Heckman, 2008). Therefore, recent studies have argued in favour of improving policies affecting younger children, such as early childhood education and care and access to quality primary education (García et al., 2017), while the need to invest in children for 'breaking the cycle of disadvantage' has also been emphasised in the national literature (Pashardes and Koutsampelas, 2014).

In this context, the chapter provides an analysis of how the economic recession and the austerity in Cyprus affected (1) child poverty, (2) families' access to early childhood education and care and (3) schools in primary education. All three dimensions are considered fundamental in shaping children's development, wellbeing and ultimately future chances in life. Furthermore, we believe that the usefulness of this analysis extends beyond offering a narrative of what happened during this turbulent period. It also provides a mapping of good practices and anti-poverty policies which policy makers can use during harsh times to counteract the adverse effects of economic recessions on vulnerable children.

Child poverty in Cyprus

Figure 8.1 shows the evolution of child poverty in Cyprus, making also comparisons with the EU average for the period 2005–2017: before the recession (2005–2009), during the recession (2010–2015) and in its aftermath (2016–2017). Child

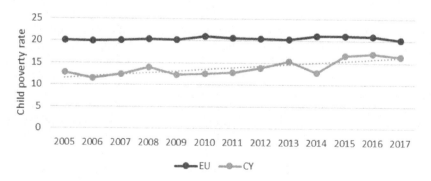

Figure 8.1 The evolution of child poverty in Cyprus and EU (2005–2017)
Source: Eurostat Online Database. Code: ilc_li02. Years refer to survey years.

poverty is measured as the percentage of children aged 17 and younger whose family income lies below the poverty threshold, which is defined as 60% of the median equivalised disposable income following Eurostat conventions. The dotted line shows the trend.

Two main points emerge from the evidence: first, the child poverty rate in Cyprus fluctuates below the EU average, though this difference has been systematically reducing the last decade or so. In 2005, the child poverty rate in Cyprus was 12.8%, 7.3 percentage points (p.p.) lower than the EU average. In 2017, this difference reduced to 3.7 p.p. Second, the poverty rate in Cyprus follows an upward trend which might have begun before the crisis, but it clearly accelerated during the crisis. In particular, the child poverty rate increased by 3.1 p.p. between 2009 and 2015 (roughly speaking between the beginning and the end of the crisis). On the contrary, the EU average does not exhibit such fluctuations or trends as it remains stable during 2005–2017.

Why did child poverty increase in a country which has been consistently characterised by low child poverty rates? According to international literature (Jarvis and Redmond, 1997; Bradshaw, 2005; Ritakallio and Bradshaw, 2006; Chzhen and Bradshaw, 2012), we can list three important factors which might drive trends in child poverty: (1) parents' participation in the labour market, (2) the generosity of income support to families with children and (3) household structure. Thus, in the next sections, the focus is placed on these factors with the aim of assessing how they were affected by the recessionary context of the period.

The impact of labour markets

The national literature has attributed the consistently low levels of child poverty in Cyprus to the good condition of the labour market, which translates to high employment rates and adequate wages for parents (Pashardes, 2007; Pashardes and Koutsampelas, 2014). In this context, parents' participation in the labour market results in substantially higher probability of lifting family above the poverty threshold (Pashardes, 2007). This argument is explored in Figure 8.2, where the child poverty rate in Cyprus is plotted against (a) the employment rate of the 25–54 age group (the overwhelming majority of parents belongs to this age group) and (b) the in-work poverty rate for the same age group.

Figure 8.2 shows that child poverty is negatively associated with the employment rate. Although causal mechanisms cannot be deduced by such simple data structures, it is reasonable to suggest that as more parents enter the labour market, more children escape from poverty. The dimension of in-work poverty is also important, for participation in the labour market alone does not guarantee exiting poverty. The right-hand figure shows that there is a strong positive association between child poverty and in-work poverty in Cyprus. This means that lower levels of in-work poverty imply a higher probability of escaping poverty in case of finding a job.

Figure 8.3 shows how these two crucial factors (in-work poverty and employment rate among the age group 25–54) shifted during the period 2008–2017. As

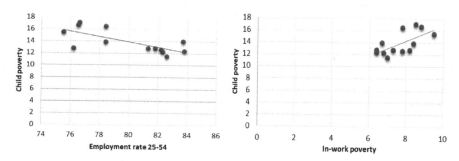

Figure 8.2 Scatterplots of child poverty with employment rate (25–54) and in-work poverty (25–54) in Cyprus (2005–2017)

Source: Eurostat Online Database. Codes: lfsq_ergan, ilc_iw01.

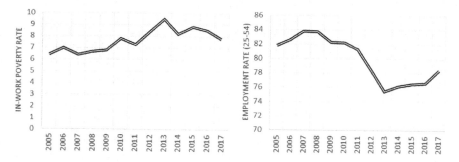

Figure 8.3 Trends in in-work poverty and employment rate (25–54) in Cyprus (2005–2017)

Source: Eurostat Online Database. Codes: lfsq_ergan; ilc_iw01.

can be seen in the right-hand graph, the employment rate was very high during the previous decade, peaking at 83.8% in 2007 (to put this figure into perspective, the EU average in that year was 79.0%). It reduced steeply the next years due to the economic recession (bottoming at 75.5% in 2013) and is currently on an increasing trajectory as the economy recovers. Similarly, in-work poverty reached a peak in 2013 (9.5%) and has been decreasing since 2013.

Taken all together, the preceding evidence shows that the recession and the austerity affected child poverty through the channel of the labour market. A proportion of parents exited the labour market while others participated with unfavourable terms (low pay). These factors had an increasing impact on child poverty.

Income support to families and family composition

The second factor identified in the literature as crucial in keeping child poverty low is family transfers to families. Table 8.1 reports evidence from the European

Table 8.1 Spending on income support to families in Cyprus (2008–2015)

	2008	2015	Change
Euros per inhabitant (at constant 2010 prices)	463.6	272.6	–€191
Million euros	355	234	–€121 million
% of GDP	1.9	1.3	–0.6 p.p.
% of total benefits	11.1	6.18	–4.65 p.p.

Source: ESSPROS, family/children function.

System of Integrated Social Protection Statistics (ESSPROS) regarding social spending on families and children in Cyprus for the period 2008–2015. The evidence clearly shows a weakening of state support to families both in relative and absolute terms. In particular, spending reduced by €121 million (from €355 million to €234 million) during this period. As percentage of GDP, spending for families reduced by 0.6 p.p., amounting to 1.3% of GDP in 2015 – a level considerably below the EU average (2.3%). The weakening of family policies can be attributed to austerity policies that were implemented during the recession years with the aim of consolidating the public budget (Koutsampelas and Pashardes, 2017).

The last factor driving child poverty trends is household composition. Although not directly relevant to austerity, it is important to highlight that in general, single parenthood and multi-child families are strongly associated with higher risk of poverty (Bradshaw, 2005; Chzhen and Bradshaw, 2012). Notably, the proportion of single-parent families is increasing across time. According to the Statistical Service of Cyprus (2016), the share of single-parent families was only 3.6% in 1982. In 2011 it reached 7.6%. On the other hand, the fertility rate stands at a low level, implying a shrinking proportion of multi-child families. The effects of these two demographic forces on child poverty most probably counterbalance.

Barriers to assessing formal early childhood education and care (ECEC) in Cyprus during the recessionary period

The provision of high-quality childcare is expected not only to increase employment participation by allowing parents to engage in employment but also to benefit the cognitive and social development of young children (Pedagogical Institute of Cyprus, 2016). These benefits are important, in particular for children from a disadvantaged background, by increasing the probability of their educational success and also improving their labour market prospects (Heckman 2006; Havnes and Mogstad, 2011; European Commission, 2014 and 2018).

In view of the benefits of formal ECEC, countries across Europe and the Organisation for Economic Co-operation and Development (OECD) have put considerable effort into encouraging participation in ECEC services, while the European Council in 2002 set specific targets with regard to the availability of high-quality and affordable childcare facilities for pre-school children.[4] Cyprus has not achieved these goals, due to problems in regard to the affordability of childcare for children aged 3 years old and younger.

Short description of the system

Formal childcare in Cyprus is provided by the public sector, local communities and the private sector, while informal childcare, mostly provided by parents and close relatives, is also common. Pre-primary education is mandatory for children aged 4 years and 8 months to 5 years and 8 months. The Ministry of Education undertakes all expenses of the public pre-primary schools and is responsible for the assessment and training of the educational staff. The community pre-primary schools are financed by the government, local authorities and parents' associations. They operate on a not-for-profit basis, usually in areas where the number of public facilities is insufficient to meet the needs of the community.

The pre-school system, in addition to kindergartens, also includes day nursery schools, infant care centres, day care and afternoon nurseries. Parents can choose the type of pre-primary school for their children between public, communal or private. Although the provision of public and communal kindergartens is adequate in Cyprus, the number of public and communal day nursery schools targeting children from birth to 3 years old is rather low. According to the last available data (Statistical Service, Republic of Cyprus, 2015/2016), out of 195 day nursery schools, only 8 were public and 60 communal, with the remaining operating in the private sector. Thus, just 4% of available day nursery schools in Cyprus are freely publicly provided, while about 31% of them are partially subsidised by the state.

Affordability of ECEC in Cyprus

The relative lack of public infrastructure for children aged 3 years and younger appears to affect participation in formal childcare in Cyprus, which lags compared to the EU average. In particular, 28.1% of children less than 3 years old received formal childcare in Cyprus in 2017, whereas the respective figure for EU28 was 34.2%.[5] As the majority of families with children below 3 years old are obliged to turn to the private sector for purchasing childcare services, the issue of affordability becomes crucial for formal childcare participation, especially for low-income households during a recession. This issue is explored in Table 8.2 using data from the Cyprus Family Expenditure Surveys (CyFES) for the years 2009 and 2015. ECEC affordability is defined as the household expenditure for childcare as a percentage of the household income. Childcare affordability is investigated for four hypothetical households (single parent with one/two children and couple with one/two children) whose incomes lie at (1) the official poverty threshold[6] and (2) the median equivalised net income.[7]

The second and third columns of Table 8.2 report the annual income for poor and median income households, respectively, as defined by Eurostat. The fourth column presents the average annual household childcare expenditure for households

Table 8.2 Childcare affordability in Cyprus (2009 and 2015)

2009	Annual income (poor households) (a)	Annual income (median households) (b)	Childcare annual expenditure (c)	(a)/(c) (%)	(b)/(c) (%)
Single parent with one child	12,832	17,538	2,118	16.51	12.08
Single parent with two children	15,794	21,586	4,236	26.82	19.62
Couple with one child	17,768	24,284	2,118	11.92	8.72
Couple with two children	20,729	28,331	4,236	20.44	14.95
2015					
Single parent with one child	10,759	15,829	2,043	18.99	12.91
Single parent with two children	13,242	19,482	4,086	30.86	20.97
Couple with one child	14,897	21,917	2,043	13.71	9.32
Couple with two children	17,380	25,570	4,086	23.51	15.98

Source: Authors' own calculations using CyFES 2009 and 2015.

with children up to 3 years old, while the last two columns show the proportions of income that is spent on childcare. For low-income families in Cyprus, the proportion of income spent on childcare ranged from around 12% to 27% in 2009 and from 14% to 31% in 2015 depending on the household's composition. As expected, these ratios are lower for median income households (9% to 20% in 2009 and 9.5% to 21% in 2015). To put these figures into perspective, the average cost for childcare is 15% of net family income in OECD countries (OECD, 2016).

The high cost of formal ECEC provision turns a large number of families to the informal sector providing similar services (European Commission, 2018). Indeed, in Cyprus 21.2% and 32% of parents report great and moderate difficulty, respectively, in affording formal childcare, while the respective figures for EU28 are 4.2% and 7.8% (EU-SILC ad-hoc module on services, 2016).

Crucially, it appears that between 2009 and 2015 the affordability of childcare worsened in Cyprus as household income fell at a faster rate than childcare cost. Indeed, Cyprus has suffered a substantial financial blow, changing the distribution of wealth among the population while also shrinking the level of real wages, especially in the private sector. This has led to steep decreases in wages reducing the affordability of pre-primary care in the absence of coherent policy framework for subsidising these services. As a result, in Cyprus, almost 40% of the population reports financial constraints as the main reason for not using formal childcare, a percentage more than double in relation to the EU28 average (16.2%). These rates are much higher for poor and single-adult households (61.5% and 67.7%, respectively), again well above the EU28 average (27.9% and 20.9%, respectively).

Future challenges of ECEC in Cyprus

Cyprus has several issues to review in relation to availability but also affordability of ECEC, particularly for children of low socioeconomic background. Childcare costs for young children (3 years old and younger) from disadvantaged backgrounds are high and can amount to almost one-third of the disposable income of a low-income single parent family in Cyprus. These problems have exacerbated during crisis. Such high costs can act as a barrier to the use of ECEC and discourage parental employment.

The low use of formal childcare has adverse effects not only for children but also for their mothers by means of underemployment, interrupted careers and reliance on non-standard employment (e.g. part-time work). Suffice to say that these phenomena become more intense during recessions and austerity and mostly affect low-income and single mothers. The increase of available formal childcare, especially for children ages 3 and younger, must be a prime objective for policy makers in Cyprus. This is not an easy task for policy, as it requires changes in the structure and organisation of ECEC services in the country. Yet the recent recession and following period of austerity highlighted the importance of childcare challenges and the need to rethink the appropriateness of delivering ECEC under market conditions (Lloyda and Penna, 2014).

The response of the primary school system in the period of crisis

The conceptual framework: schools and austerity

Austerity is linked to the reduction of both public and private spending on education bringing about significant changes in the structure of the education system and the day-to-day operation of schools. It therefore raises the question about what, and how much, schools can do to mitigate these effects. This is important because exclusionary forms of discrimination may start even from the primary school level and may be connected with students' professional future and their adult life chances (Papaloi, 2017). Thus the issue of counterbalancing educational policy against economic austerity in Cyprus will be developed herein, while also discussing the effectiveness of the measures taken and the practices adopted so as to consolidate social justice and address social and educational inequalities.

Undeniably, school is the basic unit of the education system and, according to Pashiardis (2013), it includes three basic elements: (a) the inputs (i.e. data received from the environment such as material resources, students' number and socio-economic origin and legislative interventions defining managerial, educational and other issues); (b) the so-called black box of processes (curricula, teaching methods, cultivation of students' behaviour and teacher training); and (c) the environment (the external factors that affect all the educational sub-systems).

Therefore, school functioning is based upon internal factors (teachers, administration, practices) and external environmental factors (reduction of family income and incidents of domestic violence), as well as on changes and societal challenges which affect in multiple levels the education system and, consequently, school's prosperity and effectiveness (Hoy and Miskel, 2005).

In particular, as a result of the austerity, at school level, the main factors that negatively affect outflows include the reduction of family income as well as organisational practices and behaviours that reproduce inequalities (Vryonides and Spyrou, 2014). Undoubtedly, education as an institution is never neutral and contributes to the reproduction and legitimisation of social hierarchy by promoting standards similar to power relations in society and by acting as a catalyst in student's formation of values (Bernstein, 1977).

Interestingly, income reductions highlight and exacerbate already existing negative situations within families, including interpersonal conflicts, anxiety, negative mood, insecurity, rivalry, inconsistency, alienation, conflict, psychological disorders, domestic violence, violence against children, and complete disorganisation and dissolution (Conger et al., 1992). Furthermore, it appears that the deterioration in the standard of living due to the economic crisis in Cyprus and its consequences on the daily life of children, especially the vulnerable ones, often touches the limits on the violation of the basic rights of the child. Children who are directly affected by problems within their families, such as rising unemployment and a steady decline in family incomes, experience feelings of uncertainty and ultimately anger, which foster the emergence of violent and aggressive attitudes at school (Frey et al., 2009).

Accordingly, in times of austerity, the international literature has highlighted a number of negative in-school factors including teacher dissatisfaction with wage cuts, job uncertainty, increased workload and negative predisposition of parents towards public services. It seems that all these negatively affect teacher self-sufficiency by cultivating feelings of frustration, deteriorating the relationship between parents and school, and by hindering the cultivation of a culture of mutual trust (Main, 2014; Slay and Penny, 2013).

The response of the educational system in Cyprus

Undeniably, to mitigate the effects of austerity has been a crucial challenge for the educational system in Cyprus. The state was led into a series of reforms, changes and measures which aimed at saving money and reducing costs, but at the same time with a view to cause the least possible impact on the amount and the quality of services offered.

The findings of empirical research show that the Cypriot education policy against the austerity was in general fruitful by investing in removing inequalities and in eliminating marginalisation and exclusion for disadvantaged students. Interestingly, in Cyprus, emphasis has been given to the promotion of a democratic culture and the formation of democratic dispositions and allegiances as a part of educational community's responsibility. Meanwhile, despite the sharp decline in GDP, public expenditure on primary education regarding developmental policy was not suspended, while operating expenses (consumables and other running expenses) decreased by 66.6%, resulting in a significant deterioration in daily life at school (Ministry of Education and Culture, 2017).

Moreover, the priorities in the allocation of resources seem to have drastically changed in favour of pre-primary education during the crisis years. Specifically, the children attending community and public kindergartens increased by 33.7% and 17.7% respectively during the period of crisis (2010–2015), while for the corresponding five-year period before the crisis (2004–2009) the relevant number of students remained almost stable. In primary education, the number of both students and teachers during the years of crisis has decreased by 3.1% and 3.9%, respectively; in the period before the crisis (2004–2009), Cyprus had adopted a wasteful policy reflected in an increase of teachers hired for this level by 9.3%, while at the same time the number of students was decreasing (9.8%).[8]

Apart from the reallocation of more resources to pre-primary education, during the austerity period there have been other more targeted measures mostly addressing children at risk, such as the extension of the Educational Priorities Zones (EPZ) or the 'Free supply of breakfast to needy children in public schools' programmes. The EPZ programme was first introduced in 2004 to combat early school leaving, school failure and delinquency in schools located in socially disadvantages areas. While in the school year of 2009–2010, at the outbreak of the crisis, only 21 schools participated in the programme, currently the programme is applied to 96 school units covering about 15% of the total student population. The second policy, 'Free supply of breakfast to needy children in public schools', began operation in December 2012. The provision of breakfast for deprived students is subsidised at all levels of education. Approximately 12% of the primary school population (about 13,000 students) have benefited from the programme during the crisis.

There are some indications that these policies had a positive contribution in combating child poverty and exclusion. Specifically, it seems that during the years of crisis there was a 3% increase in the number of children from migrant families who gained access to the Cypriot education system and especially the pre-primary level. At the same time, the educational psychological services recorded a slightly positive trend regarding the behavioural patterns of children living under precarious social conditions, whereas based on the trends identified in other similar cases one should have expected a sharp upturn in the number of individual cases reported for school delinquency in periods of austerity (Hannon, 2003). These rather positive effects may be connected to the national system's investment in reducing educational inequalities and the cultivation of respect, responsibility, recognition and empathy (Gewirtz, 1998).

Moreover, the investment in social justice and social inclusion should be seen as a cornerstone of Cypriot national educational policy over the crisis period. The school system of Cyprus faced significant challenges during these years, but it appears that, in general, it responded positively by increasing its inclusivity for the most disadvantaged groups of children and by increasing participation levels in the pre-primary level. In any case, it has to be underlined that schools alone cannot compensate for social inequalities. Thus emphasis must be placed on the implementation of just educational practices with significant investment and resources allocation by all stakeholders and services involved (Shain, 2015). Therefore, in times of crisis, schools have to revise their philosophy and practices, open the dialogue in socially just and constructive ways with all stakeholders (principals, teachers, students, parents, academics, the local community and non-governmental organisations), re-consider objectives and goals, and become more socially oriented according to the emerging social needs (Karakatsani and Papaloi, 2018).

Conclusions

The sheer magnitude of the recession and the extent of the implemented austerity measures makes Cyprus an interesting case for investigating the impact of these economic changes on the wellbeing of children. The general picture is that poverty among children was increased due to the reduction in parents' labour market participation and the rise in the number of working poor parents. Income support to families with children was weakened due to austerity, while the decline in family income intensified the problem of affordability of formal childcare, especially for children aged 3 and younger, thereby highlighting the inadequacies in public provision. Moreover, schools were affected in terms of budgetary cuts and increasing dissatisfaction among teachers, while the needs of the more vulnerable students increased.

However, it is reasonable to suggest that the impact on children could have been harsher bearing in mind the size of the GDP contraction (about 10% in real terms and one of the severest in Europe). Indicators of poverty and social exclusion among children have indeed recorded high levels, but not higher than those pertaining in most other European countries, including countries which have not experienced intense recessionary episodes. Providing full explanations of these developments extends far beyond the scope of the chapter. However, it can be argued that the social protection system played a crucial role in mitigating the severity of the recession, at least in the short run, despite that its redistributive capacity was weakened by austerity.

A quantitative manifestation of the preceding argument can be provided by comparing the child poverty rate (i.e. the percentage of poor children) before and after social transfers[9] (excluding pensions from the definition of social transfers). According to Eurostat calculations, child poverty in Cyprus before social transfers was 30.2% in 2015 (roughly speaking, this was the harsher year of the recession for households).[10] This figure, which is 15 p.p. above the actual poverty rate (i.e. after taking into account social transfers), might be interpreted as the poverty rate among children that would have prevailed in the absence of social protection, holding all other things constant. Additionally, Koutsampelas et al. (2013), using microsimulation techniques, demonstrate the anti-poverty impact of child benefits on specific population groups in the context of Cyprus. The analysis shows that the anti-poverty effects of child benefits are particularly large for single parents, multi-child families and low-educated parents. For example, the authors find that the poverty risk of single parents is reduced by 27.2 p.p. (from 51.2% to 24%) due to child benefits, while the poverty risk of a couple with four or more children is reduced by 15.9 p.p. (from 42.3% to 26.4%).

Another important factor was schools which in some cases operated as a cushion against child poverty by providing the place and context for the successful implementation of important anti-poverty initiatives, such as the provision of free breakfast to children. The latter point highlights the importance of compulsory public education not only in achieving educational goals but also in hosting social policy, thus promoting wider societal goals. Taken all together, a key message of the chapter is that the combination of social and educational policy might be a useful and effective tool in reducing the adverse effects of economic cycles even during periods of fiscal consolidation.

Another policy implication of our analysis is that it highlights some weaknesses of the policy framework, with the most important being the lack of provision of affordable childcare to all families. As was discussed in the relevant section, early childhood education is fundamental in child development and pivotal in reducing inequalities. Parents often purchase these services from the private sector. Yet when family incomes are compressed by austerity measures and the economic recession, the lack of adequate public provision becomes more visible, creating financing difficulties for households and especially the more economically vulnerable.

Finally, it is important to note that similar distributional changes (although of smaller magnitude) occurred in many countries which experienced recessionary episodes (according to Eurostat data, child poverty increased in 22 out of 27 member states between 2008 and 2014) and, inescapably, are going to happen again in the future. On that basis, the policy lessons derived from this case study are useful for policy-making beyond the context of the country of reference. A clear normative message is that during a recessionary period, families with children should be protected at least in relative terms while the weakening of cash or in-kind transfers to families should be avoided. To the budget-conscious, this may sound overly optimistic. Yet transfers to families are among the less costly items of social protection, accounting only for 2.4% of GDP or 8.6% of total social spending in EU28 countries,[11] thus protecting them during a recession is mostly a matter of political prioritisation. Furthermore, the chapter also highlights the importance of public education, including early childhood education, in fencing off child poverty. All the more, it is the synergy between the social policy and education that produces the best outcomes. The latter point is among the less well investigated in the fields of social and educational policy, certainly deserving more attention.

Notes

1 Average government deficit in EU28 reduced from −6.6% in 2009 to −2.3% in 2015. In Cyprus, the government deficit reduced from −5.4% in 2009 to 0.3% in 2016 (Eurostat Online Database, Code: tec00127).
2 Own analysis using Eurostat data on real GDP growth (Eurostat Online Database, Code: tec00115).
3 Eurostat Online Database, Code: [ilc_peps01].
4 The two targets are (1) 90% participation of children from age 3 until mandatory school age and (2) 33% participation of children under the age of 3.
5 Eurostat Online Database, Code: [tepsr_sp210].

6　Eurostat Online Database, Code: [ilc_li01].
7　Eurostat Online Database, Code: [Ilc_di04].
8　Processing of the relevant data included in the annual reports issued by the Ministry of Education and Culture (MOEC), downloaded from the MOEC's website: http://www.moec.gov.cy.
9　Social transfers cover the social support given by central, state or local institutional units and include old-age and survivors' pensions, unemployment benefits, family-related benefits, sickness and invalidity benefits, housing allowances, social assistance and other benefits. Eurostat Statistics Explained, Online Glossary: available at https://ec.europa.eu/eurostat/statistics-explained/index.php?title=Thematic_glossaries.
10　Eurostat Online Database, Code: ilc_li10.
11　Eurostat Online Database, Code: [spr_exp_sum].

References

Atkinson, A. B. and Marlier, E. (2010). *Income and Living Conditions in Europe*. Luxembourg: Eurostat.

Bernstein, B. (1977). *Class, Codes and Control, Vol. 3: Towards a Theory of Educational Transmissions (Primary Socialization, Language and Education)*, 2nd ed. London: Routledge & Kegan Paul.

Bradshaw, J. (2005). *A Review of the Comparative Evidence on Child Poverty*. York: Joseph Rowntree Foundation, University of York.

Chzhen, Y. and Bradshaw, J. (2012). Lone parents, poverty and policy in the European Union. *Journal of European Social Policy*, 22(5), 487–506.

Clerides, S. (2014). The collapse of the Cypriot banking system: A bird's eye view. *Cyprus Economic Policy Review*, 8(2), 3–35.

Conger, R. D., Conger, K. J., Elder, G. H., Jr, Lorenz, F. O., Simons, R. L. and Whitbeck, L. B. (1992). A family process model of economic hardship and adjustment of early adolescent boys. *Child Development*, 63(3), 526–541.

European Commission (2014). *Proposal for Key Principles of a Quality Framework for Early Childhood Education and Care (ECEC)*. Report of the Working Group on Early Childhood Education and Care under the Auspices of the European Commission, European Commission, Brussels.

European Commission (2018). *Strike a Work-life Balance for Working Parents and Bring about Sustainable and Inclusive Growth in Europe*. Report on the Development of Childcare Facilities for Young Children with a View to Increase Female Labour Participation, European Commission, Brussels, 8 May 2018, COM(2018) 273 final.

Frey, A., Ruchkin, V., Martin, A. and Schwab-Stone, M. (2009). Adolescents in transition: School and family characteristics in the development of violent behaviors entering high school. *Child Psychiatry and Human Development*, 40(1), 1–13.

Garcia, J.L., Heckman, J.J., Leaf, D. E. and Prados, M.J. (2017). *Quantifying the Life-Cycle Benefits of a Prototypical Early Childhood Program*. NBER Working Paper No. 23479.

Gewirtz, S. (1998). Conceptualizing social justice in education: Mapping the territory. *Journal of Education Policy*, 13(4), 469–484.

Hannon, L. (2003). Poverty, delinquency, and educational attainment: Cumulative disadvantage or disadvantage saturation? *Sociological Inquiry*, 73(4), 575–594.

Havnes, T. and Mogstad, M. (2011). No child left behind: Subsidized child care and children's long-run outcomes. *American Economic Journal: Economic Policy*, 3(2), 97–129.

Heckman, J.J. (2006). Skill formation and the economics of investing in disadvantaged children. *Science*, 312(5782), 1900–1902.

Heckman, J.J. (2008). The case for investing in disadvantaged young children. *CESifo DICE Report*, 6(2), 3–8.

Hoy, W. and Miskel, C. (2005). *Educational Administration. Theory, Research, and Practice*. Boston: McGraw-Hill.

Jarvis, S. and Redmond, G. (1997). Welfare state regimes and child poverty in the UK and Hungary. *Journal of European Social Policy*, 7(4), 275–290.

Karakatsani, D. and Papaloi, E. (2018). School learning architecture for active citizenship and social justice based on organizational meaningfulness. In N. Palaiologou and M. Zembylas (Eds.), *Human Rights and Citizenship Education: An Intercultural and International Perspective*. Cambridge: Cambridge Scholars Publishing.

Koutsampelas, C. and Pashardes, P. (2017). *Social Protection in Cyprus: Overview and Challenges*. Economic Policy Papers, No. 05–17, University of Cyprus.

Koutsampelas, C., Polycarpou, A. and Pashardes, P. (2013). *Child Poverty, Family Transfers, and the Effect of Economic Crisis*. Economic Analysis Papers, No 10–13, University of Cyprus.

Lloyda, E. and Penna, P. (2014). Childcare markets in an age of Austerity. *European Early Childhood Education Research Journal*, 22(3), 386–396.

Main, G. (2014). *The Impact of Austerity on Children's Well-being*. Paper presented at Questioning Austerity: Realities and Alternatives Conference, York, United Kingdom.

Ministry of Education and Culture (2017). *Annual Report 2017*. Nicosia: Ministry of Education and Culture.

OECD (2016). *Who Uses Childcare? Background Brief on Inequalities in the Use of Formal Early Childhood Education and Care (ECEC) among Very Young Children*. Social Policy Division, Directorate for Employment, Labour and Social Affair.

Papaloi, E. (2017). Leadership for social justice as an antidote to social pathogenesis. *Business Ethics and Leadership*, 1(3), 10–19.

Pashardes, P. (2017). Why child poverty in Cyprus is so low? *Cyprus Economic Policy Review*, 1(2), 3–16.

Pashardes, P. and Koutsampelas, C. (2014). *Investing in Children – Breaking the Cycle of Disadvantage*. EU Network of Independent Experts on Social Inclusion. Brussels: European Commission.

Pashiardis, P. (Ed.) (2013). *Modelling School Leadership across Europe: In Search of New Frontiers*. Dordrecht, Heidelberg, New York, London: Springer.

Pedagogical Institute of Cyprus (2016). *National Curriculum for Pre-school Education (3–6yrs old)*. Nicosia: Pedagogical Institute.

Ritakallio, V.M. and Bradshaw, J. (2006). Family poverty in the European Union. In J. Bradshaw and A. Hatland (Eds.), *Social Policy, Family Change and Employment in Comparative Perspective*. Cheltenham: Edward Elgar.

Shain, F. (2015). Succeeding against the odds: Can schools 'compensate for society'? *Education*, 3–13.

Slay, J. and Penny, J. (2013). Surviving austerity. Local voices and local action in England's poorest neighbourhoods. London: New Economics Foundation.

Statistical Service of Cyprus (2016). *2016 Demographic Report*. Republic of Cyprus.

Vryonides, M. and Spyrou, S. (2014). Cyprus. In P. Stevens and A.G. Dworkin (Eds.), *The Palgrave Handbook of Race and Ethnic Inequalities in Education*. London: Palgrave Macmillan.

9 Beyond coping

Families and young people's journeys through austerity, relational poverty and stigma

Sally Lloyd-Evans and the Whitley Researchers (John Ord, Lorna Zischka, Paul Allen, Liz Ashcroft, Aneta Banas, Sandra Clare, Sonia Duval, Naomi Lee)

Introduction

Recent shifts in the 'language of poverty' places increasing responsibility on families for their precarious circumstances and is often perpetuated through place-based stigma and discourses of othering at the grassroots (Slater and Anderson, 2012). Although existing research attends to the 'local' everyday micro-geographies of families *living in* and *through* austerity (Pimlott-Wilson and Hall, 2017; Hall 2017; van Lanen, 2018), highlighting the variegated and emotional experiences of 'getting by' (McKenzie, 2015; Hall, 2016; Hitchen, 2016), less attention has focused on the ways in which these experiences are also entangled with complex feelings around neighbourhood identities, relationality and socio-spatial stigma (Valentine and Harris, 2014; Tyler and Slater, 2018). Although it is well established that the stigma caused by poverty and exclusion can restrict people's access to services and opportunities (Sutton et al., 2014; JRF, 2018; Halliday et al., 2018), there is a need to better understand how the everyday 'micro-territories of stigma' (Verdouw and Flanagan, 2019) impact on relationality during austerity in order to reflect on how communities and policy makers might action strategies 'beyond coping'.

This chapter makes a contribution to these debates through the narrative of a participatory action research (PAR) collective called the Whitley Researchers, who engage local people in co-producing research to facilitate social change.[1] The research took place in two wards within the town of South Reading (Whitley and Church) that are often described as the 'most deprived wards'[2] in Reading, with parts of them ranking among the 10% most deprived areas in England in the domains of education, skills and training. While we did not set out to investigate the impact of austerity in South Reading's poorest communities, we researched issues raised by people who live in these communities together, and what we discovered was how people struggled to eke out a living, to survive each and every day, year in and year out. Our work highlighted the diversity of everyday pressures on ordinary people in poorer communities whose 'getting by' or 'coping' may be seen as patronising euphemisms living in a nation where almost every measure of a civilised society – longevity, health, income, childhood poverty or social mobility – has ground to a halt or regressed (JRF, 2018). Focusing on the so-called deprived community of Whitley, South Reading, this chapter reflects on five years of shared learning to highlight how place-based stigmatism simultaneously propagates, and provides a space for, resisting social inequality and relational poverty.

First, our chapter reflects on existing research that has helped us make sense of the knowledge we co-produce with local families, young people and community organisations. We then offer a snapshot of the everyday experiences of austerity facing local families through a focus on the barriers to mobility that have facilitated long-term spatial isolation and intensified stigmatisation of the local community. Third, we discuss how the misrepresentation of the Whitley community as 'deprived' and 'disadvantaged' within policy discourse has been a significant barrier to collaborative working and explore how these feelings can further damage the relationships and community-led capacity building that are essential for resisting neoliberal poverty discourses at the grassroots. Finally, we reflect on how the current disruption of top-down service delivery, support that in the past has intensified negative stigmatisation of community deprivation, can provide room for greater participation and activism.

Situating our research: relational poverty, socio-spatial stigma and precarity

Through our five-year journey as community researchers, a number of interrelated themes have emerged that help us make sense of the stories we encounter. First, that poverty and 'deprivation' is always *relational* and the everyday injustices that accompany wealth inequalities are felt, lived and connected to place (Elwood et al., 2017). Relational poverty studies look beyond economic explanations to consider how levels of poverty vary according to intersections of 'political-economic, social ordering and cultural-political processes' (Lawson, 2010: 1, 2012) and evidence how the emotional outcomes of being stigmatised and 'othered' shape access to decent work and education (Lawson and Elwood, 2018). Moreover, these relational tensions can serve to undermine communication and positive relationships between local residents and policy makers, parents and schools or young people and their wider community.

Second, so-called disadvantaged communities are often separated from the histories through which they operate and from the everyday situational geographies that shape how local families feel about their lives (Jupp, 2013). Experiences of getting by under austerity are often constituted through their encounters with 'others', family or kinship networks that are important for community resilience and resistance (Nayak, 2019), and these *everyday relational interactions* also play an essential role in shaping lived experiences of deprivation (Zischka, 2019). Austerity alters the emotional experiences of families, affecting how they live, meet, work and play across different spaces which renders a single 'social reading of austerity' meaningless if disconnected to place (Manzo, 2003; Clayton et al., 2015; Stenning, 2018: 2). Drawing on the work of Goffman (1963), the notion of territorial stigma expresses the powerful spatial dimensions of stigmatism that draw attention to a community's social characteristics and identities (Wacquant et al., 2014; Paton et al., 2017). Geographers prefer to use the term 'socio-spatial' rather than 'territorial' (Slater and Anderson, 2012; Meyer et al., 2016) in order to emphasise the fluidity of stigma through changing cultural space (Geiselhart, 2017; Tyler and Slater, 2018). There is nothing new here: the poorest at lowest end of the social hierarchy have been looked down upon for centuries as a 'problem', a threat or 'idle', and the age-old distinction between 'deserving' and 'underserving' poor (Blokland, 2012; Ridge, 2013) now transmutes into 'strivers' and 'skivers' (Valentine and Harris, 2014). The negative impacts of stigmatisation range from difficulties in finding work, address discrimination and limited access to health services (Kirkness and Tijé-Dra, 2017), and they can also weaken the *relationships* between local communities, institutions and service providers under austerity and precarity (Sutton et al., 2014; Chase and Walker, 2013).

Third, *precarity* as a concept is also being used in a range of place-based research contexts to help frame research around in-work poverty and livelihood insecurity (Waite, 2009). Notwithstanding the critiques of this concept (see Harris and Nowicki, 2018), precarity is another useful lens for framing the context of our research. A relational approach to *precarity* provides a method of inquiry into how work and life intersect, particularly in respect of the everyday stresses relating to zero-hour contracts, shift work and caring responsibilities. Of particular relevance to our research on mobility is the association between precarity and time poverty (Standing, 2011) as a result of families' complex work and care commitments with limited transport options. In the following sections we explore how austerity restricts the everyday mobility of families, exacerbating social isolation, precarity and feelings of disconnection that bring negative feelings of stigmatisation to the surface.

Research context: the Whitley Researchers collective

Participatory action research (PAR) attempts to move away from identifying and theorising the problems of 'others' towards engaging communities in co-producing their own knowledge to engender social action (Askins and Pain, 2011; Mason, 2015; Lloyd-Evans, 2016; Askins, 2018; Holt et al., 2019). Established in 2014, the Whitley Researchers is a PAR partnership between the Whitley Community Development Association (WCDA), local residents, young people and the University of Reading that engages local people in co-producing knowledge for community improvement and a more socially just society (https://research.reading. ac.uk/community-based-research/). The initial impetus for the collective was from local residents working with the Whitley Big Local, who reached out to the university to help them gather local knowledge to target a £1 million grant from the Big Local National Lottery. Since then, we have explored important issues chosen by local people including transport, financial exclusion, unemployment and youth aspiration.

In official language, Whitley in South Reading is variously described as 'working class', 'disadvantaged', 'underprivileged' or 'deprived' (see Whitley Researchers, 2018). Communities such as Whitley are mostly described in the language of 'deficiency' and interpreted as a catalogue of failings or weaknesses in the resident population (Shildrick, 2018). Less addressed is the failure of institutions or agencies, often statutory providers, to meet the challenge of internal attitudes and processes under the crushing impact of severe cutbacks at a time of austerity. As we will explore, such depictions serve to stereotype local families as either in need of 'fixing' or as partly to blame for their own socio-economic situation. Conversely, Whitley is also termed a 'community', and this conveys warm evocations of cohesion and togetherness. As a quote from a resident in the 2015 WCDA Community Plan (cited in Whitley Researchers, 2018) states: 'Whitley is a vibrant and growing community with huge potential to achieve for itself. With a single voice and community cohesion Whitley will continue to grow and challenge old stereotypes'. This is the community within which our research collective is embedded and, evident from the preceding quotes, it is a community stigmatised but with strong collective spirit.

'Getting there': a snapshot of families' everyday journeys through austerity

In 2014, we conducted research to explore the everyday travel needs and experiences of local families, identify transport barriers and suggest ways of addressing unmet needs that could be targeted by the Whitley Big Local Initiative. The research focused on family mobilities in an era of austerity, and we used the context of precarious livelihoods and time poverty (Lloyd-Evans et al., 2015) as a starting point for understanding everyday family practices around juggling work and care on dwindling incomes.

The research, which consisted of a face-to-face questionnaire with 500 households, 30 in-depth interviews with public and voluntary sector organisations and five focus groups, highlighted the central role played by mobility in connecting people to the places they needed, and more importantly, where they aspired or wanted to go to. The data gave us a snapshot of families' everyday lives that told us a story about the importance of being mobile and connected and how austerity exacerbates social isolation and restricts access to work, health services, decent food and education (see Table 9.1).

Table 9.1 Snapshot of everyday mobility from a survey of 500 households

- 45% of households had no car
- 70% shop in one local supermarket
- 72% faced transport barriers, particularly cost
- 34% travel to hospital/doctors *at least once* a month
- 50% are in paid work (many on zero-hour contracts)
- People only travel to where they can get easily – social isolation is an issue
- Everyday family practices were largely confined to Whitley
- 80% of those with a car socialise weekly compared to only 60% of those without a car (women are less likely to socialise than men)

Source: Lloyd-Evans et al. (2015).

We discovered that restricted mobility was contributing to the isolation, social exclusion and stress for local families due to three main factors. First, around half of the households we talked to relied on public transport and yet, local buses were routed around the Whitley community with no cross-community transport or direct routes to the main hospital, supermarkets and sixth form colleges. As a result, some of the most vulnerable residents in Reading needed to take two buses to access healthcare, education and adhere to the requirements of new welfare reforms that give little consideration to complex family lives:

> Under the new rules I have to keep going to the Job Centre – it's always 9am and I keep saying that '*I can't take my kids to school*' and get into the centre of town. If you're late or don't turn up, they stop your benefits for 2 weeks. They won't listen – it's 2 buses into the centre and it takes an hour with a buggy and 2 kids.
>
> (Dawn, 21, Focus Group 1)

Second, rising living costs and changes to welfare support were leaving families without the capacity to pay for bus trips. Money was the most frequently cited transport barrier, with 'not being able to get everyone in your family where they need to go with the time and money you have' (Clare, Focus Group 4) as one of the most significant problems being experienced by families.

Third, the precarious nature of job opportunities and low-paid work, combined with the everyday caring responsibilities, particularly for women, meant that families were suffering from time poverty. As discussed earlier, time poverty is often seen as a hidden condition of precarity and this particularly impacts upon women's capacity to work as 'social glue' within communities suffering from a shrinking welfare state (Hall, 2018). The complex daily family work and caring practices with children at different schools and no school transport place significant time pressures and stress on carless families in Whitley (Bowlby, 2012; Hall, 2016; Jupp 2017; Jupp et al., 2019). This was highlighted by Ann and Helen's experiences:

> It takes me all morning to get my children to school; I get back to feed the little one and I start all over again. If my Mum needs me, she has problems getting out, then *something has to give*. The oldest ends up missing school and going to help her Nan.
>
> (Ann, 23, Focus Group 3)

One of the most important issues facing local families, mainly mothers, is that they live in extended family networks with huge caring responsibilities and there's not enough support. They constantly juggle the needs of one family member over another. How can you possibly get 3 kids to different schools and then get to work or take your Dad to the hospital and back for pre-school pick up at 11.45?

> (Helen, NGO worker)

'Getting there' was often based on a series of decisions around family priorities, often made by women, with transport being one of the first 'budgets' to be cut under austerity. Lack of connectedness and social isolation was leading to rising health concerns and emotional stress, as well as restricting young people's opportunities to access education and extra-curricular opportunities that helped them make sense of their own place in the world. We did not look for austerity, but we found it in every area of the research we have conducted.

In 2015, local residents took the *Working Better with Whitley* report to the local bus company, and together they developed a new cross-community bus route that started in 2016. As well as connecting families to the hospital and supermarkets, the researchers felt a sense of empowerment that would shape the next four years of our action research. However, we found that 'fixing' the bus route was only one side of the story and that austerity and place-based isolation were interwoven to produce a local geography of relational poverty and relationality aggravated by negative external stigma. Over the next few years we explored issues around debt and financial exclusion, worklessness and youth aspirations. Through these journeys, a common story around the emotional hurt and negative impact of place-based stigma as a result of decades of 'othering' and social isolation began to emerge from each project. This was often a barrier to engaging participants in research on difficult issues as highlighted by one of our community researchers when we were discussing ways of researching financial exclusion:

> You have to be very careful as people already think they are being judged, stigma for living in Whitley, be aware that people will be defensive.
>
> (Whitley Researcher, 2017)

Despite some successes in changing bus routes and shaping service provision, negative stigma that represented local residents as 'undeserving', 'deprived' or 'in need of saving' (Lambie-Mumford and Green, 2017) continued to impact on the embodied feelings of local residents, including our research team. As our collective gained ground and austerity cutbacks on essential services took hold, our community researchers were invited to facilitate strategic policy workshops in an attempt to bring 'the local voice' to the table and do 'more with less'. Such events are often held in the evenings and this can exacerbate the everyday impacts of austerity on the Whitley Researchers and their families, particular in terms of their caring commitments and the time pressures of juggling more than one job. Meetings were often emotionally charged, not just due to tensions around cutbacks, but also because our researchers began to tire of sitting in meetings, albeit with empathetic service providers, only to hear their families and homes consistently represented as 'deprived', 'lacking in aspiration' or 'troubled'. Researchers would leave meetings feeling angered, as an extract from a field diary shows in Figure 9.1.

> "A local public sector representative is talking about the lack of young people's aspirations, a culture of poverty and why 'no-one goes to University' in the neighbourhood. Some of the community researchers start to withdraw from the discussion, moving their chairs away from the circle, angered at the continued perpetuation of what they see as a false stereotype when their children are at University! It's clear from their body language that they are uncomfortable being talked about...some leave the meeting before it finishes".

Figure 9.1 Extract from Sally Lloyd-Evans's field diary, community meeting 2016

Beyond coping: aspirations, relationships and stigma

In 2017, our collective co-produced a project with young people, schools and parents that sought to explore, understand and share the attitudes, experiences and feelings held around youth aspirations and transitions to work and further education. Our most exciting initiative was the development of a 'young Whitley Researchers' team with a group of Year 9 pupils at the local secondary school who created their own innovative methods, including an 'aspiration game' based on snakes and ladders (see Figure 9.2), and documented their attachments with place through photography (see Whitley Researchers, 2018). Based on their version of snakes and ladders, the game is a tool for opening conversations with peers around the things that hold them back in life (the snakes) and things that help them forward (the ladders). It has been played in both primary and secondary schools and is an effective way of helping students to express their feelings. Within a year, the team had undertaken 136 face-to-face interviews with local parents, played the aspiration game with over 70 pupils from local secondary and primary schools, interviewed a further 38 students and 38 teachers, and conducted several participatory events and community panels.

In keeping with existing research (Menzies, 2013; Gulczyńska, 2019) it was clear that there was no lack of aspiration in Whitley, but the findings demonstrated how strongly youth aspirations depend on *two* interlinked elements around *place and relationships*.

First, and unsurprisingly, our research found that family, school and community attitudes to 'youth aspiration' are influenced by a set of place-based conditions in South Reading. They demonstrated how the ideas and constraints young people are exposed to as they grow up shape their choices and how these choices are being curtailed under austerity (Horton, 2016). On the positive side, these include strong community bonds, a sense of togetherness and a desire for good local schooling, but on the negative side there is evidence of difficult socio-economic and emotional circumstances for some families and poor parental experience of

Figure 9.2 What helps or hinders you? The Young Researchers 'Aspiration Game'

education: socio-economic inequalities, challenging family situations and auster-ity can fracture trust, respect and damage social cohesion. Lack of confidence and money were also seen as holding children back by half of all parents. Monetary barriers included costs associated with going to university, after-school clubs, expensive local housing and austerity cuts to youth provision (McDowell, 2017).

Second, these place-based material conditions were also impacting negatively on the *relationships* between young people and adults, parents and teachers, and local residents and service providers in what Verdouw and Flanagan (2019) refer to as the 'micro-territories' of stigmatism. Positive and collaborative two-way communication with (and between) the adults in their lives made a huge differ-ence to young people's outlook and furthermore, the relationships between young people, families, schools and the wider community were key to shaping local attitudes to, and outcomes arising from, beliefs around 'aspirations' (Pimlott-Wilson, 2015). While the context of austerity shaped the everyday lived experiences of the different groups we worked with, from cutbacks in education and school provision to the overstretched and exhausted neighbourhood service providers, economic crisis was not the only factor at play. Tasked with the job of reducing social inequality and disadvantage by working with statutory service providers, community researchers and local residents have become increasingly angry at the negative representations of their communities that can fracture relationships between residents and policy makers, as illustrated in the following extract from our report (Figure 9.3).

Through their innovative board game (see Figure 9.2), the Young Researchers also talked to their peers about the things that help and hinder young people in achieving their ambitions. 'Relationships' was the most frequently mentioned issue mentioned by around 70% of young participants. In particular, around 40% of the young participants interviewed found 'it difficult to approach teachers' and the 'feeling of having no voice and that views are not understood and respected'.

Young people told us about their desires to be listened to and to challenge any negative stigma associated with the area or their own ambitions. Students were troubled by occasions on which they felt 'put down' by adults as 'they don't even listen to what you are trying to say', and they appreciated being listened to and supported. The research pointed to the need that young people have to be part of a *secure wider environment (community)* which features *positive two-way relationships* that the young people can draw on when needed, and into which they are inspired to give their own contribution. Young people's interaction with place is

---

The Whitley Big Local Community Plan (2012 – 2022) is written by Whitley residents, who are vexed about the way in which their community is portrayed e.g. it's 'crime addled' 'falling further behind' 'benefit dependant' with a 'very high concentration of single parents' (pages 9 and 10). They go on to say it is not surprising that people in Whitley suffer from '.. low expectations within ourselves' (p10). Residents have been 'talked down to' and disabled by those authorities who 'know best' for long enough with the result that residents:

".. (think) they aren't capable ... so they expect others to do things for them when in practice they could and should be making changes for themselves and their community and friends" (p10).

Figure 9.3 Extract from the Whitley Researchers *Aspiration in Whitley Report* (2018: 49), based on the Whitley Big Local Community Plan (2012–2022)

an affective relationship (De Backer and Pavoni, 2018), and around half of the students were not confident that everything that could be done is being done to help them.

In April 2018, the Young Researchers invited a panel of ten residents and agency representatives to respond to questions about how they could support the hopes and aspirations of its young people (see Figure 9.4). Key findings from the event are highlighted in Figure 9.5, and they demonstrated the desire to focus on relational matters and the language of talking about their neighbourhood.

The parents who participated in our interviews strongly felt that communication with schools and service providers can be difficult when they feel threatened or stigmatised or do not feel informed. Many parents' reluctance to engage with schools was based on their own poor experiences of education in the same area. Teachers went on to tell us what makes it easy and what makes it hard to work with parents on these issues or questions. The most common response mentioned by over 80% of teachers was to do with the *way* in which parents communicated, and they also mentioned economic pressures and external stigma, but they were less aware of their *own roles* in shaping these discourses. It was clear that deeply embedded stigmatisation of the community had weakened trust between parents/ schools and teachers, local service providers and residents, young people and teachers over a much longer period of time – austerity and crisis can bring these place attachments and raw feelings to the surface.

Figure 9.4 Community panel led by the Young Researchers, April 2018

Source: Young Researchers, John Madejski Academy.

- The importance of promoting a local culture of respect
- Addressing stigma involves changing the way that each of us talks about Whitley – there was still evidence of stigma in the room
- Getting community groups and young people together generated a real sense of goodwill and common purpose. Developing positive lines of communication in this way helps to reduce the negative commentary.
- Celebrating and learning from local role models highlights positive pathways forwards.
- Extra-curricular activities that provide hands-on learning experience also reveals pathways forwards.
- Accessibility to extra-curricular activities in Whitley is increased if they are local, free, and promoted via the school. Collaboration with schools would help with targeting the young people who might benefit the most.

Figure 9.5 Relationships and stigma matter: reflections from a student-led community panel, May 2018

What these findings from our research illustrate is a set of tense relationships, first, of all *between* Whitley residents: those who are discouraged and disengaged and those who are activist and working at community development. Second, the *links* between residents and serving agencies or institutions who may be seen by residents as patronising and/or dismissive of local capabilities. Moreover, relational tensions were sometimes being used implicitly to justify service cutbacks in an area where 'people don't work together'. Third is the view from *inside the schools* of the community they serve and the families whose children they educate.

Compounding the challenges associated with attempts to bridge differences of expectation and experience between community, families and schools is the impact of deprivation and inequality which tends to fracture bonds and undermine potential ties. The key findings and recommendations from the 'aspiration' research were widely disseminated to 12,000 households around the community in 2019 in a 'Whitley Says "Yes We Can!" ' leaflet. Four funded action groups (young people, parents, schools and community) were created by local residents to develop priorities for moving forward.

Although the parent's group were keen to replace the extra-curricular youth clubs and activities closed under austerity, a key priority was the need to challenge the stigma that negatively impacts on their everyday lives. They wanted to start this by creating local events to help support each other and build better relationships with schools and service providers from a position of confidence and empowerment. In July 2019 they organised a community fun day attended by around 2,000 local residents at the local secondary school to bring diverse groups of families and young people together as a starting point. A teachers-led group are also making plans for starting conversations around ways to disrupt wider negative representations of their schools and students, and younger residents believe that they can build resilience and make a difference to their lives through voice and activism. As a couple of the Young Researchers so clearly articulated:

'How effective would it be to put a group of children in charge, to make the greater change, to inspire a movement, to push towards a better Whitley?'

'I have really enjoyed my time as a young researcher. I have loved hearing people's different opinions and perspectives and showing that having a voice is extremely important: your opinion matters. The past couple of years have shown me that if you want *change* you need to be determined and fight for it. My main aim was to help young people have a voice and to always have an opinion no matter what age, race or gender. I never realized how big this project would be and seeing the outcomes makes me proud to be a part of it.'

Conclusions: new stories of resisting stigma, participation and activism

Recent calls for changing the language of poverty (Shildrick, 2018) requires the telling of new narratives about social inequality in the UK, and our research hopes to make a small contribution to this agenda. Austerity is a double-edged sword: on one edge it cuts people's material support and local community services disappear along with the youth club and children's centre; on the other edge it cuts by stigmatisation. However, addressing stigmatisation is a complex task, and it would be following the creeds of neoliberalism to simply address stigmatism as an image problem that needs to be 'managed'.

It is well established that structural inequality undermines community development, increases disconnection, and destabilises community relations and our collective aims to help facilitate community-led activism, voice and resistance at the grassroots. A common story that we encountered in our research journey has been the perpetuation of discourses of spatial stigma and place-based othering that has served to undermine the community relationality required to tackle important issues such as mobility, social isolation and young people's life chances. While the roll-back of public and voluntary services had exacerbated material inequalities for many local families, and we do not condone the devastating withdrawal of the welfare state, we also found that the disruption of decades of top-down public funds has created new organic spaces for local families and activists to tackle what they see as the most important issues facing *their* communities. In Whitley, local residents and young people have identified challenging stigma and fostering better community relationships as key priorities, but what is less clear at present is how this might be addressed.

Greater focus on co-producing knowledge with families and communities can help destabilise ineffective top-down 'anti-poverty' strategies and open up new academic and policy debates around participation, intergenerational poverty and social activism. Our research also underlines the importance of knowledge: top-down assumptions are that people in 'working-class' communities have little or no understanding of their situation and are quite unable to express their thoughts meaningfully. What we have demonstrated clearly in our participatory research approach is that people can articulate their perceptions and feelings and what they know is something more than the standard insights generated from top-down policy initiatives. Relational thinking refers to a politics of possibility, challenging hegemonic modes and relations of knowledge production which can act to frame social inequality in different ways. Given recent welfare reforms and austerity measures, it has never been more urgent to think of more innovative solutions to engendering grassroots community development, and we hope that our research helps develop new conversations around the possibilities for 'beyond coping' with communities and service providers.

Notes

1 The Whitley Researchers are a local participatory action research partnership supported by the Whitley Community Development Association and the University of Reading. In this chapter, we use the pronoun 'we' to refer to our collective voice and co-production of the research presented in this chapter (John Ord, Lorna Zischka, Paul Allen, Liz Ashcroft, Aneta Banas, Sandra Clare, Sonia Duval, Naomi Lee).
2 According to the Indices of Multiple Deprivation (see www.gov.uk).

References

Askins, K. (2018) Feminist geographies and participatory action research: Co-producing narratives with people and place. *Gender, Place & Culture*, 25(9), 1277–1294.

Askins, K. and Pain, R. (2011) Contact zones: Participation, materiality and the messiness of interaction. *Environment and Planning D: Society and Space*, 5, 803–821.

Blokland, T. (2012) Blaming neither the undeserving poor nor the revanchist middle classes: A relational approach to marginalization. *Urban Geography*, 33(4), 488–507.

Bowlby, S. (2012) Recognising the time-spaces dimension of care: Caringscapes and carescapes. *Environment and Planning A: Society and Space*, 44(9), 2101–2118.

Chase, E. and Walker, R. (2013) The co-construction of shame in the context of poverty: Beyond a threat to the social bond. *Sociology*, 47(4), 739–754.

Clayton, J. et al. (2015) Emotions of austerity: Care and commitment in public service delivery in the North East of England. *Emotion, Space and Society*, 14, 24–32.

De Backer, M. and Pavoni, A. (2018) Through thick and thin: Young people's affective geographies in Brussels' public space. *Emotion, Space and Society*, 27, 9–15.

Elwood, S., Lawson, V. and Sheppard, E. (2017) Geographical relational poverty studies. *Progress in Human Geography*, 41(6), 745–765.

Geiselhart, K. (2017) Call it by its proper name! Territory-ism and territorial stigmatisation as a dynamic model: The case of old naledi. In: P. Kirkness and A. Tijé-Dra, eds., *Negative Neighbourhood Reputation and Place Attachment*. New York: Routledge.

Goffman, E. (1963) *Stigma: Notes of the Management of Spoiled Identity*. London: Penguin Books.

Gulczyńska, A. (2019) Stigma and the doomed-to-fail school careers of young people from disadvantaged neighbourhoods. *Children's Geographies*, 17(4), 413–426.

Hall, S. M. (2016) Everyday family experiences of the financial crisis: Getting by in the recent economic recession. *Journal of Economic Geography*, 16(2), 305–330.

Hall, S. M. (2017) Personal, relational and intimate geographies of austerity: Ethical and empirical considerations. *Area*, 49(3), 303–310.

Hall, S.M. (2018) Everyday austerity: Towards relational geographies of family, friendship and intimacy'. *Progress in Human Geography*. https://doi.org/10.1177/0309132518796280

Halliday, E., Popay, P., Anderson de Cuevas, R. and Wheeler, P. (2018) The elephant in the room? Why spatial stigma does not receive the public health attention it deserves. *Journal of Public Health*, fdy214. https://doi.org/10.1093/pubmed/fdy214

Harris, E. and Nowicki, M. (2018) Cultural geographies of precarity. *Cultural Geographies*, 25(3), 387–391.

Hitchen, E. (2016) Living and feeling the austere. *New Formations*, 87, 102–118.

Holt, L., Jeffries, J., Hall, E. and Power, A. (2019) Geographies of co-production: Learning from inclusive research approaches at the margins. *Area*, 51(3), 390–395.

Horton, J. (2016) Anticipating service withdrawal: Young people in spaces of neoliberalisation, austerity and economic crisis. *Transactions of the Institute of British Geographers*, 41(4), 349–362.

JRF (2018) *Poverty 2018: A Briefing*. Joseph Rowntree Foundation. Retrieved from www.jrf.org.uk/report/uk-poverty-2018 on 01.06.19.

Jupp, E. (2013) 'I feel more at home here than in my own community': Approaching the emotional geographies of neighbourhood policy. *Critical Social Policy*, 33, 532–553.

Jupp, E. (2017) Families, policy and place in times of austerity. *Area*, 49(3), 266–272.

Jupp, E., Bowlby, S., Franklin, S. and Hall, S. M. (2019) *The New Politics of Home*. Bristol: Policy Press.

Kirkness, P. and Tijé-Dra, A., eds. (2017) *Negative Neighbourhood Reputation and Place Attachment*. New York: Routledge.

Lambie-Mumford, H. and Green, M.A. (2017) Austerity, welfare reform and the rising use of food banks by children in England and Wales. *Area*, 49(3), 273–279.

Lawson, V. (2010), Reshaping economic geography? Producing spaces of inclusive development. *Economic Geography*, 86(4), 351–360.

Lawson, V. (2012) Decentring poverty studies: Middle class alliances and the social construction of poverty. *Singapore Journal of Tropical Geography*, 33(1), 1–19.

Lawson, V. and Elwood, S. (2018) *Relational Poverty Politics: Forms, Struggle and Possibilities*. Athens: University of Georgia Press.

Lloyd-Evans, S. (2016) Focus groups, community engagement, and researching with young people. In: R. Evans, L. Holt and T. Skelton, eds., *Methodological Approaches. Geographies of Children and Young People*, vol. 2. Singapore: Springer.

Lloyd-Evans, S. and the Whitley Researchers (2015) *Working Better with Whitley: Exploring the Everyday Transport Needs and Experiences of Local Communities in Reading*. University of Reading and WCDA. Retrieved from https://localtrust.org.uk/wp-content/uploads/2019/03/local_trust_whitley_report_25.09.2015.pdf

Manzo, L. C. 2003. Beyond house and haven: Toward a revisioning of emotional relationships with place. *Journal of Environmental Psychology*, 23(1), 47–61.

Mason, K. (2015) Participatory action research: Coproduction, governance and care. *Geography Compass*, 9(9), 497–507.

McDowell, L. (2017) Youth, children and families in austere times: Change, politics and a new gender contract. *Area*, 49(3), 311–316.

McKenzie, L. (2015) *Getting By: Estates, Class and Culture in Austerity Britain*. Southampton: Policy Press.

Menzies, L. (2013) *Educational Aspirations: How English Schools Can Work with Parents to Keep Them on Track*. Joseph Rowntree Foundation. Retrieved from www.jrf.org.uk/sites/default/files/jrf/migrated/files/england-education-aspirations-summary.pdf

Meyer, F., Miggelbrink, J. and Schwarzenberg, 2016. Reflecting on the margins: Sociospatial stigmatisation among adolescents in a peripheralised region. *Comparative Population Studies*, 41(3–4), 285–320.

Nayak, T. (2019) Re-scripting place: Managing social class stigma in a former steel-making region. *Antipode*, 51(3), 927–948.

Paton, K., McCall, V. and Mooney, G. (2017) Place revisited: Class, stigma and urban restructuring in the case of Glasgow's Commonwealth Games. *Sociological Review*, 65(4), 578–594.

Pimlott-Wilson, H. (2015) Individualising the future: The emotional geographies of neoliberal governance in young people's aspirations. *Area*, 49, 288–295.

Pimlott-Wilson, H. and Hall, S.M. (2017) Everyday experiences of economic change: Repositioning geographies of children, youth and families. *Area*, 49(3), 258–265.

Ridge, T. (2013) 'We are all in this together'? The hidden costs of poverty, recession and austerity policies on Britain's poorest children. *Children and Society*, 27, 406–417.

Shildrick, T. (2018) Lessons from Grenfell: Poverty, propaganda, stigma and class power. *Sociological Review*, 66(4), 783–798.

Slater, T. and Anderson, N. (2012) The reputational ghetto: Territorial stigmatisation in St Paul's, Bristol. *Transactions of the Institute of British Geographers*, 37(4), 530–546.

Standing, G. (2011) *The Precariat: The New Dangerous Class*. London: Bloomsbury.

Stenning, A. (2018) Feeling the squeeze: Towards a psychosocial geography of austerity in low to middle income families. *Geoforum* (in press). https://doi.org/10.1016/j.geoforum.2018.09.035

Sutton, E., Pemberton, S., Fahmy, E. and Tamiya, Y. (2014) Stigma, shame and the experience of poverty in Japan and the United Kingdom. *Social Policy and Society*, 13(1), 143–154.

Tyler, I. and Slater, T. (2018) Rethinking the sociology of stigma. *Sociological Review*, 66(4), 721–743.

Valentine, G. and Harris, C. (2014) Strivers vs skivers: Class prejudice and the demonization of dependency in everyday life. *Geoforum*, 53(May), 84–92.

van Lanen, S. (2018) Encountering austerity in deprived urban neighbourhoods: Local geographies and the emergence of austerity in the lifeworld of urban youth. *Geoforum*, (in press).

Verdouw, J. and Flanagan, K. (2019) 'I call it the dark side': Stigma, social capital and social networks in a disadvantaged neighbourhood. *Urban Studies* (published online). https://doi.org/10.1177/0042098018817226

Wacquant, L., Slater, T. and Pereira, V.B. (2014) Territorial stigmatization in action. *Environment and Planning A*, 46(6), 1270–1280.

Waite, L. (2009) A space and place for a critical geography of precarity. *Geography Compass*, 3(1), 412–433.

Whitley Researchers (2018) *Aspiration in Whitley: Improving the Collaboration between Schools, Families and the Community*. University of Reading and Whitley Community Development Association. Retrieved from https://aspiration-in-whitley.whitley-cda.org

Zischka, L. (2019) *Giving Behaviours and Social Cohesion: How People Who 'Give' Make Better Communities*. Cheltenham: Edward Elgar.

10 Escaping from capitalism

The enactment of alternative lifeworlds in France's mountain regions

Kirsten Koop

Introduction

France has been suffering less than many other EU countries that have implemented austerity measures. The French strategy for coping with the economic crisis that followed the 2008 recession focused more on raising taxes than drastically cutting public spending, which is what happened in the UK, Ireland, Portugal and Greece (Bozio et al., 2015; Farnsworth and Irving, 2012).[1] Because of the French government's reluctance to undertake drastic and unpopular reforms of the welfare state, some historical achievements made by trade unions (e.g. unemployment benefits) are still at levels that would be the envy of people in need in many other countries. Ten years after the recession, it is clear that redistribution measures have mitigated the impact of the crisis on low-income households. According to France's National Institute of Statistics and Economic Studies, the decline in the standard of living of France's 20% poorest households would have been four times more severe without the redistributive effects of social transfers (Fourmy, 2013).

However, the social situation in France is far from unproblematic. A report by the *Observatoire français des conjonctures économiques* pointed out that the average available revenue of French households declined by 1.2% between 2008 and 2016 (Demaison et al., 2018, p. 107). During the same period, France lost more than 600,000 jobs, and the unemployment rate rose steadily to unprecedented levels. Today, inside the European Union, France's youth unemployment rate of 20.2% is surpassed only by Croatia, Spain, Italy, and Greece (EUROSTAT, 2019). As a result of these and other factors, including deterioration in the education and health systems, a growing malaise is affecting large parts of the French population. The recent protests by the 'yellow vest' movement, which followed the announcement of a carbon tax at the end of 2018, have brought to light the profound anxiety in parts of the lower and middle classes in France, which have been suffering from a constant loss of purchasing power and confidence in successive liberal governments (Algan et al., 2019). Already in the spring of 2016, the *Nuit Debout* ('Night Upright') youth movement had revealed dissatisfaction with both the political and the economic systems. This movement was an unprecedented phenomenon as it had evolved from nationwide demonstrations against a liberal labour law (the El Khomri law) towards collective reflections on precari-ousness, neoliberalism, austerity and democracy (Kokoreff, 2016). Students and pupils occupied urban public spaces during night-time for months, in order to not only contest but also have exchanges with intellectuals about societal transforma-tion and utopia, and to take collective action outside the classical political system (Syrovatka, 2016).

The *Nuit Debout* movement made it clear there is broader resistance to the capitalist system in France among the country's younger generation. The latter has already been taking concrete actions by trying to set up life projects accord-ing to their own principles. As in many other EU countries, alternative initiatives in agroecology, eco-construction and eco-housing, recycling, energy transition, local currencies, food networks and cooperatives have been mushrooming across France since the beginning of the 21st century, with a particular increase since the global financial crisis.[2] These projects differentiate themselves from capitalist modes of functioning, as their aim is to achieve greater balance between society, economy and nature. In the wake of growing critique towards neoliberalism and interest in sustainability transitions, such community-led grassroots organisations are increasingly the subject of academic research in Europe, especially among degrowth and postcapitalist scholars (e.g. Chatterton and Pickerill, 2010; Demaria et al., 2019; Fischer et al., 2017; Jarvis, 2019; Neal, 2013; Pickerill and Chat-terton, 2006; Pruvost, 2017; Seyfang and Smith, 2007; Smith et al., 2016; Yates, 2015). The everyday practices of the members of such projects are considered as coping strategies allowing to escape from the relational impacts of crisis and austerity (Holmes, 2018). At the same time, they build concrete alternatives to the crisis-prone present (Ince and Hall, 2017). According to the scope and aim of analysis, such projects of resistance bringing visions of desirable futures to the present are addressed as autonomous geographies (Pickerill and Chatterton, 2006), grassroots innovations for sustainable development (Seyfang and Smith, 2007), alternative modernities (Hardt and Negri, 2011), real utopias (Wright, 2010), nowtopias (Demaria et al., 2019) and the like. I here address them as *life-worlds*, a term coined by Edmund Husserl, to underscore their capacity to create a common consciousness of being in the world through specific ways of living together (Husserl, 1970). The notion makes it possible to grasp the ontologi-cal dimension of such projects: alternative lifeworlds come into existence when shared imaginaries differing from those of the dominant 'world' are generated and enacted in space. The everyday practices constructing such lifeworlds create safe spaces preventing from living, feeling and experiencing the impacts of crisis and austerity. It is thus important to understand *how* they come into being in the inter-stices of the dominant system, and under which conditions they can be preserved and might even transform their immediate vicinity.

This chapter addresses some feature of such lifeworlds, taking a closer look at the modes of being and doing of alternative collectivities in rural mountain regions in the southeast of France, namely in the Ardèche and Drôme depart-ments (located on either side of the Rhône Valley) and on the pre-alpine Trièves plateau. These marginal areas have attracted individuals trying to live outside the incumbent system since the 1970s, providing access to cheap land, a magnificent landscape and municipalities that have a generally welcoming attitude and are trying to combat rural depopulation. Since 2008, the number of alternative projects has more than doubled in all three areas.[3] In 2019, 27 initiatives were run in the south of Ardèche, 29 in Trièves and 43 in the Drôme, by people aged between 20 and 40. Many of them have created place-based life projects combining accommodation, work and leisure. During three years of fieldwork (2015–2017), participants in most of these initiatives were interviewed on their worldview, values, practices and innovations enabling them to build concrete alternatives to the crisis-prone present.[4]

By delving into the underlying motivations and values of the project members, the next section of this chapter shows that the actors challenge many of the fundamental principles of conventional modern society, such as capitalism, bureaucracy and the division of labour. As the dominant capitalist regime does not provide regulatory frameworks for the intended way of living together, the actors have to imagine and create the desired world ex nihilo. The third section thus illustrates how the alternative values function as a shared code, guiding them when filling the spaces they had acquired with the intended senses. The modes of doing are similar to the major features of improvisation: intuition, spontaneity, flexibility, and the assemblage of known elements to create something new are at play in everyday practice. The fourth section discusses the longevity of these alternative lifeworlds under a specific lens. As the interviewed communities experienced that their adaptation to the legal frameworks of the dominant regime[5] is an indispensable precondition for being durably accepted by the dominant system, this section gives attention to the struggle to obtain the official rights to exist within the incumbent system. The last section explores the potential for a wider transformation of the incumbent regime, focusing on the relationship with the local population and local authorities, which potentially favours the mitigation of impacts of crisis on a broader scale by transmitting alternative values and practices to the incumbent system.

Resisting the fundamental characteristics of modernity

When asked about the reasons for their involvement in alternative projects, most of the interviewees referred to their personal decision to change their lives in a major way. None of them mentioned specific personal experience with economic crisis and/or austerity as the driver for this decision, even though some had been directly affected by periods of unemployment. Instead, the interviewees expressed emotional affection by the multiple crisis and a fundamental critique of some of the major characteristics of the capitalist society, such as consumerism, individualism and environmental destruction. 'We want to transition from an out-of-breath society to a better life for all, to get out of the prison that we have created for ourselves' (Christophe, Ardèche). All respondents mentioned their aspiration towards greater self-determination and self-blossoming while reconnecting with nature and people: 'We have to agree to put things back on the table and reconsider everything: learn collectively to live according to our needs, with the local resources that are available, reduce speed and consumption . . . experiment together, share' (Bernard, Drôme).

In order to express their lack of satisfaction and to fight for change, some interviewees had been through traditional forms of political engagement – inside political parties and through activism. Yet, all of them came to the decision that political action has to start with oneself, as one of them stated:

> It's not enough to criticize; you have to embody it, you have to go get it. If you're not embodying it, it's no use going to the theories behind. It's better to go and take risks, to dare . . . rather than having this wait-and-see attitude, being crushed by the weight of the model, and feeling defeated . . . by this inertia that you feel a lot in France.
>
> (Sylvain, Ardèche)

It is worth examining what the 'it' in Sylvain's statement refers to. It comes as no surprise that the interviewees do not label their being and doing in a specific way. And yet, our analysis of the interviews reveals that, whatever their projects are, they have a set of commonly shared normative principles. Conviviality, frugality, self-fulfilment, autonomy, living with nature, caring and sharing are central issues mentioned by the participants of our study (see Figure 10.1). Such features have been reported by other studies on similar grassroots initiatives in other parts of Europe. They constitute guiding principles for coping with crisis and getting by (e.g. Ince and Hall, 2017). At the same time, they shape imaginaries and form the fundaments of counter-hegemonic practices (Mason, 2014; Pickerill and Chatterton, 2006). In fact, these principles challenge key features of (high-)modern societies, such as accumulation and overuse of natural resources, the division of labour (Weber, 2003), trust in abstract systems and the reliance on experts (Giddens, 1997) (see Figure 10.1).

Taking such self-descriptions for granted, we can interpret these principles not only as responses to neoliberalism and capitalism but also as key principles guiding the search to overcome modernity as we know it.[6] The interviewees emphasised that they do not want to be thought of as returning to the past, as is a common trope within some literature on austerity and crisis (e.g. Bramall, 2013). In fact, the analysis of their modes of doing shows that they do not blindly reject everything that appeals to modernist values. They do not refuse high technology or global networking, and they are reflexive and sometimes apply linear thinking. Therefore, their projects are to be considered not as the negation of modernity as such but rather as other, alternative modernities. The underlying principles that the interviewees mentioned function as guidelines when experimenting with new ways of doing. A parallel to improvisation in music can be drawn here: by suggesting that conventional modernist principles represent the music sheet from which musicians want to distance themselves, we can consider the aforementioned alternative principles as the collectively shared code (Lévy, 2013, p. 235), guiding the communities when improvising in order to detach

	Alternative values*	Characteristics of modern societies**
1	Living with nature, preserving natural resources	Transformation of nature, overuse of natural resources
2	Conviviality, intergenerational living, sharing, caring, not depending on money	Individualism, competition
3	Local economy	Globalized economy
4	Autonomy, independence, self-sufficiency, creativity, community, pooling of resources, and taking collective action	Division of labor, industrialism, trust in abstract systems
5	Self-fulfillment, learning by doing	Expert knowledge – expert systems
6	Frugality	Growth – accumulation – consumerism
7	Deceleration	Most effective use of time
8	More circular thinking, personal journey	Rationality – linearity – progress
9	Diversity	Standardization, homogenization
10	Horizontal trans-local exchange networks	Hierarchic structure, control, order, regulation
11	Partial local re-embedding of social relations	Disembedding of social relations from the local context
12	Reflexivity	Reflexive ordering and reordering of social relations
13	Humanized technology	Technology

* 1–9: as mentioned by the interviewees; 10–13: as analyzed by the research team

** According to Durkheim (1997); Giddens (1997); Scott (1998); Weber (2003); Werlen (1995)

Figure 10.1 Alternative values challenging fundamental principles of (high-)modern society

Source: Koop and Senil (2016).

from the dominant modernist system. Following Vladimir Jankélévitch, philosopher and musician, there is even a dual metaphor here: he proposed improvisation as an alternative to both the teleological and the rational character of modernity (Jankélévitch, 1955).

Enacting alternative principles in space through improvisation

The first step of the communities that decide to launch an alternative development project is to acquire a convenient place to settle down. In fact, having space is an indispensable precondition to put their alternative principles into practice. Many communities choose the ruins of abandoned hamlets and try to legally acquire the land. Official recognition is a crucial issue for them, as it gives them the right to exist within the dominant system. But this first step also ushers in the first conflict with the conventional regime. How is it possible to set up a legal framework recognised by a societal system that is based on the protection of individual privacy and property but also compatible with the alternative principle of collective and equitable use? (also see Jarvis, 2019). The groups have to improvise by combining various regulations to reach a legal arrangement in line with both their principles and official norms. In this context, a frequent solution is the acquisition of property through a *société civile immobiliaire* or SCI (a civil real estate company scheme), which allows plural ownership. In most cases, up to three or four people legally acquire the collective property rights. In order to avoid unequal power relations caused by ownership, the formal owners then sign an emphyteutic lease[7] with the other project members, who specifically adopt an official status (e.g., an association or cooperative) for this purpose. Thus, in-depth knowledge of formal regulations is necessary so that they can be either bypassed or recombined.

The second step is to fill the available space with the intended meaning and sense. There are more or less concrete ideas about construction, housing, farming and producing goods and services. And there is motivation and enthusiasm but no master plan. Thus improvisation is the name of the game. The alternative principles, which represent more of a collectively shared intuition and intention than a model, guide their actions. Nature preservation and frugality are clearly the major guiding principles. They are specifically tangible in an analysis of how dwellings are constructed. Using local resources in the best possible way, adapting to the landscape and preserving the environment lead the collectivities to assemble and combine vernacular knowledge[8] with modern technologies. Inspiration comes from contacting local craftsmen and from exchanging information about similar projects within transnational alternative networks they are connected to. Thus the buildings have an amazing mix of styles and materials. For instance, a timber house might be inspired by Canadian techniques but deploy only locally available resources (such as walls containing crushed recycled cork for isolation). Houses might have green roofs covered in lichen and glass-bottle floors (a technique that dates to ancient Rome and is very fashionable in contemporary ecological housing) (Figure 10.2).

Mongolian yurts are sometimes taken as a source of inspiration and adapted to local climate conditions by using wood instead of felt. The (re)construction of traditional stone houses might be inspired by a Japanese style and built in a round form for maximum light. Insulation techniques are improved by putting movable glass panes in front of a wall to maximise heat – the so-called captive wall,

Figure 10.2 Grass roof of a restored ruin at the hamlet La Mérigue
Source: Florian Lucas (2014).

which is a local innovation at the eco-village of Hameau des Buis. The principle of frugality is also evident in infrastructure, machines and products for everyday life. The communities always search for solutions to their needs and aspirations in accordance with local constraints and situations, as demonstrated by home-made solar water heaters, rainwater capturing installations, biological wastewater plants, dry toilets, washing machines powered by human energy, as well as toothpaste and soap that people make from local plants and so forth. Exploration, experimentation, adaption, hybridisation and creation are major characteristics of these modes of doing (Koop and Senil, 2016) (Figure 10.3).

The interviewees not only insisted on the specificity of their modes of *doing* but also on their modes of *being*. Paying attention and listening to each other while learning collectively is a crucial mode of conduct. The principles of solidarity and cooperation, sharing and caring (also see Hall, 2019; Holmes, 2018; Ince and Hall, 2017) are at the heart of all the activities, including economic ones. These values are always prioritised over efficiency, productivity and profit. They even influence the choice of techniques and the production of material. At Viel Audan in Ardèche, a site combining housing, agro-ecology and environmental education,

Figure 10.3 Experimenting agroecological techniques at Terre et Humanisme
Source: Kirsten Koop (2018).

the collective intentionally chose not to purchase a modern oven to bake bread because their traditional one obliges them to work collaboratively. Intergenerational activities are a guiding principle at Hameau des Buis: members of the older generation transfer knowledge to the project-related school; in turn, they can be sure to be cared for by the younger generation. Last but not least, production going beyond the needs of the group is always a relevant issue, and its market use is discussed collectively.

Besides the aforementioned principles, autonomy is also central for the collectivities. Autonomy has several dimensions. At the individual level, it takes the sense of freeing from wage labour and of self-fulfilment (Gorz, 1983), opening up ways to forgo the division of labour, which is considered to be alienating. The labour force is activated according to the desires and skills of each member. Most of the interviewees said they had chosen various jobs and tasks since the beginning of their project according to their evolving personal interests. Doing so, they reject expert knowledge and specialisation, which are fundamental characteristics of modern society. At the level of the community, autonomy is understood as material self-sufficiency and leads to self-production and consumption while using local resources as much as possible. Last but not least, it is the ability to decide their future in common without external imperatives (Castoriadis, 1987) and to respond to the collectivities' own values that break with conventional standards.

These examples give some insight into how alternative principles are enacted in space through improvisation. The collective creation of alternative modes of living leads to what some interviewees called a particular *esprit de lieu* ('spirit of place'). These places are imbued with specific meanings, culture and materiality that differ from the dominant conventional regime. They represent alternative lifeworlds in the sense that they are appropriated, shaped and governed in a different way and with different means, which gives them a different meaning (Escobar, 2008). Following John Law, we can assert that the issue is an ontological one here, as 'different realities [are] being done in different practices' (Law 2011, p. 2). The lifeworlds have the function of safe spaces, engendering feelings of belonging and protecting from relational impacts of crisis. As they are ruled by principles, regulations and relations which subvert established norms, they have a political dimension. Following Chatterton and Pickerill and Yates, turning their alternative principles into reality in everyday life with the means available can be considered as prefigurative politics (Chatterton and Pickerill, 2010; Yates, 2015). These politics are quiet politics: they consist in 'a form of engagement that emphasizes embodied, practical, tactile and creative ways of acting, resisting, reworking and subverting' (Pottinger, 2017, p. 3) and remain 'modest, quotidian and proceeding with little fanfare' (Horton and Kraftl, 2009, p. 14).

Acquiring the right to exist within the incumbent regime

What are the chances for such lifeworlds to be truly long-lasting perspectives for the younger generation? As they are ruled by principles that often diverge from the norms of the incumbent regime, these places of resistance are prone to being not tolerated and even dismantled. Most of the interviewees insisted on the necessity of struggling to have the right to exist within the conventional system. In concrete terms, this means finding ways to have their alterity recognised by the local authorities and not to be considered illegal by official laws and regulations. Collectivities quickly realise that having land at their disposal does not mean they can shape it as they wish. In fact, the acquired space cannot be understood as a container that can be freely filled with new meanings. Even such alternative places are traversed by a wide range of power networks (Nicholls et al., 2016, p. 11), including those of the dominant conventional regime in the form of numerous laws and regulations, conditioning the possibilities of construction, access to water and electricity and so on. The interviewees said they were constantly confronted with these constraints. This point is especially striking when it comes to the construction of habitats. Many of the acquired sites were officially classified as non-constructible land. Negotiations with the relevant municipalities were necessary to find viable (or at least semi-legal and tolerated) solutions. Either the municipality undertook official changes in the land use plan, or the alternative community engaged in building light constructions without foundations – not legally classified as buildings. Blockhouses or yurts can quickly be disassembled.

Their construction makes it possible to play with the legal vacuum in France concerning this type of construction.

Many other examples could be given to illustrate how the incompatibility of norms between the two worlds causes trouble, if not conflicts, but can be overcome through quiet politics aiming at preserving alterity through improvisation! A good illustration is a recent issue at Veil Audan, a training centre for environmental education that is located in Ardèche. The site is only accessible via a 400-metre footpath from the village of Balazuc. The municipality declared that, in order to be in compliance with the law, they should build a concrete road allowing access to the fire brigade in case a fire breaks out. The non-accessibility for cars, however, is part of Veil Audan's (non-conventional) concept. After discussions, the Veil Audan community decided to do fire-fighting training themselves and to install the necessary technical material directly on their site in order to comply with the law. This creative game with official regulations aimed at making alternative principles compatible with the dominant norms was described by one of the interviewees as 'administrative aikido' or the art of 'stretching the legal elastic' (Yann, Ardèche). Caring about conforming to the conventional legal system, whatever the circumventions, is essential for the interviewed communities to preserve the right to exist within the interstices of the dominant system.

The potential of alternative lifeworlds to transform the incumbent regime

In times of severe social, economic and ecological crisis, much more is at stake than simply preserving such places of difference. We might question the extent to which such places of experimentation with altermodernities can trigger broader change in the incumbent system (Smith et al., 2016). The social sciences do not provide conclusive answers to this question yet, although some research has started in the fields of social innovation, transition, and socio-ecological studies (e.g. Davies and Simon, 2013; Moore et al., 2015; Westley et al., 2014; Sievers-Glotzbach and Tschersich, 2019). Contrary to the managerial approaches of many of these studies, attention will be paid here to the modes whereby alternative principles and norms can be deployed outside alternative places.

So far, these lifeworlds have been described in a rather binary approach as bounded places within a local environment embodying the dominant conventional regime. Of course, constant interactions with the outside are at work. Especially the members of more recent projects have declared their goal of a wider social transformation and their intention to disseminate their ideas among the population of the region in which they operate. This attitude is characteristic of the transition movement that is currently spreading across Europe. The search for contact with the local population is clearly seen in the new geographical patterns of recently emerging alternative initiatives, specifically in the south of Ardèche and on the Trièves plateau: unlike older projects, the recent ones are located along main roads or close to central villages and towns, thus showing a geographical shift from the margins to the centre (Figure 10.4).

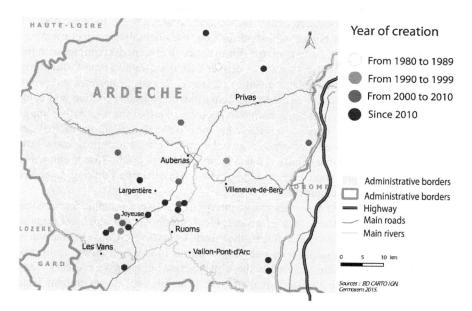

Figure 10.4 Sites of alternative initiatives in the south of the Ardèche department: the recent increase of locations along the main national road

Source: The author. Cartography: Nicolas Robinet.

These alternative communities seek geographical and social proximity, with the boundaries between the places of difference and their outside becoming more porous. Several examples illustrate the initiators' determination to interact with the local population, to make their values known and to act in favour of social transformation. The Changement de Cap association in Ardèche rented a plot of land near a traffic circle on a main road and created various types of open spaces: a 'material area' selling second-hand clothes and furniture, a 'plant area' based on the agro-ecology model, a 'reading area', a 'catering area' and so on. Autopia, a solidarity garage, offers training in autonomous car repairs as well as supplies tools and know-how, and organises public debates and concerts to spread ideas in the immediate vicinity. In Trièves, Recycl'Art offers creative workshops to the local population, enabling them to transform waste material into new objects, while raising public awareness about waste management (recycling, repair, re-use). Community food hubs that link consumers directly with local producers are also frequent. Such intersections with the conventional commodified sphere have recently attracted attention and have been analysed (e.g. Holmes, 2018; Ince and Hall, 2017; Lamine et al., 2019). In the present study, the combination of being visible in central places and proposing useful services to the local population while transmitting practices (and, consequently, values) is a current strategy and channel for broader social transformation.

A second mode that potentially allows for the transmission of alternative values is cooperation with local authorities (Koop and Landel, 2019). In some cases, a win-win situation has been established for both the alternative project members and the public authorities. Recycl'Art, for instance, has signed a contract with the local waste management authority to recover useful waste and repair, transform and resell it, thus lowering the quantity of waste. *Trièves compostage & environnement* proposes action plans to municipalities for waste reduction and composting. Public authorities have started to become aware of the alternative image 'their' territory has acquired and seem to be open to the idea. Some municipalities seek concrete inspiration and contact associations to obtain technical know-how on frugal and sustainable solutions (such as dry toilets for public spaces and waste reduction techniques) and even to engage them in collective thinking on future sustainable local development.

The aforementioned dynamics can be interpreted as (weak) signals for transformational processes. The search of geographical proximity with the local population by investing more central places, the efforts to involve citizens in alternative actions and the cooperation with public institutions indicate a scaling-up of processes in the immediate vicinity of these place-based alternative projects. They potentially favour the transfer of alternative principles to the incumbent local system; however, this study did not confirm any systemic change (the research method was not designed with this goal in mind, nor was any empirical evidence found).

Conclusion

This chapter discussed how communities of young people are turning their backs on the capitalist system by taking concrete actions and setting up projects aimed at securing more sustainable and fulfilling modes of living to better weather times of hardship. Based on an empirical study of 52 alternative initiatives in rural mountain areas in France, it explored the ways in which these communities are putting their principles into practice and creating alternative lifeworlds that differ from their immediate surroundings. No master plan exists; therefore, collectively experimenting by means of shared intentions and intuitions, using the means at their disposal, and assembling known elements to create something new are major features of the enactment of their alternative principles in space.

The chapter also examined the chances of these *places of difference* to be viable in the long term. It appears that official recognition by local authorities is essential for the communities, as it is equivalent to the right to exist within the incumbent system. But the dominant legal system often does not foresee alternative principles, such as the common use of land instead of individual property rights. Therefore, official regulations frequently have to be circumvented or creatively reassembled in order not to be considered illegal. The formalisation of (and despite) their otherness also seems to be an indispensable precondition for involving the local population in their activities, for fruitfully cooperating with local authorities and, as a result, for disseminating their values on the local scale. In times of a growing consciousness about the profound crises of neoliberal capitalism and climate change, such initiatives can no longer be considered marginal or ephemeral. Neither should they be only understood and analysed as 'counter to the mono-culture of capitalism' (Gibson-Graham, 2008, p. 623). Their potential for instigating wider transformative processes within the incumbent crisis-prone and unsustainable system structures should be further investigated (Schmid, 2019; Sievers-Glotzbach and Tschersich, 2019), looking into the content and nature of the interactions between both 'worlds'. As the findings of this research have shown, quiet politics are not only about the spatial enactment of alternative principles but also about creative engagement with conventional regulations and their holders.

Notes

1 France is known for having the highest level of social security expenditure in the EU (33.9% in 2015) (Demaison et al., 2018, p. 220).
2 For an overview on alternative initiatives in France, see https://transiscope.org/carte-des-alternatives and http://utopies-concretes.org/#/map.
3 Before 2008, nine alternative projects have been set up in the south of Ardèche, 21 in Drôme and nine in Trièves. After 2008, 18 supplementary projects emerged in the south of Ardèche, 22 in Drôme and 20 in Trièves.
4 This study formed part of a four-year program by the French Research Agency (ANR) on innovation in marginalised regions around the Mediterranean (ANR *Med-Inn-Local*) (2013–2018) and the LabEx program *Innovation and Mountain Territories* – ITEM (2013–2018) of the Université Grenoble Alpes. It is based on 52 qualitative interviews with the actors of these initiatives. I wish to thank my interns, Florian Lucas, Edward Lamy and Jeremy Caussanel, for giving a hand with these interviews, as well as transcribing and in part analysing them. Results have been published in various book chapters (Koop et al., 2019, 2016; Landel and Koop, 2018).
5 The expression of 'conventional regime' is used here to refer to the beliefs, rules and norms that are commonly shared and orient behaviour (Buclet and Lazarevic, 2015)
6 Of course, this way of thinking is rooted in a long history of protest against capitalism and the state that started with utopian socialism and anarchist and libertarian movements during the 19th century and was revived in the 1960s and 1970s with the hippie movement (Pruvost, 2017).
7 A type of real estate contract allowing the holder a long-lasting right to the enjoyment of a property on condition of proper care and payment of tax and rent.
8 It is worth mentioning that vernacular local know-how in agriculture and construction is still present among the local population. Historically, the mountainous regions of our study have stayed at the margins of national modernisation processes. Especially agricultural modernisation stayed limited due to the difficult geomorphology (slopes, poor soils, lack of accessibility). Traditional techniques are thus still present in the collective local memory.

References

Algan, Y., Beasley, E., Cohen, D., Foucault, M., Péron, M., 2019. Qui sont les Gilets jaunes et leurs soutiens? *Observatoire du Bien-être du CEPREMAP et CEVIPOF*, 1–13.
Bramall, R., 2013. *The cultural politics of austerity: Past and present in austere times.* London: Palgrave Macmillan.

Bozio, A., Emmerson, C., Peichl, A., Tetlow, G., 2015. European Public Finances and the Great Recession: France, Germany, Ireland, Italy, Spain and the United Kingdom Compared. *Fiscal Studies* 36, 405–430.

Buclet, N., Lazarevic, D., 2015. Principles for sustainability: The need to shift to a sustainable conventional regime. *Environmental, Development and Sustainability* 17, 83–100.

Castoriadis, C., 1987. *The imaginary institution of society*. MIT Press, Cambridge, MA.

Chatterton, P., Pickerill, J., 2010. Everyday activism and transitions towards post-capitalist worlds: Everyday activism and transitions towards post-capitalist worlds. *Transactions of the Institute of British Geographers* 35, 475–490.

Demaison, C., Grivet, L., Maury-Duprey, D., Mayo-Simbsler, S., 2018. *France. Portrait social*. Institut national de la statistique et des études économiques INSEE.

Demaria, F., Kallis, G., Bakker, K., 2019. Geographies of degrowth: Nowtopias, resurgences and the decolonization of imaginaries and places. *Environment and Planning E: Nature and Space* 2, 431–450.

Durkheim, É., 1997. *The division of labor in society*. Free Press, New York.

Eurostat, 2019. Unemployment statistics. URL: https://ec.europa.eu/eurostat/statistics-explained/index.php/Unemployment_statistics (website visited September 2019).

Escobar, A., 2008. *Territories of difference: Place, movements, life, redes*. New ecologies for the twenty-first century. Duke University Press, Durham, NC.

Farnsworth,K., Irving, Z., 2012. Varieties of crisis, varieties of austerity: social policy in challenging times. *Journal of Poverty and Social Justice* 20, 133–147.

Fischer, A., Holstead, K., Hendrickson, C.Y., Virkkula, O., Prampolini, A., 2017. Community-led initiatives' everyday politics for sustainability – conflicting rationalities and aspirations for change? *Environments and Planning A* 49, 1986–2006.

Fourmy, S., 2013. *The true cost of austerity and inequality*. France Case Study, Oxfam International, Oxford.

Gibson-Graham, J.K., 2008. Diverse economies: Performative practices for 'other worlds'. *Progress in Human Geography* 32, 613–632.

Giddens, A., 1997. *The consequences of modernity*, 6th pr. ed. Stanford University Press, Stanford, CA.

Gorz, A., 1983. *Farewell to the working class: An essay on post-industrial socialism*. South End, Boston.

Hall, S.M., 2019. Everyday austerity: Towards relational geographies of family, friendship and intimacy. *Progress in Human Geography* 43, 769–789.

Hardt, M., Negri, A., 2011. *Commonwealth*, First Harvard University Press paperback ed. Belknap Press of Harvard University Press, Cambridge, MA.

Holmes, H., 2018. New spaces, ordinary practices: Circulating and sharing within diverse economies of provisioning. *Geoforum* 88, 138–147.

Horton, J., Kraftl, P., 2009. Small acts, kind words and 'not too much fuss': Implicit activisms. *Emotion, Space and Society* 2, 14–23.

Husserl, E., 1970. *The crisis of European sciences and transcendental phenomenology: An introduction to phenomenological philosophy*. Studies in phenomenology & existential philosophy. Northwestern University Press, Evanston, IL.

Ince, A., Hall, S.M., 2017. *Sharing economies in times of crisis: Practices, politics and possibilities*. Routledge, London.

Jankélévitch, V., 1955. *La Rhapsodie. Verve et improvisation musicale*. Paris, Flammarion.

Jarvis, H., 2019. Sharing, togetherness and intentional degrowth. *Progress in Human Geography* 43, 256–275.

Kokoreff, M., 2016. Nuit debout sur place. Petite ethnographie micropolitique. *Les Temps Modernes* 691, 157–176.

Koop, K., Fourny, M.-C., Landel, P.-A., Senil, N., 2016. *Spatial patterns of transformative social innovation. The example of alternative initiatives in Ardèche, France.* ZSI Discussion Paper Series.

Koop, K., Landel, P.-A., Fourny, M.-C., 2019. L'étude des capacités transformatrices des innovations sociales à travers leurs formes de dissémination, in: Klein, J.L., Boucher, J.L., Camus, A., Champagne, C., Noiseux, Y. (Eds.), *Trajectoires d'innovation. Des Émergences à La Reconnaissance.* Innovation Sociale, Québec, pp. 81–89.

Koop, K., Senil, N., 2016. Innovation sociale, improvisation et développement territorial: l'expérience ardéchoise, in: Klein, J.L., Pecqueur, B., Koop, K., Soussi, S.A. (Eds.), *L'innovation Socio-Territoriale à l'épreuve Du Global: Un Défi Pour Les Acteurs.* Géographie Contemporaine, Québec, pp. 155–167.

Lamine, C., Garçon, L., Brunori, G., 2019. Territorial agrifood systems: A Franco-Italian contribution to the debates over alternative food networks in rural areas. *Journal of Rural Studies* 68, 159–170.

Landel, P.-A., Koop, K., 2018. Quand l'innovation sociale change la dynamique des territoires de montagne, in: Fourny, M.-C. (Ed.), *Montagnes En Mouvements. Dynamiques Territoriales et Innovation Sociale.* Presses Universitaires de Grenoble, Grenoble, pp. 21–43.

Lévy, L, 2013. *L'improvisation en aménagement du territoire : d'une réalité augmentée aux fondements d'une discipline pour l'action? Enquête sur un projet interdépartemental (le pôle Orly).* PhD thesis. Université de Grenoble 1, Grenoble.

Law, J., 2011. What's Wrong with a One-World World. *Heterogeneities.net,* URL: http://heterogeneities.net/publications/Law2011WhatsWrongWithAOneWorldWorld.pdf (website visited November 2011).

Mason, K., 2014. Becoming citizen Green: Prefigurative politics, autonomous geographies, and hoping against hope. *Environmental Politics* 23, 140–158.

Neal, S., 2013. Transition culture: Politics, localities and ruralities. *Journal of Rural Studies* 32, 60–69.

Nicholls, W., Beaumont, J., Miller, B.A., 2016. *Spaces of contention: Spatialities and social movements.* Routledge, London.

Pickerill, J., Chatterton, P., 2006a. Notes towards autonomous geographies: Creation, resistance and self-management as survival tactics. *Progress in Human Geography* 30, 730–746.

Pottinger, L., 2017. Planting the seeds of a quiet activism. *Area* 49, 215–222.

Pruvost, G., 2017. Modes de vie alternatifs et engagement, in: Badie, B., Vidal, D. (Eds.), *En Quête d'alternatives. L'état Du Monde 2018.* La Découverte, Paris, pp. 218–224.

Schmid, B., 2019. Degrowth and postcapitalism: Transformative geographies beyond accumulation and growth. *Geography Compass.* https://doi.org/10.1111/gec3.12470

Scott, J.C., 1998. *Seeing like a state. How certain schemes to improve the human condition have failed.* Yale University Press, New Haven, CT.

Seyfang, G., Smith, A., 2007. Grassroots innovations for sustainable development: Towards a new research and policy agenda. *Environmental Politics* 16, 584–603.

Sievers-Glotzbach, S., Tschersich, J., 2019. Overcoming the process-structure divide in conceptions of social-ecological transformation. *Ecological Economics* 164, 106361.

Smith, A., Hargreaves, T., Hielscher, S., Martiskainen, M., Seyfang, G., 2016a. Making the most of community energies: Three perspectives on grassroots innovation. *Environmental Planning A* 48, 407–432.

Syrovatka, F., 2016. Nuit Debout: Frankreich gerät in Bewegung! *PROKLA* 183, 317–323.

Weber, M., 2003. *Économie et Société*. Plon, Paris.

Werlen, B., 1995. *Sozialgeographie alltaeglicher Regionalisierung, Band 1. Zur Ontologie von Gesellschaft und Raum.* Franz Steiner Verlag, Stuttgart.

Wright, E. O., 2010. *Envisioning real utopias*. Verso, London.

Yates, L., 2015. Rethinking prefiguration: Alternatives, micropolitics and goals in social movements. *Social Movement Studies* 14, 1–21.

Part III

Community, civic and state infrastructures

11 E-government and digital by default

Normalising austerity as the new norm

Irene Hardill and Roger O'Sullivan

Introduction

In this chapter we focus on the impact of the move to deliver more and more public services online. This transformation in public service delivery has gained pace post-2008 (cf. HMSO, 2017). The impact of 'digital by default' on citizens was highlighted powerfully in the 2016 film *I, Daniel Blake* by Ken Loach. It provided a dramatic depiction of austerity measures in the UK, best illustrated when the lead character Daniel was advised at a government benefits office that 'We're digital by default', to which he replied, 'Yeah? Well I'm *pencil* by default'. The film underscores a real concern of how online systems such as Universal Credit can impact hardest upon the most vulnerable in society. This chapter will focus on older people resident in the island of Ireland to illustrate the policy context and the practical implications for citizens of this drive. The focus on the island of Ireland enables us to examine public policy making relating to e-government in two jurisdictions: the Republic of Ireland and Northern Ireland.

'Digital by default' was examined by Stephen Armstrong (2017) in a book which marked the 75th anniversary of the publication of the Beveridge Report (Beveridge, HMSO (1942)). Armstrong (2017) explored the digital barriers facing the unwaged in searching for jobs online via Universal Jobmatch. In 2018, Professor Philip Alston, United Nations special rapporteur on extreme poverty and human rights, published a statement on his visit to the United Kingdom. He commented in particular on the human impact of the 2017 Government Transformation Strategy (HMSO, 2017), which aims for government services to become 'digital by default': 'we are witnessing the gradual disappearance of the postwar British welfare state behind a webpage and an algorithm' (Alston, 2018, 7). The Republic of Ireland (RoI) is also embracing the drive towards digital, across local and central government. For example, information about the introduction of the 'household' charge in 2012 was available only online and the charge could not be paid in a post office, a route familiar to many older people (Hardill, 2013).[1]

'Digital by default' is dependent on citizens accessing public services online, and for this to happen, access to the necessary infrastructure (computer and

Internet connection) is required along with a level of competency in using information and communication technologies (ICTs) (West, 2004). The entitlement to access public services and fully participate in a society are key aspects of social citizenship (Marshall, 2009[1950]), which Dwyer (2000) suggests provides a benchmark against which it is possible to assess the status of certain individuals and groups in relation to access to agreed welfare rights and resources.

In this chapter draw on research with older adults in urban and rural areas on the island of Ireland (the Republic of Ireland and Northern Ireland) to illustrate the impact on citizens of the move to deliver more and more public services online. There is an increasing separation between those who have the skills, knowledge and economic resources to do so and those who do not; how we ensure full citizenship for all remains unanswered if not too often unconsidered (Hardill and O'Sullivan, 2018). While it is true that across the European Union the percentage of households having access to the Internet, via one of its members, is increasing, including older adult households, the proportion using public authority websites is limited. The chapter is divided into four sections in which we first focus on e-government, followed by an examination of citizenship. This is followed by an examination of living with e-government on the island of Ireland and then a concluding reflection.

E-government

E-government defined

While many different definitions of e-government (short for electronic government) exist, the underpinning principle is the use of ICTs[2] by governments to deliver public services online as well as aiming to improve the working of government itself (Northern Ireland Assembly, 2001; West, 2004). Online public service delivery takes a number of forms (Asgarkhani, 2005), ranging from websites as static mechanisms for the display of information, with little interactivity through to the electronic interconnection of services, such as a single web portal to access all online government services and information (West, 2004). The transformational potential of e-government was highlighted in a Northern Ireland Assembly report as early as 2001, which conceived of e-government as involving a progression from the simple provision of information electronically to full integration across government of electronic service delivery. O'Donnell et al. (2003) and colleagues argued that in the Republic of Ireland e-government had been primarily motivated by a genuine desire to make government more efficient, citizen-oriented and customer-friendly, with the goal of achieving seamless client-centred service delivery. Online information services were organised around the 'life events' of individuals and businesses with a 'user' focus, rather than around the structures of government, but not all citizens in the Republic, or in other jurisdictions, have the skills and resources to access these online services.

However, the period of austerity has seen the driver of e-government increasing with the purpose to reduce government budget deficits as the primary focus.

In this section we set the context for understanding e-government in the Republic of Ireland (RoI) and Northern Ireland (NI). In both jurisdictions there has been a long-standing commitment to e-government; we first explore the policy context for e-government and then examine the development of e-government in the two jurisdictions. Responsibility for e-government rests within NI – it is a non-reserved power – but the NI strategy must be fully compatible with the UK approach (cf. Paris, 2005). While the direction of travel of e-government is determined nationally, the spatial scale for the delivery of many services is local. E-government, at the national level, centres on providing information on government services and benefits with some interaction such as completing benefit forms, tax submissions, and paying fines and charges. At the local level, e-government is more about providing services, with an emphasis on improving service quality (Asgarkhani, 2005), and integration between organisations to ensure better management (Rahman, 2010).

At the time of writing there is a third spatial dimension, international, as NI and RoI both form part of the European Union (EU), where there has also been a renewed commitment to e-government post-2008 (EC Directorate for Information Society and Media, 2010). The fifth Ministerial E-government Conference and the Malmö Declaration of 2009 gave rise to a new e-government action plan (2011–15), which supports and complements the European Commission's A Digital Agenda for Europe (2010). The European Commission[3] also runs an annual benchmarking project across member states, one of the flagship studies in measuring public sector performance.[4] The EU e-Government Action Plan 2016–2020 highlights the importance of the digital transformation and sets out 20 principles that member states are recommended to observe. We now turn to chart the development of e-government, first in RoI and then in NI.

RoI e-government policy context

Responsibility for e-government and digital inclusion in RoI rests in two different departments. Since 2008, the Department of Public Expenditure and Reform is responsible for e-government and the Department of Communications, Energy and Natural Resources for digital inclusion. Since 2001, the single main portal in RoI[5] which was developed and is maintained by Citizens Information,[6] is under contract to central government. The portal has a number of access points from different government departments and agencies and several 'referral on' points. Similar to NI, the website is organised thematically and includes older people.

In 2011, a Fine Gael–led administration aligned its strategy to A Digital Agenda for Europe, and published a policy document on e-government in 2012 as part of the Public Service Reform Plan, with e-government playing an important role in economic recovery plans. The National Digital Strategy was launched in

July 2013. The main focus of the strategy was on 'Doing More with Digital' and encouraging RoI to reap the benefits of a digitally enabled society (Department of Communications, 2013). A number of strategies have been launched, including the e-Government 2012–2015 Strategy, the Public Service ICT Strategy (2015) and the e-Government Strategy 2017–2020 which aligns with the EU e-Government Action Plan.

Running alongside e-government have been schemes promoting digital inclusion, including the Access Skills and Content scheme which was established in 2006 (www.taoiseach.gov.ie). In 2009, Technology Actions to Support the Smart Economy was published as part of RoI's Knowledge Society Strategy (Department of Communications, Energy and Natural Resources, 2009), which centred on motivating people, particularly older people, to learn how to use the Internet and other new technologies. Under the aegis of this strategy, BenefIT 3 was launched in June 2011 to provide one-to-one training for 40,000 non-ICT users across RoI. The training (about six hours) was largely provided in community facilities by voluntary and community organisations, and within the first year 36% of the people who received training were aged 65 or over (Department of Communications, Energy and Natural Resources, 2012). Between 2008–2014 the BenefIT programme provided over 129,000 training places (www.dcenr. gov.ie/). At the time of writing, the most recent programme, the Digital Skills for Citizens Scheme, provides basic digital skills training to those who have never used the Internet. The scheme was launched in 2017 and aimed to train 50,000 people by the end of 2018.

NI e-government policy context

In NI the Department of Finance is responsible for both digital inclusion and e-government. In 2002, the Office of the First Minister and Deputy First Minister launched a public consultation, Bridging the Digital Divide in Northern Ireland, at a time when 53% of NI citizens (16 years old and over) were without access to the Internet (OFMDFM, 2002). To bridge this divide, the executive wanted to build awareness, to ensure ICT education for all citizens and expand access to ICTs for all citizens (OFMDFM, 2002, p. 25). This consultation document was followed by a digital inclusion strategy and the creation of a Digital Inclusion Unit within the Information Strategy and Innovation Division in the Department (Department of Finance and Personnel, 2003).

A UK-wide digital strategy was launched by the Westminster (Great Britain) New Labour government in 2005 (Prime Minister's Strategy Unit, 2005), which noted achievements in improving broadband access but the persistence of a digital divide. A range of barriers was identified including cost, lack of confidence or ICT skills, people not seeing the relevance of the Internet to their needs and people not seeing how ICTs could transform their lives. The role of government in helping to promote and increase public awareness about the Internet was also emphasised (Prime Minister's Strategy Unit, 2005).

In March 2009, a public-facing website providing information and services to people across NI was launched, modelled on the Direct Gov website for Great Britain. Nidirect[7] was developed by, and was administered by, the then Department of Finance and Personnel which also housed the Digital Inclusion Unit. Nidirect, like the RoI website, is organised thematically, with cross-departmental themes such as money, tax and benefits (Northern Ireland Executive, 2009), and the option for interactivity is via the 'Contact Us' page (HMSO, 2014).

In May 2010, the then Department of Employment and Learning announced the introduction of free-of-charge entry-level classes for anyone wishing to improve their computer skills (NI Direct, 2010).[8] In addition, the Digital Inclusion Unit offered several services aimed at getting more people using ICTs, as well as improving the convenience and efficiency of public services by driving online delivery.

In summary, e-government is at broadly the same stage of development in NI and RoI and the drive towards e-government is part of a wider efficiency plan, cost saving for government and streamlining administration function and to a lesser degree about the 'e-empowerment' of the individual or e-inclusion. In the following section we examine the implications of the move to e-government on social citizenship.

Citizenship and e-government

In an offline world, access to public services is based on manual form-filling, letter writing and/or the submission of official documents (passport, driving licence or birth certificate) as proof of entitlement. Entitlement to public services is derived from the administrative principle of 'equality under the law': equity in terms of contents (equal service outcome for similar cases) and procedures (equal treatment during the service process) (Lips, 2006). But an online world entitlement to public services increasingly necessitates completing forms online, leading Philip Alston to comment that the welfare state is 'behind a webpage and an algorithm' (Alston, 2018, 7).

We have previously explored the impact of e-government on citizenship in the UK (Hardill and O'Sullivan, 2018) building on T. H. Marshall's (200 [1950]) conceptualisation of citizenship and especially the relationship between the individual citizen and the state. Marshall (2009) defined citizenship as full membership of a community, where membership entails the participation by individuals in the determination of the conditions of their own association in that community; citizenship is bestowed on those who are full members of a community (Marshall, 2009, 149), and it requires a direct sense of community membership (p. 151). Marshall's theory links three elements: civil (rights to liberty and equality in law), political (the right to vote and participate in the political process) and social (rights to basic welfare and full participation in society). The ability to fully participate in a society are key aspects of social citizenship, ensuring the inclusion and full participation of all members of society. Building on Oldfield (1990), Lister (1997) identifies citizenship as a status that brings with it the enjoyment of civil, political and social rights and citizenship as a practice that requires the acceptance and performance of wider communal responsibilities and duties.

Dwyer (2000) suggests that social citizenship provides a benchmark against which it is possible to assess the status of certain individuals and groups in relation to access to the agreed welfare rights and resources that are generally available to all those who are regarded as citizens within a specific community. Social citizenship offers the capacity for an exploration of a number of dimensions (class, gender, race, disability, age) when assessing both the levels and causes of inequality within a society, which we extend to include digital inclusion. Building on the work of Lash (2002) and Graham (2002), Burrows and Ellison (2004) have examined access to digital technologies in urban areas to understand the changing nature of citizenship. They recast social citizenship as 'engagement', pointing to new categories of social inclusion and exclusion that could emerge because of differentiated access to digital technologies through 'urban splintering' (Burrows and Ellison, 2004, 335), a theme which Armstrong (2017) and Alston (2018) have also developed.

In summary, differences in ICT skill levels and a lack of the means (ICT equipment) and economic resources to access information play major roles in RoI, NI and beyond, in terms of the divide between people having the potential to benefit fully from e-government and those who cannot (UN Department of Economic and Social Affairs, 2012). In the UK, a 2015 House of Lords Select Committee report concluded that the government should define the Internet as a utility service, available for all to access and use, thereby reinforcing the connection with citizenship (HMSO, 2015). In RoI, progress on the National Broadband Plan has received much criticism especially as it relates to provision in rural areas. We now turn to examine the impact of e-government in the RoI and NI.

Living with e-government

In this section we draw specifically on a study of the impact on older citizens (men and women aged 50+ years) of the move to deliver more and more public services online across the island of Ireland (Hardill 2013). A mixed-methods approach was employed, which included an analysis of published materials (policy documents, grey literature and academic literature) alongside relevant published statistical data. Twenty-one in-depth interviews were undertaken with key stakeholders in the statutory and non-statutory sectors in RoI and NI,[9] and four focus groups (with a total of 31 older adults with varying levels of IT competency) were held in urban and rural locations about using ICT and accessing public services online (see Table 11.1). Levels of digital skills and literacy start to decline with people aged 65+; differences in digital skills reflect income and housing tenure inequalities as well as a digital gender divide in favour of men, and the highest rate of digital exclusion was found to be in rural areas, especially in RoI (Hardill, 2013).

While the focus group participants recognised that e-government is inevitable and that older people will have to get on board, they also identified a

Table 11.1 Focus group participants

Location	Age range	Computer/ Internet in own home	Users	Non-users	Total participants
ROI – Urban	55–65	7	3	4	7
NI – Urban	75+	5	4	3	7
ROI – Rural	65–75	6	4	5	9
NI – Rural	65–75	8	6	2	8

Fear of using computer. 'If you can get over the fear factor of using, you are halfway there. People have a fear' (Urban focus group – male participant).

Fear of internet safety: 'Never use it for anything to do with my credit card. Buy everything with cheques. I have a deep ingrained distrust' (Urban focus group – male participant).

Cost 'They are going to give you good ideas and give you recommendations but expect you to pay for it. A good idea is a good idea if you can afford it. If someone had the choice between a bag of coal and computer I know what they would pick' (Urban focus group – male participant).

Lack of skills and lack of confidence: 'I imagine I can't do it so I won't do it. I probably could do it but I think it does take over your life. My daughter is on it constantly' (Urban focus group – female participant).

Figure 11.1 E-government barriers

number of barriers that need to be addressed in order to achieve e-inclusion. These barriers are summarised in Figure 11.1 and include lack of interest/relevancy, fear, costs and lack of skills/confidence. As can be seen from Figure 11.1 there was a genuine fear and distrust of the Internet; for example, 'there is a criminal element abusing the internet – scams etc. You never really know when you are secure' (Rural RoI focus group – male participant). There is a remarkable similarity with the barriers identified in other studies (e.g. Hardill, 2013; Hardill and Olphert, 2012), at a number of spatial levels, elsewhere in the EU, the UK, RoI and NI. These barriers all relate to older people and highlight lack of interest/relevance, financial considerations and knowledge. There was a perception from both the NI focus groups that e-government as a strategy is more about serving government's needs rather than those of individuals, particularly older people. Regarding *lack of interest and relevance*, the non-users in the four focus groups indicated that the main barrier for them was the fact that they could not relate to the Internet and therefore did not see where or how it would be relevant or useful in their own lives. Turning to *costs* incurred, 'there is also the issue of cost for older people – cost is a barrier' (Urban RoI focus group – female participant). Residents in rural areas were perceived to face added barriers: 'there is a feeling people will be disadvantaged. In rural areas . . . not

100% coverage' (Urban RoI focus group – male participant). Participants from rural areas raised concern about the quality of Internet and speed of service; this remains an ongoing issue, especially in RoI. Broadband provision was not raised as an issue in urban areas. The first hurdle older people have is to overcome getting connected to the Internet (the cost and availability of service); the second hurdle is developing the skills, confidence and support to sustain ICT usage and stay connected (Hargattai, 2008).

The language and computer jargon and terminology used were seen to be off-putting in relation to participants' lived experience of government websites: for example, 'some Council sites will ask you to download their cookies. Can you tell a 75 year old what a cookie is?' (Urban NI focus group – female participant). Those who had experience of using the government portal held mixed views: one noted that 'you have to be very dedicated and patient to work your way through it – press the right button' (Urban NI focus group – male participant). A RoI resident felt that the 'Department of Finance is quite good. Jobs, census, house price index are all quite good' (Rural RoI focus group – female participant), while another said that the 'Department of Finance is not user friendly' (Urban RoI focus group – male participant). A participant in the Urban NI group commented on the Housing Executive website which they had looked at in relation to housing benefit and noted, 'it was all too much . . . the only way they will make a computer system work is to simplify it' (Urban NI focus group – male participant).

One male participant summed things up: 'simplicity is the secret – if it is simple, people will use it' (Urban RoI focus group – male participant). In summary, the Internet is normal for many people but alien to others, especially those who did not have ICT as part of their working lives. Government websites were seen as a source of information: 'you can go online and get information anonymously' (Urban NI focus group – male participant), thereby reinforcing the findings of Denvir et al. (2014) for England. But for particularly sensitive or more complex issues, including those requiring discussion of personal or financial information, users and non-users preferred to have face-to-face contact: 'I like to speak to a person' (Urban NI focus group – male participant).

Implications for austerity

Ireland, north and south, entered the period of austerity at different stages and it impacted upon different groups (socio-economic) to varying degrees. In both RoI and NI, the lowest paid and those with fewest qualifications have been most adversely affected by austerity. RoI is deemed to be post-recession, but the affordability and availability of housing remains a key concern. In NI, like the rest of the UK, the human impact of austerity is seen in the rise in the number of foodbanks, which are being used by those in paid work as well the traditional low-income groups (Alston, 2018; Armstrong, 2017). It is also feared that Brexit is adding to the uncertainty generated by austerity.

While e-government involves the transformation in the way in which public services are delivered, it is also dependent on transferring the responsibility to the individual: it is changing the way services are accessed and changing behaviours, with important implications for social citizenship. While the number of older adults in households across the two jurisdictions with a computer and the Internet is increasing, the proportion remains below those for other age groups. A spectrum of 'onlineness' should be recognised, rather than simply categorising people as being online and offline. For e-government to succeed, it is dependent on citizens being confident Internet users, possessing a specific skill set, owning or having access to the correct equipment and an Internet connection and learning how to navigate the Internet.

E-government offers the potential to help governments balance budgets through cost savings, and it has been a key element of post-2008 austerity programmes, but these cost savings will only be achieved by moving the cost to the consumer (i.e. when increasing numbers of citizens access public services online). It must be recognised that e-government is not cost-neutral to citizens. The move to online government replicates and compounds existing inequalities, and a digital divide persists and is linked strongly to educational attainment, gender, income and age. Added to this is the speed of change in ICT, which has implications for usage, skills, social citizenship and inequality (Hardill 2013).

There are important implications for social rights (rights to basic welfare and full participation in society) (Marshall, 2009[1950], 1972), as citizens have to access public services online rather than rely on paper-based access. The ability to fully participate in a society is a key aspect of social citizenship, including accessing public services as and when they are needed (Dwyer, 2002). Burrows and Ellison (2004) identify social citizenship as 'engagement' and point to new categories of social inclusion and exclusion that are likely to emerge as a result of differentiated access to digital technologies.

Conclusions

In this chapter we have presented a case study of the impact on older people of the increasing move to deliver public services online (e-government) across the island of Ireland, especially within the context of austerity and e-exclusion. We have argued that accessing public services online is dependent upon overcoming two digital divides, the acquisition of the required infrastructure and a specific skill set, 'Internet self efficacy' (Hargattai, 2008), or at the very least ensuring that others are supported by 'proxy' ICT users to access e-government. Austerity has traditionally been depicted as a short-term measure to correct a budget in balance, however it increasingly seems to be a norm in today's society. The ambition of e-government is impressive, but it needs to be balanced not just towards those who are educated and online but also towards those who are offline, excluded and vulnerable on low incomes without networks of support. We must consider if e-government and digital by default are normalising austerity and compounding inequalities.

Notes

1 In 2011 the EU/IMF Programme of Financial Support for Ireland committed the government to the introduction of a property tax. As a result, a €100 charge was introduced by the Local Government (Household Charge) Act 2011. It was payable by owners of residential property for the year 2012. It was superseded by the introduction of a valuation-based local property tax in 2013.
2 ICTs include telecommunications technologies, such as telephony, cable, satellite and radio, as well as digital technologies such as computers, information networks and software (Damodaran and Olphert, 2006, p. 6). Using ICTs enable people to access an ever-increasing range of information, goods, services, entertainment/leisure, educational and social networking opportunities.
3 The United Nations also conducts an annual survey on e-government which highlights which countries are the best performing and the innovative solutions to e-government they provide that can be copied by others.
4 By 2010, RoI achieved a 100% rating for all the services included in the benchmark and was ranked first of 32 countries for online provision of information and services, for the online sophistication of its services, for e-procurement availability and for integrating services as 'life events' for both businesses and citizens.
5 This site can also be accessed via www.citizensinformation.ie.
6 Agency of the Department of Social Protection.
7 www.nidirect.gov.uk.
8 www.nidirect.gov.uk.
9 Interviews were undertaken with representatives from key government departments, representatives from local authorities alongside representatives from a range of organisations in the voluntary and community sector, and organisations that fulfil an advocacy role for older adults from the two jurisdictions.

References

Alston, P. (2018, 16 November) *Statement on visit to the United Kingdom, by Professor Philip Alston, United Nations Special Rapporteur on extreme poverty and human rights London*. Retrieved 25 January 2019, from https://www.ohchr.org/en/issues/poverty/pages/srextremepovertyindex.aspx

Armstrong, S. (2017) *The new poverty*. London: Verso (Beveridge). HMSO (1942) *Social insurance and allied services: Report by Sir William Beveridge*. Cmd. 6404. London: HMSO.

Asgarkhani, M. (2005) 'The effectiveness of e-service in local government: A case study', *Electronic Journal of e-Government*, 3, 4, 157–166.

Burrows, R. and Ellison, N. (2004) 'Sorting places out? Towards a social politics of neighbourhood informatization', *Information, Communication and Society*, 7, 3, 221–236.

Department of Communications (2013) – *Doing more with digital. The national digital strategy for Ireland 'phase 1 – digital engagement'*. Dublin: Department of Communications.

Department of Communications, Energy and Natural Resources (2009) *Technology actions to support the smart economy*. Dublin: Department of Communications, Energy and Natural Resources.

Department of Communications, Energy and Natural Resources (2012, 1 June) *Minister Rabbitte extends basic digital skills training*. Retrieved 23 July 2012, from www.dcenr.gov.ie

Department of Finance and Personnel (2003) *A digital inclusion strategy for Northern Ireland*. Belfast: Department of Finance and Personnel.

Dwyer, P. (2000) *Welfare rights and responsibilities: Contesting social citizenship* Bristol: Policy Press.

Fine Gael; Labour Party (2011) *Towards recovery: Programme for a national government 2011–2016*. Dublin: Fine Gael; Labour Party.

Hardill, I. (2013) *E-government and older people in Ireland North and South*. Belfast: CARDI.

Hardill, I. and Mills, S. (2013) 'Enlivening evidence-based policy through embodiment and emotions', *Contemporary Social Science*, 8, 3, 321–332.

Hardill, I. and Olphert, C. W. (2012) 'Staying connected: Exploring mobile phone use amongst older adults in the UK', *Geoforum*, 43, 6, 1306–1312.

Hardill, I. and O'Sullivan, R. (2018) 'E-government: Accessing public services online: Implications for citizenship', *Local Economy: The Journal of the Local Economy Policy Unit*, 33, 1, 3–9.

Hargattai, E. (2008) 'Whose space? Differences among users and non-users of social network sites', *Journal of Computer-Mediated Communication*, 13, 276–297.

HMSO (2014) *UK digital inclusion strategy*. London: HMSO.

HMSO (2017, 9 February) *Government transformation strategy*. Retrieved 25 January 2019, from www.gov.uk/government/publications/government-transformation-strategy-2017-to-2020

Lips, M. (2006) *E-government under construction: Challenging traditional conceptions of citizenship*. Paper retrieved 31 August 2016, from www.oii.ox.ac.uk/archive/downloads/research/files/Identity_e-Gov_chapter.pdf

Marshall, T. H. (1972) 'Value problems in welfare capitalism', *Journal of Social Policy*, 1, 15–32.

Marshall, T. H. (2009, first published 1950) 'Citizenship and social class', in Manza, J. and Sauder, M. (eds.), *Inequality and society*. New York: Norton, pp. 148–154.

NI Direct (2010, 17 May) *Bridge the digital divide – for free!* Retrieved 23 July 2012, from www.northernireland.gov.uk

Northern Ireland Assembly (2001) *E-government research paper*. Belfast: Northern Ireland Assembly Library and Research Services.

Northern Ireland Executive (2009, 7 May) *Government services and information are being made more accessible to the people of Northern Ireland*. Retrieved 17 October 2012, from www.northernireland.gov.uk

O'Donnell, O., Boyle, R. and Timonen, V. (2003) 'Transformational aspects of E-government in Ireland: Issues to be addressed', *Electronic Journal of e-Government*, 1, 1, 22–30.

OFMDFM (2002) *Bridging the digital divide in Northern Ireland: A consultation document*. Belfast: OFMDFM.

Paris, M. (2005) 'Local E-government and devolution: Electronic service delivery in Northern Ireland', *Local Government Studies*, 31, 3, 307–319.

Rahman, H. (2010) 'Framework of E-governance at the local government level', in G. Reddick (ed.), *Comparative E-government*. New York: Springer, pp. 23–47.

UN Department of Economic and Social Affairs (2012) *E-government survey 2012. E-government for the people*. New York: UN Department of Economic and Social Affairs.

West, D. M. (2004) 'E-government and the transformation of service delivery and citizen attitudes', *Public Administration Review*, 64, 1, 15–27.

12 Requesting labour activation without addressing inequalities

A move towards racialised workfare in Slovakia

Daniel Škobla and Richard Filčák

Introduction

In this chapter we explore labour practices that shape the everyday experience of unemployed and poverty-stricken Roma in Slovakia. We use the term 'labour activation' throughout to refer to the range of activities aimed at enhancing motivation and incentives to seek employment and improving job readiness and help in finding suitable employment. In the context of our study,[1] labour activation consisted usually of unqualified, menial and low-skilled work (sweeping streets, cleaning pavements, mowing grass, watering vegetables, maintenance of parks and cemeteries, simple maintenance of mechanisms, etc.). Only rarely were activation workers requested to undertake more qualified work, such as masonry or instalment of electrical wiring and water pipes. There are more types of programmes under which labour activation is carried out. Due to administrative terms (labour activation is partially funded by the EU structural funds and partially by the national government), each type of program has been implemented by a different entity: state Labour Office, regional government or municipality. Unemployed people can qualify for activation also through participating in training or education. With the latest social assistance reform (2013), however, benefit recipients are requested to work at least 32 hours of activation a month. If they refuse, or if they do not work the required number of hours, a reduction in the total amount of social benefit follows.

Overall, the average annual number of persons performing activation work decreased from approximately 59,000 in 2013 to 47,000 in 2018 (79% of the initial figure) (Ministry of Labour, Social Affairs and Family of the Slovak Republic 2019). This might be a consequence either of more available jobs since the economic cycle is in boom, because many benefit claimants were forced to exit the welfare system, or a combination of both. However, labour activation has had some unintended consequences. One of the possible costs for the poor was that there has been a growing stigma against the activation in general as constantly failing to deliver the original goals (i.e. activating people for re-entering the labour market). This way of reasoning not only generated the stigma but also aggravated discourse in which the jobless and unemployed 'Gypsy' are pictured as the truly 'undeserving poor'. Thus labour activation does not contribute to integration and inclusion of the poor into the society, but rather it reinforced social disparities and discrimination along the ethnic lines. This chapter therefore focuses on labour activation as a means of exacerbating racial inequality, particularly regarding Roma, in Slovakia.

More broadly, the social implications of neoliberalism have been increasingly analysed outside of the realm of the economy. Martinez and Garcia (1996) emphasise neoliberalism's role in the elimination of notions such as 'public welfare' or 'community' and their replacement by concepts such as 'individual responsibility'. Narrowed-down recipes on the economics and society professed by neoliberalism thus lead to social exclusion of the less educated, less skilled or otherwise disadvantaged people from society. In the context of Slovakia, there is perhaps not a more apt case to study adverse impacts of inequalities than the situation of the Roma ethnic minority; they are the last in and the first out of the labour market, and they are structurally discriminated against regarding access to jobs, education, healthcare and housing (UNDP 2009; EU FRA 2016).

The onset of neoliberal governance in Slovakia was manifested by the major changes that took place in the Slovak welfare regime in 2004 (Gerbery 2011; van Baar 2017; Škobla et al. 2017). Social assistance system with this reform came to be internally more fragmented and labour activation, in the form of a supplement to the basic social income, came to be a fundamental component of the whole system. Receipt of the labour activation surcharge was contingent on extra work undertaken or on enrolling in active labour market policy measures such as training or education. The basic social income was cut to a low level and was supposed to be 'motivating' enough for claimants voluntarily to engage with the programme in order to supplement their income. In the second wave of welfare reform, with its neoliberal thrust that swept across the country in early 2010s, the government introduced further cuts and changes. These were aimed at more effectively 'pushing' the long-term jobless into the labour market. The main novelty was the obligation towards labour activation, which made the work activity a mandatory condition to qualify for the basic social income. Activation was supposed to contribute to an improvement in the participants' employability and increase their re-employment prospects. At the time of fiscal consolidation and austerity, one of the side effects of mandatory activation is the poverty stricken and unemployed provide some municipal services for free, which would otherwise be difficult for municipalities with tight budgets to obtain on the market. Thus on the one hand, municipalities have a direct economic benefit from the labour activation. On the other hand, activation somewhat paradoxically prevents the creation of regular local low-skilled jobs, as it is cheaper for a municipality to cover cleaning services by activation work at a fraction of the cost which would otherwise have to be paid to employees on a salaried, full-time basis (Lajčáková et al. 2017).

The mainstream discourse on policies regarding employment and welfare has been particularly racialised in Slovakia. There are around 400,000 Roma in the country (approximately 8% of the total population), who suffer profound institutional discrimination and face widespread unemployment and poverty (UNDP 2009, 2012). They are often scapegoated and blamed by right-wing populists for general social problems and economic misery. Research by Mušinka et al. (2014) identified almost 800 segregated Roma settlements in the territory of Slovakia, with extremely poor living conditions characterised by dilapidated housing and an absence of physical infrastructure such as water and sewerage (Filčák et al. 2017). Many Roma families face rampant unemployment, are trapped in debt and are dependent on social assistance. According to surveys, 87% of the Roma live below the poverty line (EU FRA 2016) and are the victims of unequal treatment and victimisation by the majority population, politicians as well as the media (Amnesty International 2017; ERRC 2017). The prime minister did not hesitate to publicly declare that the unfavourable unemployment statistics were deformed by the large size of the jobless Roma population (Nový Čas 2013), thus reproducing popular prejudices about the Roma, who are portrayed as scroungers in the welfare system.

To explore these issues further, in the first part of this chapter we briefly discuss our methodology and introduce the discussion on the welfare versus workfare regimes. The dichotomy between these two approaches lies in the different perspective on what are the drivers and what are the barriers regarding access to the labour market. In the second part of the chapter, based on our fieldwork we describe perspectives of main actors on activation and the implementation practices regarding activation at the local level. In doing so we examine the power asymmetries at the local level and suggest that as a social practice, labour activation takes on certain 'disciplining' and 'punitive' qualities in relation to the local Roma. Finally, we summarise our findings and discuss labour activation and its impacts in a wider social-political context. We argue that labour activation has considerably racialised the social assistance system since it extended racial meaning to a previously racially unclassified relationship and policy practice. Labour activation also emerged to have uneven outcomes for the ethnic majority population and for the Roma minority.

Methodology

This chapter is based on short-term field research in two administrative districts in the eastern regions of Slovakia. These areas are characterised by an above-average share of the long-term unemployed and an above-average share of the Roma population. The research consisted of visits to two district capital towns and 15 villages in the area, observation and a total of 37 semi-structured interviews and group discussions in the Labour Offices and municipal governments and with Roma participants of activation works. Interviews and discussions were not recorded but notes were taken during the interview, which allowed for the creation of an atmosphere of mutual trust, even when dealing with things that might be considered by the officers or labour activation participants to be 'sensitive'. After each working day, the researchers met and discussed findings and compared and consolidated opinions. Our research also rested on publicly available statistical data on the labour market (for the period 2013–2018) and literature about the active labour market policies and the effects of the workfare programmes. This chapter is primarily based on the findings from particular fieldwork; however, contextualisation of wider patterns of power asymmetries, Roma marginalisation and discrimination are based on our long-term sociological research on Roma and social exclusion in Slovakia.

From welfare to workfare

Welfare regimes are sometimes called passive systems, since they are characterised by transfers and services to the unemployed without reciprocity or conditionality. In contrast, workfare regimes consist of measures conditioning a payment of social benefits on carrying out some activity. The crucial pillar of workfare regimes concerns the active labour market policies as social expenditure programmes, which are aimed at the improvement of beneficiaries' prospects of finding gainful employment or otherwise increase their earning capacity (Peck and Theodore 2000). When we examine global workfare programmes more closely, they are characterised by three important elements: they are mandatory, they are mainly work-related and they are fundamentally tied to social aid, the lowest stratum of the social protection system. In theory, these programmes are aimed at the improvement of jobless individuals' prospects of finding gainful employment. They are meant to constitute labour that helps people to obtain future paid work. The defining moment is the element of constraint: it can be in a form of a request, which one cannot refuse without serious consequences in the broadest sense (Lødemel and Trickey 2000).

Social assistance in Slovakia consists of seven different supplements, benefits and allowances. The labour activation surcharge represents a significant source of income for jobless households and is available only to people who are registered as jobseekers (Kureková-Mýtna et al. 2013). With changes to the Act on Social Assistance in 2013, all recipients of social assistance have to accept at least 32 hours of labour activation per month, which typically includes unqualified, demeaning menial and low-level labour (street cleaning, grass mowing, maintenance of cemeteries or parks, etc.). If they refuse to do so, or if they for various reasons do not work the required number of hours, a punishment in the form of a cut in the total welfare income follows. Mandatory labour activation has affected general involvement in a short time, as is obvious from the continuous decrease in the number of activation participants and in the substantial outflow of clients from the welfare system (Škobla et al. 2017). This might be either because some unemployed people opted to exit the system in order to avoid stigmatising outdoor labour activities or because of the economic growth, since there have been more available jobs in the labour market – albeit mostly jobs requiring some qualification (*Skills Panorama* 2015). Thus while some were pushed back into employment, those without the right skills are still struggling.

According to the state Central Office of Labour, Social Affairs and Family, registry sanctions in the form of reduced social income for those who refused the labour activation affected approximately 4,000 recipients each month. While the share of the punished recipients was higher than 10% in the more economically developed western Slovakian regions, it never exceeded 4% in economically disadvantaged eastern Slovakian regions, where most of the poverty-stricken Roma population lives (Škobla et al. 2017). It might thus indirectly suggest that those unemployed and unskilled, who live in economically less developed areas, could not afford to refuse labour activation since they did not have chance to find any jobs on the 'shadow' or regular labour market.

Entrapment on the margins of labour markets

Analysis of workfare policies in the UK reveals that they failed to transcend the constraints of earlier forms of active responses to unemployment, and this approach has only limited potential. Workfare policies either depend on their 'fit' with the existing policy-making heritage or remain merely symbolic, while there are other aspects which are of crucial importance. Economies increasingly based on automation and computerisation do not provide many low-end jobs in services. Success of the programmes depends on dismantling the structural barriers in the labour market, such as racial discrimination or low mobility of the workforce (Dostal 2007). Measuring the effectiveness of job creation programmes in the public sector in Hungary and Poland confirms limited contributions of these programmes. In 1998, participation in active labour market measures reached 26.3% in Hungary and 7.9% in Poland (O'Leary et al. 1998, 2001). Participants were losing their motivation to look for a job during the duration of the programme, and undertaking small jobs for the municipality did not significantly improve their skills or their chances of finding an unsubsidised job.

Despite the declared goals of the labour activation programmes, such as sustaining or acquiring work habits and skills, according to some authors labour activation has only a limited impact on participant's chances of obtaining an unsubsidised job (Card et al. 2010; Ingold and Stuart 2015; Messing and Bereményi 2016). As pointed out by Raffass (2017), implementation of workfare policies has not resulted in bringing down rates of unemployment, combating long-term unemployment, reducing poverty or empowering jobseekers as consumers of public services, which were the goals of the 'activating state'. Instead, activation has been working as a mechanism of entrapment on the margins of liberalised labour markets. The activation turn has thus failed to achieve its direct objectives, and its social impact has been regressive and repressive.

Recent analysis of administrative data on registered jobseekers revealed that the probability of leaving the jobseekers' database for those participating in any form of activation work was negative for the clients of the social system in Slovakia (Lubyová et al. 2014). Clients who were awarded an activation supplement were engaged in the labour market to a lesser extent than were their peers who were selected for the control group. Thus, the activation measure paradoxically reduced the chances of finding jobs in the labour market. Labour Force Survey data indicate little evidence of the positive impact of activation on the long-term unemployed and suggest that in reality, the biggest beneficiaries of these programmes are towns and villages acquiring a cheap workforce for cleaning services while saving municipal budgets (IFP 2011).

Researching labour activation: the views and perspectives of officers

In what follows, we explore practices of labour activation in the eastern regions of Slovakia characterised by an above-average share of the long-term unemployed and the above-average share of the Roma population. Opinions on labour activation from the side of the social actors we interviewed, inevitably and to a large extent, depended on their positionality based primarily on class, ethnicity and their social and professional trajectory. The most important differential in views and optics about the labour activation we identified along the line of 'those in power (Labour Office officers and mayors/municipality officers) vs. unemployed Roma'. Diversification of positions along this line was apparent when we discussed the significance and impacts of labour activation. Mayors and Labour Office employees often appreciated a certain punitive charge encapsulated in labour activation: 'At least they [unemployed] learned that they have to wake up in the morning and go to work!'; 'It helps them to maintain work habits'. The mandatory activation was viewed positively and as a measure resulting in positive outcomes and as a step towards meaningful engagement of the unemployed in the labour market: 'It allows them [Roma] to acquire working skills and contacts'; 'When someone sees them working, maybe he/she will hire them for regular job'; 'They have a better chance of finding a job . . . because they are acquiring skills'. However, it must be noted that ideas about Roma as individuals without any previous work experience are often false. Many of the Roma activation participants were skilful workers prior to neoliberal economic restructuring in the 1990s. The older generation in particular had a significant amount of work experience (see also Hurrle et al. 2012).

Due to the scope and variety of labour activation activities, adequate management and infrastructure was required. In practice, the introduction of labour activation entailed the establishment of new local institutions. So-called activation centres with positions of activation coordinators established by central government were supposed to mediate between the state Labour Offices and municipalities in order to assist with organising activation works. Activation coordinators regularly (several times a week) visited villages and supervised activation works in the districts assigned to them. The practice of labour activation started in the morning with the 'command', as municipalities' representatives informally call it. The so-called command comprised the morning gathering of activation workers, usually in front of the town hall, with the presence of the mayor. It was almost a military procedure, a ritual which symbolically underlines the disciplining character of labour activation. As a mayor we interviewed indicated: '[At the command] I yell out the names. If someone's absent, he/she gets an absence record'. After the command, the mayor along with the activation coordinator would visit the municipality office, sign official daily records and briefly check the list with workers' names and whether workers were properly assigned to streets or zones of the village or town. As was obvious, the ritual of the command, besides its abominable symbolic military connotations, served not only to check the presence of activation workers but also to legitimate and maintain the very institution of labour activation and public display of power.

However, the coordination of labour activation often overlaps between more institutions. Besides the activation centres established by central government, towns or larger villages set up their own activation centres to organise and supervise labour activation. For instance, a district capital town's activation centre we visited had 16 employees, five of whom were in the position of manager. The activation centre located in the municipal house has its subsidiary office in the immediate vicinity of a large Roma neighbourhood with almost 4,000 inhabitants.

Since labour activation measures were introduced in 2004, there have been some negative economic consequences, including the destruction of regular jobs in the local service sector. The provision of municipal cleaning services has been eroded, impacting upon elementary occupations. For instance, cleaning and maintenance services used to be carried out by municipal companies with employees on regular, salaried job contracts. With the introduction of labour activation, there is a workforce available to municipalities for free since it is paid for by social assistance from the state, thus reducing the costs of maintenance services for local government. It also has the side effect of depriving the local economy of its important pillar that provided salaried jobs with health and pension insurance (see also Lajčáková et al. 2017). Interestingly, this phenomenon was captured by the statement of one of our municipalities' representatives: 'Activation workers are useful to us . . . now who else would mow the lawns when we do not have municipal firm?' This statement also illustrates the point that labour activation is not considered by the municipalities to be a transitory phase for unemployed but rather to be permanent state and state-sponsored work for the municipality.

We noted also a discrepancy in perspectives between municipalities and Labour Office representatives regarding the labour activation policies. On the one hand, Labour Office employees oftentimes complained that mayors were 'bending the rules' in complicity with local Roma and non-Roma social assistance recipients to achieve some unlawful advantages in order to ease mandatory activation obligations. On the other hand, the mayors had the feeling that they were proceeding fully according to the law, albeit sometimes a bit 'flexibly' with the aim of not harming their clients by blindly executing administrative rules.

In general, the unemployed Roma have been perceived to be a very specific and problematic group by all mayors, local government officials and Labour Office representatives. This perception was often filtered through the social and professional trajectories of our participants but also by widespread prejudices against the Roma which prevail in public discourse and the media. Most of the mayors whom we interviewed reiterated anti-Roma stereotypes regarding the specific dispositions of the Roma and their culture: 'They [Roma] live with a short-term perspective, from day to day'; 'They live only for today'; 'They are not used to working'; 'Generous social benefits teach them irresponsibility'. The Roma often were seen as 'spoiled' by the welfare system, believed to be preferring social benefits rather than engaging in the formal economy. Moralising and patronising, as well as flaunting with the use of 'a firm hand' with respect to the Roma, were widespread among representatives of municipalities. Common were statements such as 'They [Roma] need discipline', 'They need to be taught some manners' and 'They need to be educated'. However, in our opinion, what mayors interpreted in terms of habitual, psychological and cultural dispositions only illustrated their inability to reflect on the larger matrix of socioeconomic and structural inequalities in society.

The labour activation 'carousel'

Labour activation was officially designed 'to support acquisition, sustaining, deepening, or improving knowledge, professional skills, practical experience, and work habits, for the purpose of improving applicability in the labour market' (*The Act*, 2013). However, not even the Labour Office employees, with their experience which allowed them to see the results over a longer period of time, really believed in the meaningfulness of activation. According to them, labour activation does not meet its purpose 'because it is not really activating people'. In the opinion of Labour Office employees, many Roma clients have been receiving an activation supplement for 15 years, are permanently in the unemployment registers and are rotating between various programmes: 'We rotate them, they are like on a carousel'. A widespread practice in Labour Offices thus consists of changing position of the unemployed between various types of labour activation: from activation administered by municipalities through activation administered by the state to subsidised work for a limited time period of nine months (funded by the European Social Fund). Clients finish a cycle and then start a new one. However, the higher levels of this carousel, namely subsidised work, are not for everyone, but only for those who are viewed as 'reliable' and 'deserving'. Because of widely shared negative stereotypes, this almost by default excludes the ethnic Roma. Moreover, since salaries in subsidised work projects exceed a legal protection threshold against confiscation by debt collectors (approx. €200/month), and given the pandemic of indebtedness of low-income households, only a few of the long-term unemployed without debts can afford to be involved.

Labour Office representatives repeatedly indicated that only a few of the unemployed Roma obtained salaried jobs following involvement with a labour activation programme. If they did, it was in various seasonal work, or they migrated abroad to the UK or the Czech Republic and later returned home and re-entered the social assistance system. They also pointed out the fact that the chances of finding jobs are also worsened by intensified automation and mechanisation, causing a reduction in elementary jobs, specifically in the low-skilled segments. In this respect, our respondent mayor put in contrast the current situation with the situation prior to the 1990s, during socialism, when the Roma had regular jobs in agricultural cooperatives, in factories, and many were employed in the public transport company as car pullers on the railroads.

The unemployed Roma themselves tend to refer to labour activation in the Romany language as *butjis pro vyboris* ('work for the municipality') and also distinguish between what they consider to be 'normal' work for money and labour activation work (for more on this, see Grill 2014, 2018). The Roma undertaking labour activation often also shared a feeling of injustice, especially because of what are from their perspective unclear rules of how they are assigned to different work. We also noted that Roma activation workers often perceived the allocation of duties to be unjust, favouring local 'white' citizens who have good connections with the mayor or with activation coordinators. Those advantaged by the system were assigned easier or more pleasant activities (e.g. cutting grass in front of their own house). It is also often the case that the mayor prioritises and treats more leniently those Roma who have shown loyalty towards him, who vote for him in elections, who inform on other Roma, or with whom he had previously developed good ties. In contrast, those Roma families who lack social capital or connections are often marginalised and more likely to encounter problems in activation or generally vis-à-vis the municipality. In the context of a society with a vast marginalised Roma population, the popularity of workfare in mainstream political discourse and policy practice stems more from the populist attempt to demonstrate to the majority an 'iron fist' approach and 'control' over the Roma population rather than a real belief in their potential.

The most definite form of avoiding stigmatising and demeaning labour activation involves claimants exiting the welfare system. However, there were more 'soft' options which claimants could pursue in order to avoid the mandatory labour activation. The frequent strategy regarding avoiding mandatory activation and securing the activation supplement became going on sick leave. In a district town, out of 209 individuals engaged in mandatory activation at the time of our visit, 42 people (approx. 20%) were currently on sick leave. As an interviewed labour activation coordinator commented: 'We always worked with sixty percent of the eligible people and I don't have the feeling that this is decreasing with time'. This type of coping strategy, however, has been almost exclusively reserved for the non-Roma who have substantial social capital in order to interact relatively equally with doctors, negotiate the symptoms and seriousness of their sickness and make some kind of agreement. Thus ethnic Slovaks sought and are allowed alternative strategies regarding avoiding activation, meaning that menial and dull labour remains with the local Roma.

Conclusions

Labour activation as a social practice has acquired certain 'disciplining' and 'punitive' qualities in relation to the local Roma. This feature of labour activation was reinforced with the introduction of mandatory activation in 2013. Despite the formal possibility to refuse activation works, those who are socially marginalised and with few social connections are coerced into participation, because otherwise they may be negatively sanctioned. Although the labour activation was designed with the aim of pushing welfare recipients into jobs, the empirical evidence showed that the results were ambivalent in this respect. While total unemployment decreased and employment increased following the 2008 crises, the long-term unemployed Roma, although engaged in labour activation, continued to face considerable barriers in entering the labour market. Labour activation has also failed to address deeper structural inequalities between classes and ethnic groups, resulting in a very modest participation of the Roma ethnic minority in the official labour market (OECD 2019). While the unemployed non-Roma got jobs or were allowed to choose alternative strategies to qualify for welfare benefits, menial and stigmatising outdoor activation work was carried out mostly by the local Roma. For example, non-Roma clients were often on sick leave or participated in 'higher levels' of the labour activation 'carousel' with supplements or in the work-subsidised programmes organised by Labour Offices and funded by the European Social Fund.

Despite creating 'space' for socialisation and interaction of long-term unemployed, labour activation did not strengthen social and symbolic capital of participants. Rather, it was quite the opposite: in the municipalities that we visited, the unemployed Roma were grouped into teams for labour activation on an ethnic basis; 'white' workers always held the roles of supervisors. Participation in labour activation, which involves menial, demeaning outdoor activities, thus did not help to improve the social and symbolic capital of the participants; quite the contrary, it acted to stigmatised them in the eyes of the public or potential employers, marking them with a stamp of 'passivity' and inability to find 'normal' work. Thus from this point of view, the Roma activation participants became victimised and stereotyped as being 'dependent' on labour activation and the state. It is also worth noting that the poverty-stricken unemployed activation participants at the time of fiscal consolidation and austerity provide municipal services for the municipalities. These services would otherwise be difficult for local government to afford on the market. Activation thus prevents the creation of jobs, as it is cheaper for municipalities to cover cleaning services by activation work at a fraction of the normal costs.

Barriers and obstacles which prevent better results in terms of employment for the long-term unemployed Roma are in our opinion linked to the fact that the logic of workfare is oriented only towards aspects narrowly related to paid work. Other forms of support within these neoliberal-inspired schemes are not thoroughly applied. Only half of the unemployed in the social assistance system are eligible for the housing allowance. Such a narrow and exclusionary design of the workfare regime proves especially detrimental when considering the unrealistic expectations of the government that extremely materially deprived Roma, who live in shacks without running water and toilets, can be transmuted via labour activation into neat, disciplined, salaried factory workers (e.g. in the flourishing car assembly industry). Thus workfare programmes should necessarily involve also housing support, physical infrastructure support and facilitation in access to health services. Since long-term Roma unemployment is caused mostly by structural problems and barriers such as sectoral economic changes and institutional discrimination, labour activation does not address the core of problems and serves only to 'discipline' and marginalise the Roma at the local level. While the impact of labour activation is inconclusive in terms of employment results, the punitive element which is inseparably entwined with the workfare programme plays an important role in activation practice.

From a broader human rights perspective, the setting of labour activation creates unequal opportunities for various groups of clients. Despite conceptually and technically being of a universalistic nature, labour activation is too dependent on particular local conditions such as the economic power of regions, towns and villages; the size of the impoverished or unemployed population; the availability of public transport; politics, attitudes and abilities of the mayors and municipal councils; and local history and the quality of interethnic relations. Social assistance claimants meeting the same formal eligibility criteria for labour activation are in reality exposed to significantly diverse situations in localities in which they live, which in turn produce unequal results. Many long-term unemployed Roma have been receiving the activation supplement for many years and, instead of obtaining regular jobs, have only continued rotating on carousel, between different activation programmes, perhaps leaving the system for a while but returning after some time. It could be that some drop out of the system because they temporarily find jobs in seasonal work or they obtain a short-term job abroad, but finally they return and re-enter the assistance system. Labour activation as a policy and practice has not addressed structural barriers in the labour market but has instead strengthened the power of the Labour Offices and municipalities vis-à-vis the local Roma population, thus further reinforcing and reproducing marginalisation and inequalities.

Note

1 This research was supported by grant APVV-17-0141.

References

Act on Assistance in Material Need and the Amendment and Supplementation of Certain Acts, No. 417/2013 Coll., Paragraph 12 (Activation Payment). Available at: www.epi.sk/zz/2013-417#p12
Amnesty International (2017): *Slovakia: A Lesson in Discrimination.* Segregation of Romani Children in Primary Education. Available at: www.amnesty.org/download/Documents/EUR7256402017ENGLISH.PDF
Card, D., Kluve, J., Weber, A. (2010): Active labour market policy evaluations: A meta analysis. *Economic Journal*, 120, 548, 452–477.
Dostal, J. M. (2007): The workfare illusion: Re-examining the concept and the British case. *Social Policy Administration*, 42, 1, 19–42.
ERRC (2017, November): *ERRC Submission to UN CERD on Slovakia.* Available at: www.errc.org/uploads/upload_en/file/slovakia-cerd-submission-5-november-2017.pdf
EU FRA (2016): *Second European Union Minorities and Discrimination Survey. Roma – Selected Findings.* Vienna, European Union Agency for Fundamental Rights.
Filčák, R., Szilvasi, M., Škobla, D. (2017): No water for the poor: The Roma minority and local governance in Slovakia. *Ethnic and Racial Studies.* https://doi.org/10.1080/01419870.2017.1291984
Gerbery, D. (2011): Minimum income protection in Slovakia. In minimum income protection in Slovakia. In: Bahle, T., Hubl, V., Pfeifer, M.: *The Last Safety Net. A Handbook of Minimum Income Protection in Europe.* Bristol, Policy Press.

Grill, J. (2014): *Butji pro výboris: Activation (works) without Mobility, Labour and Structural Vulnerability in Neo-liberalizing Slovakia.* Bratislava, United Nations Development Programme. Manuscript.

Grill, J. (2018): Re-learning to labour? 'Activation works' and new politics of social assistance in the case of Slovak Roma. *Journal of the Royal Anthropological Institute.* https://doi.org/10.1111/1467-9655.12802

Hurrle, J., Grill, J., Ivanov, A., Škobla, D., Kling, J. (2012): *Uncertain Impact: Have Roma in Slovakia Benefitted from the European Social Fund?* Findings from an Analysis of Employment and Social Inclusion Projects in the 2007–2013 Programming Period. Bratislava, United Nations Development Programme. Available at: www.undp.org/content/dam/rbec/docs/Have-Roma-in-Slovakia-benefitted-from-the-European-Social-Fund.pdf

IFP (Institute of Financial Policy) (2011): *Evaluating the Efficiency and Effectiveness of Benefits on Active Labour Market Policies in Slovakia.* Bratislava, Ministry of Finance Slovak Republic. Available at: www.finance.gov.sk/Default.aspx?CatID=7837 [Accessed 1 July 2017].

Ingold, J., Stuart, M. (2015): The demand-side of active labour market policies: A regional study of employer engagement in the work programme. *Journal of Social Policy*, 44, 3, 443–462.

Kureková-Mýtna, L., Salner, A., Farenzerová, M. (2013): *Implementation of Activation Works in Slovakia: Evaluation and Recommendations for Policy Change.* Bratislava, Slovak Governance Institute. Available at: www.governance.sk/assets/files/publikacie/ACTIVATION_WORKS_REPORT_SGI. pdf [Accessed 3 September 2019].

Lajčáková, J., Gallová-Kriglerová, E., Kadlečíková, J., Balážová, Z., Chudžíková, A. (2017): *Solving the Roma Unemployment. From Myth to Practice and Back.* Bratislava, CVEK. Available at: http://cvek.sk/wp-content/uploads/2017/04/Nezamestnanost-Romov_studia.indd_.pdf [Accessed 1 July 2017].

Lødemel, I., Trickey, H. (2000): *An Offer You Can't Refuse – Workfare in International Perspective.* Bristol, Policy Press.

Lubyová, M., Štefánik, M., Dovaľová, G., Karasová, K. (2014): Analýza účinkov nástrojov aktívnej politiky trhu práce: výstup v rámci aktivity A3-T5: Problematika trhu práce podľa regionálnych a odvetvových rozdielov. Impact evaluation of interventions of active labour market policy. Bratislava: Centrum vzdelávania Ministerstva práce, sociálnych vecí a rodiny SR. 222 pp.

Martinez, E., Garcia, A. (1996): *What is Neoliberalism? A Brief Definition for Activists.* Available at: www.corpwatch.org/article.php?id=376

Messing, V., Bereményi, B.A. (2017): Is ethnicity a meaningful category of employment policies for Roma? A comparative case study of Hungary and Spain. *Ethnic and Racial Studies*, 40, 10, 1623–1642. https://doi.org/10.1080/01419870.2016.1213402

Ministry of Labour, Social Affairs and Family of the Slovak Republic (2019): *Report on the Social Situation of the Population of the Slovak Republic for 2018.* Available at: www.employment.gov.sk/files/slovensky/ministerstvo/analyticke-centrum/2019/material_sprava_o_soc_situacii_obyvatelstva_2018_angl_verzia_final.pdf

Mušinka, A., Škobla, D., Hurrle, J., Kling, J., Matlovičová, K. (2014): *Atlas rómskych komunít na Slovensku* [Atlas of Roma Communities in Slovakia]. Bratislava, United Nations Development Programme Bratislava. ISBN 978-80-89263-18-9

Nový Čas Daily (2013, 6 June): Available at (in Slovak only): www.cas.sk/clanok/252480/velka-pravda-z-ust-roberta-fica-keby-nebolo-romov-nezamestnanost-by-bola-8–9/ [Accessed 15 September 2019].

OECD (2019, February): *Economic Surveys Slovak Republic*. Available at: www.oecd.org/economy/slovak-republic-economic-snapshot/ [Accessed 12 September 2019].

O'Leary, Ch., Kolodziejczyk, P., György, L. (1998): The net impact of active labour market programs in Hungary and Poland study. *International Labour Review*, 137, 3, 321, 346.

O'Leary, Ch., Nesporova, A., Samorodov, A. (2001): *Manual on Evaluation of Labour Market Policies in Transition Economies*. Geneva, International Labour Office.

Peck, J., Theodore, N. (2000, November): Beyond 'employability'. *Cambridge Journal of Economics*, 24, 6, 729–749. https://doi.org/10.1093/cje/24.6.729

Raffass, T. (2017): Demanding activation. *Journal of Social Policy*, 46, 2, 349–365.

Skills Panorama (2015): Available at: https://skillspanorama.cedefop.europa.eu/sites/default/files/EUSP_AH_Slovakia_0.pdf [Accessed 15 September 2019].

Škobla, D., Csomor, G., Filadelfiová, J. (2017): *Zmeny v systéme pomoci v hmotnej núdzi a prieskum dopadov zmien v poskytovaní príspevku na bývanie v rámci pomoci v hmotnej núdzi*. Bratislava, IVPR.

UNDP (2009): *Report on the Living Conditions of Roma in Slovakia*. Bratislava, United Nations Development Programme. Available at: www.undp.org/content/dam/rbec/docs/Report-on-the-living-conditions-of-Roma-households-in-Slovakia-2007.pdf [Accessed 15 September 2019].

UNDP (2012): *Report on the Living Conditions of Roma Households in Slovakia*. Bratislava, United Nations Development Programme. Available at: https://issuu.com/undp_in_europe_cis/docs/romalivingconditions [Accessed 15 September 2019].

Van Baar, H. (2017): Contained mobility and the racialization of poverty in Europe: The Roma at the development – security nexus. *Social Identities*. https://doi.org/10.1080/13504630.2017.1335826

13 How to keep control? Everyday practices of governing urban marginality in a time of massive outmigration in Hungary

Cecília Kovai and Tünde Virág

Introduction

This chapter explores how different waves of outmigrations from a middle-size town situated in the periphery of a country can be interpreted as a consequence of cyclical economic crisis. We show how these migrations have led not only to significant population loss but also to the fragmentation of local urban societies. Based on a case study of a shrinking Hungarian town (which we name Kallóbánya), we analyse attempts by local government to manage different aspects of this fragmentation, such as social and ethnic relations, the demographic composition of the local population, mobility aspirations of the citizens, urban marginality and political sympathies.

Our case study[1] is based on fieldwork in Kallóbánya, a former mining town characterised by decades-long population loss. Using this example, we present the changing structure of local society and the relations between local institutions and marginal groups embedded in broader political, economic and social cycles and processes. Definitions of shrinking cities generally focus on demographic change (Bernt 2016) and describe urban areas that experience significant population loss because of substantial selective outmigration and/or low fertility rates, combined with the effects of economic downturn and employment decline and social problems, as symptoms of the structural crisis (Martinez-Fernandez et al. 2012).

The population of the investigated town has been decreasing for three decades. However, somewhat complicating the concept of 'shrinkage', behind this long-term negative demographic trend there are alternating, cyclical socio-economic processes that have different effects on different social and ethnic groups of the local society. In the first part of the chapter, we analyse how the aforementioned cyclical processes influence the capacities of local authorities to manage/control diverse social groups. We suggest that the primary objective of the local government is to maintain social order within its jurisdiction, and that it is in constant search for the means to achieve this end. Among the multiple mechanisms concerning social order, the issue of marginalisation is a crucial one, strongly connected with the issue of perception of ethnicities (namely Roma and non-Roma) embedded in local social histories. At the same time, the possibilities and constraints of the local authority for governing the town, and within that marginality, are also influenced by national- and supra- national-scale economic processes and development policies. However, we explore how local governments have only limited tools and opportunities to control the effects of the decades-long population loss caused by selective outmigration.

In the second part of the chapter, we explore everyday practices of the governance of marginality during the global economic crisis after 2008 and the subsequent economic growth. After the global economic crisis, Hungary faced the difficult task of addressing large debt burdens in an increasingly difficult economic environment. On the household level, the growing unemployment rate among youth and people with low educational attainment interplayed with indebtedness and a rapid increase in the real estate market (Bartha 2011; Pósfai and Nagy 2017). This also entailed that the mortgage crisis affected not only the poorest and least educated social groups but also the middle class. This resulted in growing social inequalities and further polarisation processes (Branyiczki and Gábos 2019) also induced a migration outflow, mainly from peripheral regions where our examined locality is situated (Váradi 2018). Due to a new wave of massive, class-based outmigration of workers who have sought work abroad, the demographic dominance of marginalised social groups has been growing and may strengthen the anxieties of less marginalised groups.

In Hungary, one of the most significant public policy reactions to the crisis after 2008 and the most important policy tool for local authorities was the introduction of the Public Works Scheme (PWS) (Kovai 2016; Szőke 2015; Váradi 2016) in order to handle these anxieties at local level. PWS is a typical workfare policy, which fundamentally defined local authorities' room for manoeuvre in controlling marginality during and after the crisis. At the same time, an increase in the proportion of marginalised social groups (mainly Roma) resulted in a growth of the importance of these groups in preserving local political power. The local government uses the loyalty of minority leadership groups and Roma non-governmental organisations (NGOs) to maximise their potential voters at the elections through the everyday practices of political clientelism (Auyero 2000).

In summary, our chapter explores the possibilities and constraints of the local authority for governing marginality in different economic cycles, mainly during and after the crisis of 2008, against a context of decades-long demographic loss which fragmented and polarised the local society. The local governments have a narrow room for manoeuvre to balance the interests of different groups whilst maintaining social order, in a context in which complex ethnic and social positions are being reproduced.

Possibilities and constraints of the local government for managing marginality

The way of life in Kallóbánya and the history of the town were determined in the twentieth century by coal mining. The town can be considered a typical product of global industrialisation tendencies after World War II. The planned development of the mine started after World War II, and the process accelerated in the late 1950s. The population of the town in 1949 remained below 6,000 even after the nearby villages were annexed. The development of the mine, the increase of miners' wages, higher levels of worker safety and mechanisation, and the development of service sector economies locally attracted a growing number of workers to the town. As a result, the number of residents increased to 23,000 by 1960 and to 30,000 by 1980. The development of infrastructure, especially housing, could not keep pace with this rapid population growth. Near the larger mineshafts, 'colonies'[2] were built with dwellings of different sizes and comfort levels according to the social status of workers inhabiting them. These colonies functioned as spatially and functionally separate units from the town as they have own infrastructure: besides the store and the bar, there were also local schools and libraries. Additionally, as a response to the housing shortage, barracks and temporary buildings were constructed for the workers on the edge of the town, who used it for decades as social housing for the most vulnerable social groups.

But who were the inhabitants of the mining colonies and barracks? During the 1960s, when there was a shortage of workforce, the majority of able-bodied workers were employed in the mines, both Roma and non-Roma, regardless of their ethnicity. Due to their generally lower levels of educational attainment, Roma men were typically employed as unskilled workers in the mine in unhealthy, often dangerous physical circumstances, but their ethnicity was perceived and constructed in a given everyday situation in a particular community through personal interactions. In other words, ethnicity evolved in a series of interactions between different ethnic and social groups. The perception of ethnicity was not constant but perpetually changing, while their production and transformation depended on particular economic and historical circumstances and they were necessarily embedded in the relations of the local society (Brubaker 2002). The mine as a hierarchical, dangerous and strictly regulated space of production demanded that every co-worker cooperate and show solidarity. Workers, even if they were forced to do so, had to adjust to each other. In the mine, reliability and disciplined work determined everyday relations that after a while, even if only temporarily and spatially connected only to the workplace, could prevail over the ethnic background. Underground, the role of Roma ethnicity was not accentuated, complicating or hiding spatial segregations that existed on the surface.

Since the early 1990s the gradual closure of the mine, the fear of losing employment, actual unemployment and a generally increasing scarcity of local resources have brought the Roma/non-Roma distinction to the forefront again. The construction and transformation of symbolic and social boundaries between ethnic categories can be understood a result of a struggle for resources, for legitimating social and spatial positions, for reaching higher social status and for the institutionalisation of these relations. The construction and consequences of ethnic categories appeared in socially determined differences between access for scarce resources (Wimmer 2008). We emphasise that the perceptions and distinctions of Roma in Kallóbánya (and in the whole country) depend on unequal social status and power relations. The Roma category is constructed locally as a result of a discursive processes, during which the more powerful and resourceful groups produce nega-tive connotations of the terms applied to lower status groups. However, decades-long lived miner identities, which determined the everyday life of these families, still have relevance in social relations today. This produces a chance to reduce demand for ethnic delimitation and the Roma/non-Roma distinction in times of economic growth and make ethnic limits more permeable than in other contexts.

Nowadays ethnic categorisation is reinforced by the dual fear of demographic change. Since the peak of the urban population in the 1980s, the number of resi-dents has been constantly decreasing, from 30,000 to 24,000 today (back to the level of the 1960s). According to estimates of employees working in municipal institutions, the real number is significantly lower than that, hardly reaching 22,000. This pessimistic estimate can be explained by the decades-long outmi-gration of the town that was experienced by almost every family, starting in the 1980s with the selective outmigration of well-to-do, educated younger people and the everyday experience of international labour migration that has become ever more prevalent lately. As one of our interviewees put it, 'We are going to be like the village'. As the proportion of the Roma population in the town increased eve-ryday encounters on the street, shops and institutions became unavoidable and the strategy of 'creating invisibility' to control and contain the marginal population became a more difficult task for the local government (Wacquant 2012).

Parallel to three decades of population loss, the society of the town was embed-ded in multiple economic processes of varying directions and intensity that demanded different reactions from the local power. In the middle of the 1980s, due to the miners' relatively stable wages, consumption and life standards were relatively high in the town. Accumulation of wealth created the possibility for the children of miner families to enter higher education and also to leave the town. Children of better-off miner families migrated to the central town of the region or the capital city after finishing higher education. The selective outmigration process has continued in the period of economic transformation connected to the closure of the mines during the 1990s.

Since the mid-1990s, one of the most important tasks of the town administration was to 'manage' those who experienced long-term exclusion from the job market after the mine closed and used social institutions and social care intensively. 'We as a local government only experienced the burden of what actually constituted this town' was the discourse of interviewees from local government. The pres-sure on the municipality caused by social problems and conflicts was relieved by foreign direct investment in the region from the mid-2000s. The assembly plant established near the town employed a significant number of unskilled workers. At the same time, smaller enterprises, first established in relation to mining, could also employ a growing number of workers.

The global economic crisis of 2008 meant another turn in the history of the town. On the one hand, the assembly plant closed and unemployment increased significantly. On the other hand, the subsequent mortgage crisis affected not only the poorest and least educated social groups but also the local middle class (Bar-tha 2011; Branyiczki and Gábos 2019). The local government tried to solve this complex social crisis, relying on national level resources in the framework of the PWS. At the same time, the families' own strategy was frequently international labour migration, mostly to Western Europe. As in other areas in Hungary, it was primarily (but not exclusively) the younger and better educated people who were involved in this migration process (Váradi 2018). Through PWS the local government was able to control marginalised social groups and to stabilise the position of the lower classes in a downward spiral, maintaining the status quo. At the same time, international migration for employment was widely realised with individual strategies and works through formal and informal networks independent from local power. Since 2015, in a period of economic growth, unemployment decreased and money flowing in from working abroad decreased indebtedness. However, the effects of the 2008 crisis are still detectable in the local society today. In the following section, we focus on the period of the 2008 crisis and the economic growth period after 2015 and present the everyday practices of govern marginality through the public work schemes and political clientelism.

Managing marginality in times of crisis and after

The 2008 crisis meant a rather sharp turn in Hungarian public policy towards workfare types of social policy. The economic crisis did not mean simply the increase of unemployment but also the growth of class-based ethnic tensions. These were mostly felt in the disadvantaged regions of the country, in villages and smaller towns such as Kallóbánya. The public policy reaction to these tensions and unemployment was the widening of PWS from 2009. PWS was introduced in 2009 by the socialist-liberal government and was redesigned as the largest public policy of the new right wing Orbán government in 2011. The Hungarian Public Work Scheme is a typical workfare framework in which unemployed people are expected to perform eight hours of labour a day in order to receive their benefits, which are less than the minimum wage. Although the population involved in the PWS is highly stratified and lower educated, long-term unemployed Roma people living in villages are over-represented among them. PWS was supposed to deal with unemployment and at the same time with class-based ethnic tensions between the formally employed and those who were excluded from employment over the long term.

Most social scientists and experts interpreted PWS as a typical workfare policy which more or less fits into international trends of neoliberal governance (Asztalos 2014; Kovai 2016; Szőke 2015). We also view PWS as part of these trends, but in our study we follow the arguments of Powell and van Baar (2018) and do not equate neoliberalism with the withdrawal of the state. Instead of looking at it as deregulation, it can be understood as a way of re-regulation. In this way of governance, local institutional power and the state have a central role similar to welfare systems. The PWS is good example of neoliberal decentralisation (Peck 2001) in social policy, since it delegates the burden of managing unemployment and poverty on the local level. In our case, this means that the local government allocates government funding received for PWS and decides who could work in the program and who receives the even less generous benefits. In settlements with high unemployment, this setting increases substantially the power of the local government over the local society. In everyday practices, PWS means a dependent relationship between the unemployed and local power, and it institutionalises the already existing informal paternalism.

However, this relation between people and local power can give also a certain feeling of security, it gives the illusion of the integrated local society where everybody works and where political leaders can control economic and social processes concerning locals (see Szombati 2018). According to a number of recent studies, PWS is able to mitigate the negative effects of long-term unemployment and the growing ethnicised class tensions and stabilise the hierarchy of local class and ethnic relations (Asztalos Morell 2014; Kovai 2016; Szőke 2015; Váradi 2016).

After the alleviation of the crisis, PWS has gradually started to lose significance since the number of public employees fell back almost by half by the first quarter of 2019. Based on our empirical evidence, however, there is a new power technique receiving an increasing significance in the relationship between local or even national political power and the marginalised population – a new kind of political clientelism among the poor Roma communities (see Auyero 2000). The expansion of political clientelism could imply that due to the outmigration of the local middle class, the population – which had been marginal earlier – gained increased significance at the elections. In other words, in order to maintain local political power, there has been a growing need for their votes.

Through the case of Kallóbánya, we would like to present the mechanisms of the PWS on the one hand and those of political clientelism on the other in the following sections. Even though the significance of two institutions in the life of these marginalised communities has been different within particular periods, they have been generally functioning either in parallel to each other or with overlaps.

Public Work Scheme as a tool for managing urban marginality

Kallóbánya provides us with an illustration of the way in which PWS as a workfare policy adopts to economic cycles. In 2012, the town employed almost 1,200 people under PWS, which is a remarkable number considering the town's population of 23,000 inhabitants. This has made the local government into the largest employer in town. However, the number of PWS employees has progressively decreased each year since 2015. In 2019, only 300 workers participated in the program. Nearby factories, the construction industry and work outmigration absorbed the 'surplus' population, which had grown during the crisis. By the end of the 2010s, therefore, PWS has become a programme involving primarily the most vulnerable groups of the town, from a structural point of view, while it affected broader strata throughout the years of crisis. During the years of crisis, stratified levels of PWS were formed in Kallóbánya. These included public sanitation projects, which required no qualification, or works maintaining the infrastructure of the town that did require qualification, up to statuses at local civic organisations, which have often been fulfilled by highly qualified public scheme employees. This has become possible due to the fact that there were unemployed people waiting to be involved from almost all social strata.

PWS thus not only ensured a cheap labour force for maintaining the town's physical infrastructure but also replicated the stratification of local class relations and stabilised them into a particular hierarchy. All these also meant the stabilisation of ethnic relations. The works with the lowest prestige that were most exposed to the control of the town and authorities have been overwhelmingly fulfilled by Roma people with low education. At the same time, it is difficult to find employees of Roma origin among work of higher prestige, such as office work. Ethnicising the hierarchy of statuses, however, reflects precisely the local social relations. Class positions of lower status and long-term unemployment are attached to the Roma minority, while higher positions are rather associated with 'Hungarianness'. Even if only symbolically, PWS reproduces local class relations, which is increasingly important at a time of crisis, when the high rate of unemployment endangers the hierarchy of class and ethnic relations in local society (see Szombati 2018).

In Kallóbánya, one can observe how PWS, as a typical workfare social policy, controls and manages the unemployed population through local power at a time of crisis. PWS is adjusted to the workfare social policy, related to the neoliberal turn on a discursive level too: the structural vulnerability of the population that has become unemployed is represented as an individual failure or an 'ethnical specificity'. Thus, the program, like workfare programs generally, appears within a given locality as a development activity that motivates work morals, as an institution representing the hegemonic work ethos (Clarke 2005; Grill 2018; Muehlebach-Shoshan 2012; Szőke 2015; Powell and van Baar 2018). For the case of Kallóbánya, as a former industrial small town this means the validation of the norm of permanent, formal wage labour, the protection of the 'work ethos' attached to it, which is important particularly in crisis periods, when its realisation is less possible, due to the lack of sufficient work places. Consequently, demanding the ethos of formal, permanent wage labour is an important element in controlling the unemployed population, just like formulated in one of the slogans accompanying the program: 'To lead the unemployed back to the "world of employment." '

The everyday mechanisms of PWS are defined by a tension between the norms of stable, permanent wage labour and its practicability. Throughout the years of crisis, there were even fewer permanent formal workplaces available compared to earlier years, thus the structural reality implies that it is not possible to lead these people back anywhere. As Jan Grill mentions in relation to a PWS program in Slovakia, this tension can be resolved through 'pretending', through the phenomenon of mock labour (Grill 2018: 109–125). This holds for our case, too, since all participants of the program have to pretend to take part in the formal labour market, although this is reflected neither in the level of payments nor in the structure of production. Employees have to structure their time and work potential in a way that would enable them to earn money also outside the PWS, which forces them to constantly outsmart the system.

Managers and leaders of the PWS are expected to put through the norms of formal wage employment, while they are unable to ensure conditions that would guarantee its credibility. Providing people with meaningful jobs means a serious challenge for local governments too, while the managers are supposed to constantly emphasise the importance of doing their work, and this contradiction in itself threatens to question their credibility. One of the most important instruments in establishing trust is the system of control and discipline. In Kallóbánya, PWS works through the controlling of personal relations by the local government, which has turned the spaces in the town into one singular space of production. All this affects lower status workers primarily, who are being controlled several times a day; moreover, sometimes it is the local inhabitants themselves who report to the town's administration that they have seen public scheme workers sluggishly hanging around. Even though the system of control originates from the town's leadership it is still the managers who have to actually organise it through everyday interactions with the workers.

The managers are employees of the local government whose vocation provides them not only with minimal existential security but also offers them the responsibility that they can manage the system. This system actually rewards the 'right' work morals, however scarcely, as opposed to the 'messy circumstances' of the primary labour market. These right work morals, as outlined earlier, proclaim the norms of a permanent, stable wage labour, presuposing employees who not only make their living from this wage but also take responsibility for their work, counting with a predictable stability of their workplaces. Clearly, in case of the PWS, none of these criteria is met. Therefore, putting forward the work ethos of a stable wage labour is constantly confronted with the facts of a disappointing reality. One of the most important elements of this disappointing reality is that workers regard PWS as a kind of temporary phase, a stage in the circulation within the different types of work, a time to be spent, after which they can engage in more important activities, such as informal ways of making money or family issues.

Accordingly, many people do not feel too engaged with their work. Even if they do, they explain it in terms of the habit of working and being autonomous, and not by the importance of the work they do. Therefore, while a large part of public workers adjust themselves to the precarious character of the work, it is exactly the managers of this work who expect them to pretend to have wage labour with a permanent status, one that secures their living. This basic contradiction needs to be resolved by the organisers, and outside the tools of control and discipline they can rely on possibilities lying in informal relationships for this purpose. Most of the organisers engage in the role of paternalistic caretakers and try to become strict but understanding bosses who make concessions to the workers: for example, they would let them go if they have a possibility to earn money or if they have family issues.

After 2015, however, the mock labour market of the PWS has been gradually replaced by 'real' jobs. The majority of public scheme workers have found jobs at the nearby factories or have taken jobs in Western Europe as commuter workers, and the functions of PWS have changed accordingly. It has become an alternative for those who cannot or do not want to comply with the exploiting demands of the primary labour market. These are the ones living with chronic illnesses, caregivers of ill relatives, mothers of small children, those who are either single or whose spouses work abroad, workers of age who are unable to take physical work in the factories, the ones who make their living through informal economic activities, or those who need the security of a permanent, official income. As we can see, PWS can no longer take its role of controlling the marginalised population, but its role in the practice of everyday political clientelism has increased.

Political clientelism

The form of political clientelism that we have studied resembles the phenomena described by Javier Auyero (2000) on the poorest districts in Buenos Aires in many ways. As he claims, the institution of political clientelism is not simply a social practice that can be narrowed down to the time of elections. It is rather a power technique which determines everyday survival strategies of the inhabitants of the poverty areas as well as their views on political power and advocacy. At the same time, Auyero emphasises that these are not one-way processes, as political clientelism works through mediators, the so-called brokers who bring resources into these communities, in exchange for votes. For that, however, these brokers have to have a good knowledge of the valid power dynamics of the local communities and their political views in general, and they have to adjust to those (Auyero 2000: 55–81; Auyero and Benzecry 2017: 99–119).

Similarly, in Kallóbánya, the institution of political clientelism affects primarily one of the poorest neighbourhoods in the town, where Roma people with a low education outside the formal employment scheme are over-represented. Ethnic representation, as we will show, makes the mechanisms of political clientelism even less unidirectional. The everyday practice of political clientelism is related primarily to the Roma local government. This means not so much a formal representation but much rather a type of social capital, which is related to the local government of which the elected minority local government leaders can take advantage. Our informants, Roma leaders of the local government, claim that Roma advocacy or representation can only be party political, and any result can only be reached within the national and local political institutions in power, in cooperation with them. Throughout our discussions the Roma population, whose interests they are supposed to represent, have come up as a collective 'us', but at the same time, the meaning of this 'us' is constantly changing. What does the 'us' include? Is it the entire Roma population? Is it the relevant political interest group and its clientele? Or is it the extended Roma family, which tries to protect its interests in a similarly vulnerable structural situation? The answer is never clear, as these three levels are intertwined. All of this is possible because the leaders themselves have emerged from the local Roma communities, and their life paths were identical with that of the Roma social history of Kallóbánya.

Robin, a local key actor in the political clientelism, is a Roma man in his early forties who grew up in a mining family and worked as a miner himself in his young years. He was affected by the closing of the mine, therefore the issue of Roma advocacy has been strongly intertwined with his own existential problems. For Robin, just like other Roma young people who have remained without a job, politics has become a field of mobility, promising beneficial contacts. By the 2000s, Robin and his brothers and their allies had organised the Roma local governments of the county, where Robin took a leading position. Since the late 1990s they have taken part in the work of the local government too. Robin keeps tight relationships with the current leadership and openly supports the mayor. Our informants, however, emphasise that taking benefit from both the symbolic and the social capital is only possible by ensuring the appropriate number of voters, because this is how local Roma leaders can get into a bargaining position at the local bodies of the town. Ensuring votes, just like keeping the positions at the minority local government, requires a good knowledge of the local marginalised Roma community and a permanent presence. Even though our informants interpret the apolitical attitude of civic organisations and NGOs most of all as a weakness, this permanent presence is guaranteed by a Roma association, which is based in the poorest part of the town and is led by Robin.

Along with Robin's social capital, the association fulfils a mediator role between the institutional power and the local community, and Robin is a type of mediator that the literature would call a broker (Auyero 2000; James 2011). The association engages in diverse activities, such as giving out donations, different types of adult education, educational programs for children, cultural programmes, organisation of Roma days and providing individual help in several areas; Robin is at the centre of all these activities. Through his connections, these diverse activities of the association have facilitated a movement of resources into poor neighbourhoods. When locals need help from the local government (such as PWS, extraordinary social aid or social housing), they would often say, 'I will talk to Robin'. At the same time, these people seeking help all know what Robin wants in exchange: the reaffirmation of his position, which allows him to get access to these resources, that is their votes. Depending on the interpretation of Robin's activities, the level of political power into which the votes get attached can vary from the minority local government elections to the local elections or the national parliamentary ones, and it is not even clear to the ones seeking help which level Robin's resources come from. Robin, as a broker, functions at the same time as a gatekeeper of the resources and as their operator. He is not merely a mediator but also the one who produces the local dynamics and interpretation of power and morals, in the process of mediation (Auyero 2000; Koster and Lenyseele 2012; James 2011).

The relationship of the inhabitants (i.e. his 'target group') to Robin's activities is rather ambivalent. On the one hand, his intervention is one of the most evident tools of getting access to help and resources. From this aspect, Auyero's and Benzecry's conclusions on political clientelism and the role of the broker seem relevant for our case. In these social contexts, politics do not mean a collective fight for centralised power, and not even a 'dirty' business, but a supportive and useful practice, a potential access to central power. Meanwhile the figure of the broker is also not a representative of collective interests and will. He does not appear as an egoistic, corrupt character, but a relatively efficient problem-solver (Auyero 2000: 55–81; Auyero and Benzecry 2017: 99–119). On the other hand, however, in this context the practice described above receives heavy criticism, which is partly due to the fact that the clientele of Robin does not support a permanent circle of people but people who get into a particular situation. Once this particular situation gets solved, loyalty might decrease. The major argument against this practice is that Robin would use people according to his own interests, and his activities serve only the reaffirmation of his position and his economic status. Converting permanent presence into votes is therefore by no chance a clear process, and it depends on several factors such as the political and economic situation of the country, the evaluation of the local government or the mobilisation skills of the broker. It is certain, though, that the practice of political clientelism in past years has become an increasingly widespread phenomenon, which determines the relationship between local power and the marginalised population, through the figure of the broker.

Conclusions

In this chapter, we aimed to present the effects of economic crisis and decades-long population decline on local social structures in Kallóbánya, Hungary, considering how they change relationships between the local institutional power and the marginalised population, through the case of a former industrial town. The chapter did not aim to study population decline in itself but as embedded into national and global processes, on different scales, which means that we have interpreted the population decline within the context of different political, economic and social processes. Even though the population of the town has been declining for about three decades, the long-term demographic trends are also affected by cyclically changing economic and political processes, which affect the different societal groups to different extents. Alongside an ongoing demographic shrinkage, there are different social conflicts and strategies that surface in a period of economic growth followed by a recession. This way, local governments have to handle and solve various problems within the frames of the altering development and support policies of the national government. In past years, the national and global political processes, predominantly from the semi-periphery towards the central states, or as in this case, the increasingly significant labour outmigration towards Western European countries shrinks the space of local authorities for influencing local social processes.

The central claim of this chapter is that the aim of the local government is to sustain a local social equilibrium. The most significant (though not the only) point of this problem is the management of marginality, which in our case correlates with the mechanisms of the ethnic (Roma-Hungarian) differentiation. The perception of ethnicity is embedded into the local social history; here it is related to the miners' way of life, which has determined social relations and the perception of marginal social groups for decades. The long-term process of outmigration, which predominantly concerns the better educated young people, not only changes societal structures but also amplifies the fear of the demographic prevalence of the Roma groups who are over-represented among the undereducated, marginalised population.

The tools of local power for the control of marginalised social groups are always affected by the national and supra-national economic processes and development strategies. In the second half of our study, we presented the everyday mechanisms of the management of marginality in different economic periods: during the 2008 crisis and after. As a reaction to the crisis we could observe the extension of the PWS as a turn towards workfare policies in the Hungarian social policy. In our case study, we showed that the primary function of PWS is a certain kind of consolidation to maintain balance in the local society. At the same time, this reproduces the ethnicised class relations that are especially central in times of crisis, when the reproduction of these relations is endangered. We also highlighted that besides the maintenance of urban infrastructure, PWS also maintains the ethos of formal wage labour that is less self-evident in a structural situation such as the crisis. We conceive PWS as a reaction to the crisis and this is why the importance of this policy has decreased after the end of the crisis when political clientelism came to the fore. In our study we outlined the everyday mechanisms of political clientelism and showed the complex trade of votes and resources. Through these insights we explained how economic, social and political processes of different scales affect the reproduction of social relations and the management of marginality in a demographically shrinking former mining town.

Notes

1 This research has been implemented with the support provided from the National Research, Development and Innovation Fund of Hungary, financed under the K-16 funding scheme (project No. 119465) and under the PD_16 funding scheme (project No. 121058). Empirical evidence for the article was combined qualitative and quantitative research. Besides the statistical analysis of the National Census between 2017 and 2018, our research team carried out more than 60 stakeholder interviews in different institutions and organisations in the chosen town. Besides the interviews, ethnological fieldwork will help us to gain an insight into the daily lives of families

2 In Hungarian the word *kolónia* has a specific meaning of settlement. The etymology of this word connects the practice of companies creating worker settlements to the colonial practice of imperial states. For this reason we will use the literal translation of *kolónia* (colony) in this text to name these specific worker settlements.

References

Asztalos, Morell Ildikó (2014): Workfare with Human Face? *Metszetek* (4): 3–24.

Auyero, Javier (2000): The Logic of Clientelism in Argentina: An Ethnographic Account. *Latin American Research Review* 35 (3): 55–81.

Auyero, Javier and Benzecry, Claudio (2017): The Practical Logic of Political Domination. Conceptualizing the Clienteist Habitus. *Sociological Theory* 35 (3): 179–199.

Bartha, Attila (2011): A válság hatása az esélyegyenlőség és a társadalmi kirekesztés szempontjából. In: Mester, D (szerk.): *Köztár.hu: Közszolgáltatás, esélyegyenlőség, önkéntesség*. Budapest and Magyarország: Nemzeti Család- és Szociálpolitikai Intézet (NCSSZI), pp. 103–143, 199.

Bernt, M. (2016): The Limits of Shrinkage: Conceptual Pitfalls and Alternatives in the Discussion of Urban Population Loss. *International Journal of Urban and Regional Research* 40 (2): 441–450.

Branyiczki, R. and Gábos, A. (2019): Poverty Dynamics during the Economic Crisis in Hungary. In: Tóth, I. Gy. (ed.): *Hungarian Social Report 2019*. Budapest: Tárki, pp. 176–194.

Brubaker, R. (2002): Ethnicity without Groups. *European Journal of Sociology* 43 (2) (August): 163–189.

Clarke, John (2005): New Labour's Citizens: Activated, Empowered, Responsibilized, Abandoned? *Critical Social Policy* 25 (4): 447–463.

Grill, Jan (2018): Re-learning to Labour? 'Activation Works' and New Politics of Social Assistance in the Case of Slovak Roma. *Journal of Royal Anthropological Institute* 24: 105–119.

James, Deborah (2011): The Return of the Broker: Consensus, Hierarchy, and Choice in South African Land Reform. *Journal of the Royal Anthropological Institute* 17 (2): 318–338.

Koster, Martijn and Leynseele, Ynes van (2018): Brokers as Assemblers: Studying Development Through the Lens of Brokerage. *Ethnos. Journal of Anthropology* 83 (5): 803–813.

Kovai, Cecília (2016): Önellátó függőség: a közfoglalkoztatás társadalmi beágyazottsága egy tolnai megyei faluban. In: Katalin, Kovács (szerk.): *Földből élők: polarizáció a magyar vidéken*. Budapest: Argumentum.

Martinez-Fernandez, C., Audirac, I., Fol, S. and Cunningham-Sabot, E. (2012): Shrinking Cities: Urban Challenges of Globalization. *International Journal of Urban and Regional Research* 36 (2): 213–225.

Muehlebach, Andrea and Shoshan, Nitzan (2012): Post-Fordist Affect: An Introduction. *Anthropological Quarterly* 85 (2): 317–343.

Peck, Jamie (2001): *Workfare States*. London: Guilford Press.

Pósfai, Zs. and Nagy, G. (2017): Crisis and the Reproduction of Core-Periphery Relations on the Hungarian Housing Market. *European Spatial Research and Policy* 24 (2): 17–38.

Powell, Ryan and van Baar, Huub (2018): Invisibilization of Anti-Roma Racism. In: *Securitization of Roma in Europe*. Palgrave Macmillan, Cham.

Szőke, Alexa (2015): A Road to Work? The Reworking of Deservedness, Social Citizenship and Public Work Programmes in Rural Hungary. *Citizenship Studies* 19 (6–7): 734–750.

Szombati, Kristóf (2018): *The Revolt of the Provinces. Anti-Gypsyism and Right-Wing Politics in Rural Hungary*. New York: Berghahn Books.

Váradi, Monika (2016): Értékteremtő közfoglalkoztatás periférikus vidéki terekben. *Esély* 1: 30–56.

Váradi, Mónika (2018): Elméleti kaleidoszkóp – a migrációs tapasztalatok értelmezési lehetőségei. In: Mónika, Váradi (szerk.): *Migráció alulnézetből*. Budapest: Argumantum Kiadó.

Wacquant, L. (2012): A Janus-Faced Institution of Ethnoracial Closure: A Sociological Specification of the Ghetto. In: Hutchison, R. and Haynes, B. D. (eds.): *The Ghetto. Contemporary Global Issues and Controversies*. Boulder, CO: Westview Press, pp. 1–32.

Wimmer, A. (2008): The Making and Unmaking of Ethnic Boundaries. *American Journal of Sociology* 113 (4): 970–1022.

14 Care, austerity and citizenship

Story-telling as protest in anti-austerity activism in the UK

Eleanor Jupp

Introduction

Both in the UK and elsewhere across Europe, the past ten years have seen profound cuts to welfare state services and expenditure in the name of 'austerity'. Much research has examined the reshaping of ideological and policy discourses around this project, and of course the impacts of cuts on everyday lives (e.g. Farnsworth and Irving, 2015). More recently, research has begun to trace the contours of anti-austerity politics springing from within communities and the everyday lives of citizens experiencing cuts. As Vaiou and Kalandides (2017) point out in relation to austerity cuts in Greece, there are different ways to 'read' or analyse the politics of the community projects, movements and experiments which have arisen as the state retreats, for example collective spaces of food and welfare organised at a neighbourhood level. Such projects might be seen as examples of 'resilience' or 'innovation', in some ways an expression of the ability of communities to organise and survive in the face of state restructuring. However, as Vaiou and Kalandides (2017) argue, an alternative and more critical reading would see instead at stake questions of urban citizenship and public space in ways that might 'pre-figure' or enact wider progressive and transformative politics (Chatterton, 2010). Of relevance to this chapter is the call to treat localised, perhaps temporary forms of activism and organising as nonetheless making interventions into the sphere of politics, as I go on to explicate.

This chapter builds on other emergent research on resistance to austerity among communities in the UK, including among women of colour and associated voluntary sector organisations (Bassel and Emejulu, 2017), in response to housing pressures and crises (Watts, 2016), the loss of disability benefits (Gibbs, 2018) and library closures (Robinson and Sheldon, 2019). Although some coalitions of such movements have come to national attention, such as Sisters Uncut (Ishkanian and Peña Saavedra, 2019), campaigning against cuts to domestic violence services, in general such resistance has been localised and time-limited, often petering out in the face of the wearying and repetitive experiences of encountering austerity (Hitchen, 2016; Wilkinson and Ortega-Alcázar, 2019).

To return to questions of how to 'read' or analyse the politics of such activism, this chapter will argue, through analysis of local activism around closures of Sure

Start Children's Centres, that we can see resistance to austerity cuts as involving 'acts of citizenship' (Isin and Nielsen, 2013). The forms of citizenship at stake are gendered and based on embodied and felt experiences of care (Erel, 2011), care that is often seen as taken for granted, as 'invisible' and non-political aspects of everyday lives. As such the formation of political subjectivities involved is somewhat complex. Before moving on to this analysis, I first introduce some debates on citizenship and care and then the Sure Start programme via which the centres under threat were established.

Citizenship, gender and care

Within academic studies of citizenship, there has been a turn to models of citizenship based on participation and process, rather than formal legal or political rights, for over 20 years (Kymlicka and Norman, 1994). Isin and Nielsen (2013) proposes a conception of 'citizenship acts', which more concretely links particular embodied practices to political subjectivity. In seeing citizenship as comprising practices rather than states of being, a diversity of practices come into view as potentially politicised, but also the contingent nature of political participation and voice is emphasised. Experiences of citizenship may be associated with particular spaces and times that may be transitory, emergent or interrupted.

Somewhat in parallel to these debates has been a set of debates about gendered experiences of citizenship, especially for women. Classical civic republican models of citizenship, based on notions of rational debate within a 'public sphere' (Pateman, 2016), have long been critiqued for marginalising spheres of domestic labour and care, spheres which have historically been predominantly occupied by women (Lister 2003a). Commentators in the United States in particular (e.g. Howard, 2014), which has traditions of 'community organising' tied to racialised urban poverty, have proposed modes of citizenship and activism which speak to disadvantaged women's experiences of care and everyday lives. These include modes of citizenship based on 'getting by' in difficult circumstances, building networks of support as well as making demands of those in positions of power (see Jupp, 2012).

Alert to the dangers of essentialising women's identities and claims to political participation within such spheres, there has been less recent attention to women-centred experiences of citizenship – exceptions would include Erel's (2011) research on 'migrant mothers' and how their practices of care can in themselves be seen as 'citizenship acts' – establishing political subjectivities in often hostile and marginalising contexts. More recently, gendered analysis of citizenship has been re-animated by a context of austerity which clearly disadvantages women, and more particularly poorer and ethnic minority women. Bassel and Emejulu's (2017) analysis of austerity politics and women of colour discusses a politics of 'survival and resistance' which includes an argument about how an attention to 'care' might form the basis of a new transformative collective politics.

Indeed, beyond an attention to gendered experiences, anti-austerity activism more broadly has been seen as potentially re-working processes and meanings of citizenship. Gerbaudo (2017), in an analysis of anti-austerity activism in Spain and Greece, points out that unlike the anti-globalisation movements which have been seen as precedents, the citizenship claims emerging from these contexts were not anti-state. Instead they sought to defend, reclaim and open up state institutions, described as 'mending the system'. While Gerbaudo does not pay attention to gender, it can be argued that women have historically been more dependent on the welfare state, their everyday lives more intertwined with aspects of it, making an anti-state position less tenable (Fraser, 2013).

In a UK context, the 'social investment' state, exemplified by the 'New' Labour government 1997–2010, can be seen as one which offered particular benefits for women. While the politics of such a state has been critiqued for an ultimately economically instrumental approach to care and welfare (Lister, 2003a), it remains the case that the dynamics of feminism from the women's movement formed part of policy programmes in new ways. As Newman (2012) documents, women moved from activist and third-sector organisations into spheres of government and power, creating rather ambiguous alignments that cannot simply be reduced to the alignment of feminism with neoliberalism (Fraser, 2013). Instead, New Labour policy evidenced an often uneasy mix of rationalities, combining neoliberal managerialism and instrumentalism, with more radical and welfare-orientated impulses. As aspects of this welfare settlement are cut, such a politics becomes more apparent.

Sure Start Children's Centres and the politics of care

The Sure Start Children's Centre programme can be seen as exemplifying this uneasy mix between a programme providing welfare-orientated care and support to families, particularly mothers of young children, and a more instrumental and interventionist programme seeking to shape children's (and parents') subjectivities in certain ways, for example around 'school-readiness' (Lister, 2003b). The programme, initially only in the most 'disadvantaged areas', provided centres where families with children under 5 could access drop-in play sessions and a range of health, education and employment advice and support. The programme was later expanded to provide one such centre 'in every neighbourhood', with the idea of walking or 'pram-pushing' distance as key (Eisenstadt, 2011).

In some of my earlier research (Jupp, 2013), I characterise the spaces of Children's Centres as 'hybrid spaces' in which policy targets and imperatives were combined with other kinds of rationality and identification, especially around friendship, care and everyday help or support. Yet the collective values of care, friendship and community support that service users often valued were not necessarily recognised within the discourses under which the centres were planned and evaluated. Horton and Kraftl (2009) similarly point to the hidden benefits of the centres that were not valued in policy frameworks, interwoven as they were into everyday interactions and relationships. Indeed, findings from the national evaluation of Sure Start, which set out quantitative indicators under which the success of the programme was measured, were highly politicised, with politicians often pointing to less positive findings as evidence of the failure of the programme as a whole (Belsky et al., 2007).

Of course, it is not only within a space such as a Sure Start Children's Centre that the practices and orientations constituting 'care' can be rendered invisible. 'Care', as a set of everyday embodied practices undertaken largely by women in society, is tied up with the long-standing divisions between public and private spheres referred to earlier, a division that has functioned to marginalise women's everyday lives (Pateman, 2016). Second-wave feminism in particular drew attention to the taken-for-granted nature of care, re-framed by feminist analysis as 'social reproduction' (Fraser, 2013). Such a phrase draws attention to the productive and societal value of care beyond the individual family. Yet while care is no longer at the centre of most feminist analysis and activism, the inequalities it produces remain persistent and widespread, and its invisibility persists. Many aspects of care are not easily named or represented, and may not be articulated by either carers and those being cared for. Most care does not have a beginning or an end; it cannot be easily subdivided into ethical, emotional, practical and embodied elements (de la Bellacasa, 2017). It often involves ambivalence and conflict as much as the more positive qualities associated with care; and its accomplishments and achievements are rarely apparent. Care may furthermore be invisible within a family or household, within society more broadly and within policy and political discourses (Jupp et al., 2019).

All this has implications for how responses to austerity based on care might emerge. The issues at stake and at the centre of such a politics are hard to articulate. It may be hard to connect individual experiences with collective concerns. Unlike, perhaps, schools and hospitals and their clear connections to areas of national politics and policy, Sure Start Children's Centres have never been seen as sites of politics (Horton and Kraftl, 2009). In what follows, therefore, I trace a process of politicisation with regards to the centres, via discussing the experiences of some women involved with the protests against closures, focusing on two women. I show how women participated in different kinds of 'citizenship acts' to resist austerity cuts, focusing particularly on forms of story-telling.

Sure Start Children's Centres: researching and tracing austerity activism

The material that follows is drawn from a project undertaken in 2017–2018, focusing on two regions of South East England where Children's Centre services were heavily cut, in common with other parts of England, where it is estimated that over 1,000 centres have closed since 2009 (Smith et al., 2018). A recent report (Smith et al., 2018) described the Children's Centre service nationally as currently falling off a 'cliff edge', with many other closures currently under consideration. The two areas studied represented contrasting localities, economically and demographically. Area A is a largely affluent county, with high levels of social and cultural capital due to the position of higher education institutions alongside pockets of deprivation. Area B is a smaller urban borough and has more widespread deprivation. Both areas underwent a similar process, albeit a couple of years apart, whereby 'service restructuring' was proposed by local authorities for Sure Start Children's Centres. The processes of restructuring were shaped by the need to reduce spending in the face of massive reductions in the central government funding (Smith et al., 2018), but also by the statutory or legal obligations local authorities were subject to in relation to the centres. These obligations require local authorities to provide 'sufficient Children's Centre Services' to meet local need (Smith et al., 2018). Any substantial changes to the service (such as the closure of a centre) have to be subject to public consultation, and changes have to 'protect the most vulnerable families'.

At stake here were questions of need and of vulnerability, as well as what the service constituted and what might make it 'sufficient'. In both areas, the service restructuring involved the closure of the majority of local centres, and the redesignation of a small number of centres as 'Hubs', suggesting a concentration of resources and services in certain centres, with other centres either shutting or becoming 'satellite' centres offering much more limited services. In both areas the final number of 'hubs' was around a quarter of previous centres, shutting approximately 40 centres between them. As should already be apparent then, the closures were themselves presented via a language of restructuring and indeed service improvement, such that it made it hard to actually understand that what was proposed did involve centre closures (Jupp, 2018). The campaigns that sprung up to protest the closures therefore were partly involved in making visible the fact that the centres were shutting at all.

The campaigns that arose in both areas were local and not initiated by any particular political party or organisation, although in both cases there was some support from local left-wing politicians, and in Area A, from a trade union network. At the centre of both campaigns were service users, overwhelmingly mothers, who sought to speak out about the value of the centres and fight their closures. Various means of organising were used, both online and offline, including Facebook groups and blogs, public meetings, protest gatherings and picnics, the temporary occupation of public spaces, and in the case of Area A, a legal challenge to a centre closure. The campaigns are indicative of many other similar campaigns elsewhere. However, to my knowledge, such campaigns have been temporary and localised and have not translated into wider networks of resistance to closures on a national level. My research traced processes of closures and activist responses, involving interviews with decision makers, centre staff and services users involved in protests. I was interested in austerity politics not simply as a process of cuts but as a more complex political process which produces new political rationalities, alignments and subjectivities.

Enacting citizenship through telling stories around Sure Start Children's Centres

In this section, using data from interviews with service users, I discuss how mothers' everyday practices of using the centres became re-represented through modes of story-telling, and how such story-telling constitutes 'acts of citizenship', within a wider understanding of the politics of care and austerity. I approached these interviews based on my observation that forms of story-telling had become key to the campaigns, as will be discussed further. In order to access service users, I advertised on social media and used snowballing through existing contacts for interviewees who wanted to speak about the value of the centres. I used an unstructured interview approach in order to enable the interview encounter to capture the 'stories' (Cameron, 2012) as service users wanted them to be told. Eight such interviews were undertaken altogether, and I focus here on two in particular.

In order to consider how such story-telling can be thought of as acts of citizenship, I suggest that such an enactment has a number of different modalities. These include an attention to, and articulation of, aspects of the existing centres that were of particular value to those telling the stories, and also to other service users, within their experiences of caring for young children. This therefore involved reflection on their own experiences and making connections to the experiences of others. This process also involved reflecting on the proposals for service closures and reductions that were being discussed in both locations, in order to articulate how they would diminish the centres' values. And from a more overarching perspective, such story-telling involved giving a shape, or narrative, to the shapeless and diffuse practices and experiences of care for young children.

Of course, the shape of such a narrative was framed by the context in which it was told, who was listening, and how and where they had been told before. My interviewees brought different experiences of telling their stories into the interview encounters (Cameron, 2012). For those who had taken an active role in the collective campaigns against the closure of the centres, the telling of these 'stories' had become a key mode of activism, something they had undertaken a number of times in campaign meetings and when meeting councillors, press and decision makers, albeit generally in a shorter, more condensed form than the interviews offered. For example, at the end of one of the interviews, a service user (Sara) who had told her story in a number of such spaces asked me, 'Was that ok? I'm out of practice, a few months ago I was doing this all the time'. Interviews with these women who had been activists involved the re-telling of these stories but also moments such as these of reflexivity about the telling of these stories at other times and in other spaces.

Other interviewees had not told their 'stories' before in a public forum but said that they wanted to take part in the research in order to make them more visible. The interviews themselves could be thought of as performative acts of citizenship or interventions into a kind of public sphere. Indeed, after undertaking the interviews I worked with the interviewees to produce a digital animation using parts of their stories, as a further method to render visible and public their experiences. Figures 14.1 and 14.2 are images taken from the animation 'Save our Sure Starts', depicting moments from these stories about the everyday lives of participants and the importance of the centres.

Figure 14.1 Katie's story about her struggle with mental health and the support offered to her at the Sure Start Children's Centre

Sources: Images from Save Our Sure Starts animation, available at www.youtube.com/watch?v= tKb1NWVNFIw. Still from animation by Eleana Gabriel and Yee Hui Wong, School of Engineering and Digital Arts, University of Kent.

Figure 14.2 Sophie's story about the repetitive and claustrophobic nature of her home life

Sources: Images from Save Our Sure Starts animation, available at www.youtube.com/watch?v= tKb1NWVNFIw. Still from animation by Eleana Gabriel and Yee Hui Wong, School of Engineering and Digital Arts, University of Kent.

In what follows, I focus on interview data. I briefly discuss the 'stories' of two mothers who spoke to me during the research, to demonstrate how the processes of articulating these stories can be seen as enacting citizenship.

Karen

Karen was a prominent activist in the campaign against closures in Area A. Her story centred on the key role that a Children's Centre had played in enabling her to leave a violent and abusive relationship that she had been in for eight years. At the Children's Centre she met and connected with a health visitor (a form of family nurse) who became the catalyst for the end of her relationship. This was how she described what happened:

> So they basically pulled it out of me and they helped keep me safe, I actually met my health visitor that would actually help me escape, she staged an intervention, she basically dragged a social worker into it and staged an intervention to get him out of my home. . . . But yeah, I met her at, because I was going to baby group, I met her at a go and weigh your baby, health visitor drop-in that was on at the same time as the baby group. I wasn't getting on with my own health visitor, they put me with her and my life started to change, and then a few months after I got him [i.e. abusive partner] out, I started doing The Freedom Programme, which is a course to help people that have either just got out or are still in those situations. And then I did the follow on course recovery tool kit, which is like it says, it helps you put your life back together and covers everything from counselling your children to, yeah, absolutely everything, which is vast.

This meeting at a health drop-in, which was taking place at the same time as the baby playgroup that Karen was attending, was therefore a key turning point in her life. Karen had clearly reflected extensively on this encounter, and how it was the presence of a trained professional, able to involve other services ('dragged a social worker into it') within an informal drop-in community space, that had been so important for her. She was then able to extrapolate the importance of the centres for others, based on a connection with her own experiences:

> But it's like that sort of open door, it's all access, so that's a really, really important part of it, it's not just about referred services it's all access. And because of that people might come just to weigh their baby or to just ask a question or they might not have time to arrange an appointment with their health visitor, whatever, or they might come to a first aid course, baby massage, whatever draws people in. And then if it's someone who's struggling you've then got well trained people as opposed to a toddler group run by volunteers, you've got well trained people that can see those signs and direct those, well get to know those people first, so they feel comfortable, *it's exactly what happened with me* [my emphasis], and then direct them towards

help . . . like the woman in the middle of summer that's got really, really long sleeves because she's covering up either self-abuse or someone else's abuse and things like that. So, the trained staff and the open access are key, and then of course there's the doorway to all the other services whether it be breast feeding support or post-natal depression.

Karen was making these points within the context of service restructuring proposals that would result in 'hubs' that were not 'open access' or available to all, but rather would involve referral from another professional, framing much more formal spaces where people might not feel 'comfortable'. At the same time, the council were suggesting that informal drop-in baby groups of the kind originally used by Karen could be run by volunteers, meaning a loss of the trained professionals with other service networks. Indeed in this and other stories, the centres emerged as places where mothers were able to speak about intimate experiences that might be considered shameful or taboo in many spheres of their lives.

Karen said that during the period of her life while she was still living with her abuser: 'I didn't tell anyone what was going on, because that's how it is in a controlling relationship'. Karen's story therefore combined a very emotional and intimate narrative with a considered and reflexive analysis of the value of the centres. Karen had told her story many times, and while it clearly played a performative role in her activism, it remained a story that ultimately pointed to her own vulnerability. Therefore it had an exposing quality, and as such its reception mattered, both politically and personally.

Karen told me about a number of other mothers who had used their stories in this way as part of the campaign, and also a teenage child who had witnessed the impact of the support from a Children's Centre had had on her mother, who had also escaped an abusive relationship because of such support. Karen spoke about a council meeting where this teenager had spoken to powerful effect:

> But yeah, so she'd made this amazing speech, half the Tories were in tears, which is, you don't see that much, and they actually had a break, they actually went out for a break, which is the first time it's happened since 1990 something or whatever. And they ended up coming together with almost like a coalition budget with £2 million extra to children's centres, like I said that was the day that they all the councillors were sat there, leafing through our paperwork instead of the council paperwork on that day, so yeah.

On the other hand, if such personal stories were ignored or misunderstood, it could be very hard. For example, Karen told me about an occasion when number of the activists went to speak to a different council body:

> When I went to speak to them, the line was, which made me so angry I had to leave because I was going to throw a chair, 'if you help people they will never help themselves'. And I was just, well essentially 'we're not in Victorian times' so, and this was after myself, my friend that I said about that her

daughter spoke really passionately, her situation, she was, there was armed police when she left her situation, it was pretty bad. And obviously you know my situation and then someone else who'd had really bad PND [post-natal depression] with three young children, we all stood up and made heartfelt speeches each and then that was what they said.

The three women had clearly made themselves vulnerable and visible in this forum and they were essentially humiliated in response. Another of my interviewees, Sophie in Area B, had a similar experience in a council meeting where she had spoken about her own mental health problems, and was also very upset by responses to local newspaper reports online:

> It does feel like – 'oh those mums, they can't have everything', people that don't understand, what value they have to your lives, just keeping you sane, just keeping you and your child active and social, and the support you get, so seeing the negative feedback, 'you can't have everything, times are tough', was really really hard.

Sophie moved from a central role in the campaign to essentially withdrawing from it, I think primarily because of such feelings. Indeed I became aware that many other service users had not told their stories in the 'public' spaces of the campaign for whatever reason, but nonetheless felt they had stories they wanted to tell. This was the case with Linda, whose story I turn to next.

Linda

The context of Linda's story, in Area B, was very different from Karen's, in that she had not been actively visible in the local campaigns against closures and had not made her 'story' public before. However, it became apparent during the interview that she had followed the proposals for closures and responses to them closely in the local press. It was also clear that she saw her interview with me as, in itself, a political act, a contribution to the campaign against closures. She contacted me having seen my call for interviewees and had e-mailed, explaining that she had a story about the importance of the centres for her and her son. As will be explained, this story involved her being in poor health. Her decision to attend an interview with me was a practical and embodied challenge for her, in that she came to meet me away from home, which was hard for her.

In common with others who had not been involved in such performative storytelling as an activist, Linda took longer during the interview to develop a clear narrative about the benefits of the centres to her and her child, with more fragmentation and moving around chronologically. However, at the centre of her story was her developing a rare autoimmune condition that made exposure to common childhood illnesses extremely dangerous, indeed life-threatening. As in Karen's story, it was meeting a worker from a Children's Centre which was the catalyst for a dramatic change in her life, and a different kind of escape from the home space:

> So, trying to get out, but also staying safe was difficult, so to start with, when I was newly diagnosed, we didn't go out, we stayed in the house so it was just me and my son, we just played indoors together, for maybe, probably about a year, because I hadn't worked out how we were going to go to a group and not get poorly – very difficult. So it was a health visitor that put us in touch directly with the Children's Centre, and they arranged a one to one visit to come out to my house, and then discussed with us what we were going to do . . . so obviously, being stuck indoors with mummy, isn't great for his development, so I really needed to do something about that but also keep safe, so one of the managers from the Sure Start centres came to visit us at home a couple of times. . . . And they put in a complete plan in place to facilitate us leaving the house and going to a couple of the local groups and so . . . it worked really really well.

Essentially the Children's Centre developed a procedure to screen everyone attending the group she was going to check for the particular illnesses that put her at risk. The inclusion that this enabled for Linda was clearly life-changing and involved not just attending the sessions themselves but the sense of freedom and escape that came from travelling to the centre too.

> So to be able to walk down, with the pram, is amazing, that we got that where we lived, to get out in the fresh air as well, to have that walk, to talk to other people on the way there and back, maybe pop to the park afterwards with people from the session, that you've met is amazing.

Her reference to walking with the pram may also have referred to the fact that in the new plans, service users would have to travel further to access services, rather than the walking or 'pram-pushing' distance which had been key to the design of the centres and overall service. Other service users also spoke about the sense of escape offered by the centres, the need to get away from the claustrophobic and repetitive quality of caring for young children at home.

While Linda's story had a particularly dramatic quality therefore, having been trapped at home for an extended period, her experience spoke to more everyday experiences of care too. Linda felt an enormous sense of gratitude to the staff at the centre, perhaps especially because, as she expressed, she had not seen herself as the 'sort of family' that would need professional and welfare support. This phrase suggests a sense of herself as more financially but perhaps also socially resourceful than families that might be seen as needing need 'more help'.

> So they came out to our home, and that was really, just so, kind of them, 'cause I wouldn't have thought we were the sort of family that needed home visits and care visits, and it seems like, they done so much, just for one family,

they've made such a difference just for one little family, it made you think what else have they been doing, for all the other families that possibly need more help.

Her experience therefore made her aware of the complexity of needs around care, in the face of plans for moving to the kind of 'targeted' services which ranks needs and rations support in new ways. She also spoke about the overall invisibility of the centres and the lack of wider awareness of their importance in families' lives:

I don't think people realise how much good they do, what a place of refuge they are for mums and dads, it's a bit of a shock becoming a parent, for any-body, no matter what age or background you are from, it is a shock and you can go mad at home, and if it wasn't for these groups running – where would you be – really – where would you go for advice, or a shoulder to cry on?

This quote again makes the point about the universal needs experienced by parents of young children, 'no matter what age or background'. Needs and vulnerabilities become politicised under austerity, as universally accessible services become ever more rare and categories of need become ever more rigid.

Conclusions: telling stories of austerity and the politics of care

The stories emerging from the interviews in this chapter, and the wider themes they speak to, provide one case study of austerity politics and citizen responses. Considering the stories and experiences that emerge shows how matters of cuts to the welfare state take us into gendered and often invisible spaces that can be hard to speak about (Jupp et al., 2019). This chapter has shown how 'story-telling', both online and offline, can offer ways to resist austerity cuts to services. I have argued that the story-telling under discussion can be seen as an 'act of citizen-ship' (Isin and Nielsen, 2013), involving reflection on personal experience, con-nections to others' experiences and reflection on the values and benefits of the services under threat. Such story-telling, as others have argued (Cameron, 2012), is not just a matter of narrative but is also performative, relational and embodied, operating on affective as well as discursive registers. Such acts of citizenship offer ways for 'small stories' (Cameron, 2012) to speak to much wider-scale issues of political and economic change, and therefore this approach offers resources to those resisting austerity in diverse contexts.

However, as should be clear, such processes of story-telling involve quite complex emotional and reflective work, and there are also questions to consider around whose voices and experiences might be heard within such a politics. The two women I have focused on in this chapter were motivated to speak out by dramatic, and indeed life-changing, experiences associated with the centres. Such dramas were also in the past and had been, to some extent, been resolved; they had become narratable. It was perhaps this distance, as well as the possession of certain emotional and personal resources, that enabled these women to speak publicly about distressing and private experiences.

This raises questions about the experiences of those who are not able to articulate such stories in this way, who may be in the midst of crisis or who may lack the personal resources to speak about them. It also raises questions about those who do not have such dramatic 'stories' but struggled with the day-to-day embodied and emotional labour of care. Matters of care are mainly ordinary and banal, albeit intertwined with crisis and drama (Jupp et al., 2019). When battling austerity cuts, making the case for the importance of 'ordinary' care and support may be more difficult, when it does not necessarily lend itself to narrative and drama. This remains a challenge both for activists and for researchers who may wish to advocate on their behalf. Austerity does not always effect people in dramatic or life-changing ways. There is a danger of researchers seeking out the drama of pain and suffering caused by austerity in a voyeuristic way that overlooks the everyday impacts of austerity. A challenge to researchers therefore is to consider the modes of representation and articulation which allow the many everyday stories of the impact of austerity to be told.

References

Bassel, L., & Emejulu, A. (2017). *Minority women and austerity: Survival and resistance in France and Britain*. Bristol: Policy Press.

Belsky, J., Melhuish, E. C., & Barnes, J. (Eds.). (2007). *The national evaluation of Sure Start: Does area-based early intervention work?* Bristol: Policy Press.

Cameron, E. (2012). New geographies of story and storytelling. *Progress in Human Geography, 36*(5), 573–592.

Chatterton, P. (2010). Seeking the urban common: Furthering the debate on spatial justice. *City, 14*(6), 625–628.

de la Bellacasa, M. P. (2017). *Matters of care: Speculative ethics in more than human worlds* (Vol. 41). Minneapolis, MN: University of Minnesota Press.

Eisenstadt, N. (2011). *Providing a sure start: How government discovered early childhood*. Bristol: Policy Press.

Erel, U. (2011). Reframing migrant mothers as citizens. *Citizenship Studies, 15*(6–7), 695–709.

Farnsworth, K., & Irving, Z. (Eds.). (2015). *Social policy in times of austerity: Global economic crisis and the new politics of welfare*. Bristol: Policy Press.

Fraser, N. (2013). *Fortunes of feminism: From state-managed capitalism to neoliberal crisis*. New York: Verso.

Gerbaudo, P. (2017). The indignant citizen: Anti-austerity movements in southern Europe and the anti-oligarchic reclaiming of citizenship. *Social Movement Studies, 16*(1), 36–50.

Gibbs, J. (2018). *The politics of vulnerability: Affect, relationality, and resistance in UK austerity* (Doctoral dissertation, London School of Economics and Political Science (LSE)).

Hitchen, E. (2016). Living and feeling the austere. *New Formations, 87*(87), 102–118.

Horton, J., & Kraftl, P. (2009). What (else) matters? Policy contexts, emotional geographies. *Environment and Planning A, 41*(12), 2984–3002.

Howard, A. L. (2014). *More than shelter: Activism and community in San Francisco public housing*. Minneapolis: University of Minnesota Press.

Ishkanian, A., & Peña Saavedra, A. (2019). The politics and practices of intersectional prefiguration in social movements: The case of sisters uncut. *Sociological Review*. https://doi.org/10.1177/0038026118822974

Isin, E. F., & Nielsen, G. M. (Eds.). (2013). *Acts of citizenship*. London: Zed Books.

Jupp, E. (2012). Rethinking local activism: 'Cultivating the capacities' of neighbourhood organising. *Urban Studies*, *49*(14), 3027–3044.

Jupp, E. (2013). Enacting parenting policy? The hybrid spaces of Sure Start Children's Centres. *Children's Geographies*, *11*(2), 173–187.

Jupp, E. (2018). Children's centres are disappearing. *Conversation*, 11 April. Available at https://theconversation.com/childrens-centres-are-disappearing-heres-what-it-means-for-the-under-fives-and-their-parents-94792

Jupp, E., Bowlby, S., Franklin, J., & Hall, S. M. (2019). *The new politics of home: Housing, gender and care in times of crisis*. Bristol: Policy Press.

Kymlicka, W., & Norman, W. (1994). Return of the citizen: A survey of recent work on citizenship theory. *Ethics*, *104*(2), 352–381.

Lister, R. (2003a). What is citizenship? In *Citizenship: Feminist perspectives* (pp. 13–42). London: Palgrave Macmillan.

Lister, R. (2003b). Investing in the citizen-workers of the future: Transformations in citizenship and the state under new labour. *Social Policy & Administration*, *37*(5), 427–443.

Newman, J. (2012). *Working the spaces of power: Activism, neoliberalism and gendered labour*. London: A&C Black.

Pateman, C. (2016). Sexual contract. *The Wiley Blackwell Encyclopedia of Gender and Sexuality Studies*, 1–3.

Robinson, K., & Sheldon, R. (2019). Witnessing loss in the everyday: Community buildings in austerity Britain. *Sociological Review*, *67*(1), 111–125.

Smith, G., Sylva, K., Smith, T., Sammons, P., & Omonigho, A. (2018). *Stop start: Survival, decline or closure? Children's centres in England, 2018*. Sutton Trust.

Vaiou, D., & Kalandides, A. (2017). Practices of solidarity in Athens: Reconfigurations of public space and urban citizenship. *Citizenship Studies*, *21*(4), 440–454.

Watt, P. (2016). A nomadic war machine in the metropolis: En/countering London's 21st-century housing crisis with focus E15. *City*, *20*(2), 297–320.

Wilkinson, E., & Ortega-Alcázar, I. (2019). The right to be weary? Endurance and exhaustion in austere times. *Transactions of the Institute of British Geographers*, *44*(1), 155–167.

Index